Good Housekeeping

AGA Winter
Cookbook

Good Housekeeping

AGA **Winter Cookbook**

OVER 150 RECIPES FOR AGAS & OTHER RANGE OVENS

EBURY PRESS
LONDON

First published in 1999

1 3 5 7 9 10 8 6 4 2

Text and photography © 1999 Ebury Press or the National Magazine Company Limited

AGA is a registered trade mark of Glynwed International plc

First published in the United Kingdom in 1999 by
Ebury Press
Random House, 20 Vauxhall Bridge Road,
London SW1V 2SA

Random House Australia (Pty) Limited
20 Alfred Street, Milsons Point, Sydney,
New South Wales 2061, Australia

Random House New Zealand Limited
18 Poland Road, Glenfield, Auckland 10, New Zealand

Random House South Africa (Pty) Limited
Endulini, 5a Jubilee Road, Parktown 2193, South Africa

Random House UK Limited Reg. No. 954009

A CIP catalogue record for this book is available from the British Library.

ISBN 0 09 187165 4

Project editor Gillian Haslam
Designed by Christine Wood
Special photography by James Murphy and Laurie Evans
Illustrations by Madeleine David
Recipes adapted for the Aga by Miranda Hall

Printed and bound Tien Wah Press, Singapore

COOKERY NOTES

Both metric and imperial measures are given for the recipes. Follow one set of measures throughout, as they are not interchangeable.

All spoon measures are level unless otherwise stated. Sets of measuring spoons are available in metric and imperial for accurate measurement of small quantities.

These recipes are suitable for both 2-oven and 4-oven Aga cookers. Where the cooking instructions differ for a recipe, both are given. The following symbols apply:
■ ■ for a 2-oven Aga
■ ■ ■ ■ for a 4-oven Aga

Where a stage is specified for freezing, the dish should be frozen at the end of that stage.

Large eggs should be used except where otherwise specified. Free range eggs are recommended.

Use freshly ground black pepper and sea salt unless otherwise specified.

Use fresh rather than dried herbs unless dried herbs are suggested in the recipe.

Stocks should be freshly made if possible. Alternatively buy ready-made stocks or use good quality stock cubes.

THE GOOD HOUSEKEEPING INSTITUTE

The Good Housekeeping Institute was created in 1924 to provide readers of *Good Housekeeping* magazine with expert consumer advice and delicious, classic and contemporary easy-to-follow recipes. These ideals still hold true today. The Institute team are all experienced cooks, home economists and consumer researchers. They test the latest products in purpose-built, modern kitchens, where every recipe published in the magazine and its range of best-selling cookery books is developed and rigorously tested so that you can cook any GH recipe with confidence. When any new ingredient appears on supermarket shelves, you can be sure that GH has tried and tasted it way ahead and interpreted a food trend into a workable, stylish recipe.

Television crews and radio broadcast units are regular visitors to the renowned Institute kitchens, which have become a popular location for leading food and consumer programmes.

Good Housekeeping magazine's authority and experience go well beyond the kitchen and cooking. The Institute can also tell you the best buys in anything from wine to computers and luxury lingerie. The Good Housekeeping Institute is synonymous with quality and impartial advice, offering good value for the consumer. You can trust the authority of *Good Housekeeping*'s word on health, careers, holidays, family matters and fashion and beauty. Over two million people buy it, read it and live by it.

CONTENTS

6 Introduction

12 Soups

20 Fish and Shellfish

28 Poultry and Game

44 Meat Dishes

66 Vegetarian Dishes

76 Accompaniments

84 Christmas Dishes

106 Desserts

122 Baking

138 Preserving

144 Index

ABOVE: BUTTER AND RUM BAKED APPLES

ILLUSTRATED ON PREVIOUS PAGE: SWEET AND SOUR SPICED PORK

INTRODUCTION

The Aga is a cast-iron heat storage cooker which was invented in 1922 by the Swedish physicist, Dr Gustaf Dalen. It was introduced into England in 1929, and has become so popular that 'Aga' is now an established household name.

An Aga is an excellent investment, as it serves many purposes and will last a lifetime if properly used and maintained. Its timeless, classic design has changed little over the years, although you can now choose from a range of vitreous enamel colours to co-ordinate or contrast the cooker with the rest of your kitchen.

You will find that the Aga immediately becomes the focus of the kitchen, creating a special, all-year-round warm and welcoming atmosphere. Ensure that your cooker is positioned to take full advantage of this, especially if you eat in the kitchen – which you will almost certainly want to do once your Aga is installed!

HOW AN AGA WORKS

The Aga cooks by radiant heat emitted by the cast iron, which is different from a conventional oven. Radiant heat does not dry out the food. The fuel for your Aga may be natural gas, propane (LPG – liquid propane gas), solid fuel, oil or off-peak electricity but, whatever the heat source, all Aga cookers basically function in the same way. The heat is generated in the burner unit and conducted around the walls of the cast-iron ovens and hot plates. The cast-iron surfaces store heat and release it as radiant heat at a steady rate when needed. As you cook, the heat lost is automatically restored because the Aga is thermostatically controlled. Different areas of the cooker are maintained at different temperatures in order to provide a range of cooking options. Food smells and vapours are conveniently ducted away from the ovens to the external flue.

TWO-OVEN AND FOUR-OVEN AGA COOKERS

Aga cookers are available in two different sizes: two-oven and four-oven models. The two-oven Aga has a roasting oven and a simmering oven. In addition to these, the four-oven has a warming oven and a baking oven. These ovens are deceptively large, with a capacity of nearly 45 cu cm (2 cu ft) and every part of the ovens can be used. On top, both appliances have a fast boiling plate and a gentle simmering plate, protected by insulated lids. The four-oven cooker also has a gentle warming plate. Again, the hot plates are large, each allowing room for up to four pans. The most popular model in this country is the two-oven cooker.

Some Aga models will also provide domestic hot water. Your choice of model will obviously depend on your individual requirements. The Aga is assembled in your own home by the manufacturer's engineers.

DIFFERENCES BETWEEN USING AN AGA AND A CONVENTIONAL COOKER

■ The Aga is a constant source of heat: there's no need to wait for the oven or hob to heat up.

■ The Aga operates on the principle of heat storage and is surprisingly efficient to run.

■ The Aga has no dials or knobs to adjust for a change in temperature. Once you are used to your Aga, you will find this simplification an advantage.

■ The Aga does not have a separate grill, but grilling takes place at the top of the roasting oven, or in a grill pan on the boiling plate.

■ Because most Aga cooking takes place in the large, versatile ovens rather than on the hot plates, condensation and cleaning are minimised.

■ The Aga is vented through a flue, so there are virtually no cooking smells from the ovens.

■ Because the cast-iron walls of the Aga ovens retain heat so well, you don't need to worry about losing heat as you open the door, to peep at a soufflé or cake for example. With a conventional oven, this can cause such a drop in temperature that a soufflé or cake may collapse.

CONSERVING HEAT IN THE AGA

The secret to success with an Aga is to cook inside, rather than on the top with the lids up, whenever possible – this way you conserve heat. Few foods need to be cooked entirely on the hot plates and those which do, such as stir-fries and green vegetables, cook quickly. Many dishes which would be cooked on the top of a conventional cooker, such as soups, stews and steamed puddings, are started off on the hot plates, then transferred to the appropriate oven. The following tips on conserving heat may help:

■ Always keep hot plate lids shut unless they are in use.

■ When using the hot plates, cover as much of the surface area as possible, with one large pan or several smaller ones.

■ Allow chilled items to stand at room temperature (for 1-2 hours) before placing in the ovens, especially turkeys, joints, casseroles, soups, etc.

■ Thaw frozen food before cooking. Ideally leave in the refrigerator overnight, then at cool room temperature for 1-2 hours.

INTRODUCTION

■ Plan your menu carefully when you are entertaining or cooking for large family gatherings to avoid trying to cook several dishes at the same time which all need a very hot oven. This is particularly important if you have a 2-oven Aga. Of course, many dishes can be cooked in advance and reheated to serve.

■ If you are batch baking, bread for example, at a high temperature, allow up to 2 hours for your oven to return to temperature if you need maximum heat for your next batch of cooking. Alternatively, take advantage of the slightly cooler oven to bake cakes and biscuits after cooking family meals.

■ When there is going to be a heavy demand on your cooker, turn up the Aga heat dial slightly, about an hour in advance, remembering to return it to the normal setting before going to bed.

■ Some flue outlets are affected by high winds so you may wish to turn up the heat dial as before.

■ An Aga which heats water may cool a little if a lot of water is run off, e.g. for baths. You may wish to boost the water heat with an immersion heater if this affects your Aga when entertaining.

THE HEAT INDICATOR
The gauge on the front of your cooker indicates whether your Aga has the correct amount of heat stored.

■ When the heat indicator is on the thin black line, your Aga has the right amount of heat stored and is operating at its optimum.

■ If the indicator is towards the black shaded area, there is less heat stored and cooking will therefore take longer.

■ If the mercury reaches the red area, there is more than the required amount of heat stored and it is possible that there may be something wrong. Before calling your local approved Aga engineer, check that the control dial hasn't been altered.

■ During cooking, the temperature will fluctuate a little, but should soon return to its normal setting. If you've been using the hot plates extensively, the cooker may take 2-3 hours to recuperate.

GETTING TO KNOW YOUR OWN AGA
Each Aga is slightly different from the next: its position in the kitchen, whether situated between units or free-standing, on an inside or outside wall; the type of fuel used, and whether or not your Aga also supplies the hot water; these factors will all add to its individuality. You may find it takes a little time to get to know and love your Aga with its own personality!

BASIC PRINCIPLES OF AGA COOKING
■ As different areas of the Aga are kept at different temperatures, you simply need to choose the right

position for the dish you are cooking, depending upon whether it requires a low, moderate or high temperature, fast or slow cooking.

■ Each oven presents a range of options, because the temperature varies slightly within each oven, from top to bottom, front to back, and side to side. The top is the hottest part; the back will be a little hotter than the front; the side nearest the burner unit will be hotter than the opposite side.

■ Temperatures are a guide only as food is cooked by radiant heat, not by temperature.

THE ROASTING OVEN
Apart from roasting and baking, this versatile hot oven is used for shallow-frying, grilling, steaming and simmering. The oven has four shelf positions; the floor of the oven, and the grid shelf placed on the floor of the oven give two more cooking positions.

THE COLD PLAIN SHELF supplied with the Aga allows you to use the roasting oven for baking items which require a more moderate temperature. You simply slide in the cold shelf, usually two sets of runners above the food being cooked, to deflect the top heat and create a moderate heat below. With the 2-oven Aga, this is an important function. If your cold plain shelf is already in use, the large Aga roasting tin can fulfil the same function; to maintain the lower temperature throughout longer cooking, half-fill the tin with cold water after 20-30 minutes.

COOKING IN THE ROASTING OVEN
The recommended shelf positions for the recipes in this book are, of course, provided, but you may wish to adapt conventional recipes from elsewhere. You can, of course, purchase an oven thermometer to check the operational temperature of the different positions within your oven, if you wish. As a rough guide, the roasting oven shelf positions are used as follows:

TOP (OR FIRST) RUNNERS
Grilling (on oiled preheated rack over roasting tin)
SECOND RUNNERS
Browning dishes, gratins, roast potatoes, scones
THIRD RUNNERS
Fast-roasting, bread-baking, jacket potatoes
BOTTOM (FOURTH) RUNNERS
Medium-roasting, pastry
GRID SHELF ON OVEN FLOOR
Slower-roasting (e.g. pork, poultry)
OVEN FLOOR
Crisp pastry bases (flans, etc); to crisp roast potatoes, frying, fast reduction of sauces, preheating griddles and frying pans

THE TWO-OVEN AGA

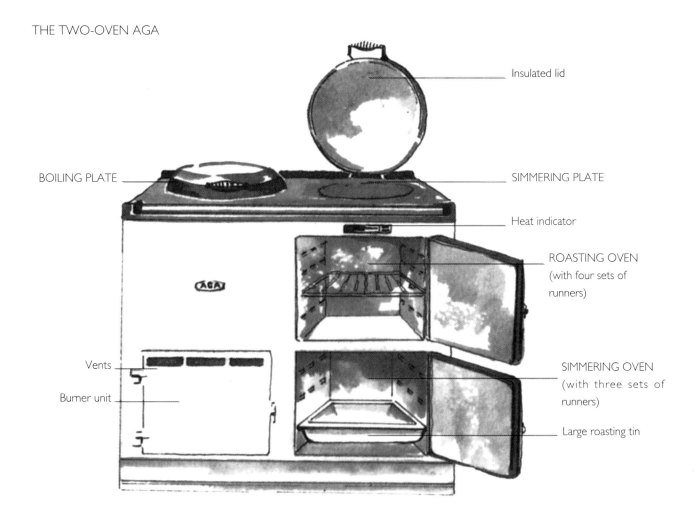

Insulated lid

BOILING PLATE

SIMMERING PLATE

Heat indicator

ROASTING OVEN
(with four sets of runners)

Vents

Burner unit

SIMMERING OVEN
(with three sets of runners)

Large roasting tin

GRID SHELF ON OVEN FLOOR
WITH COLD PLAIN SHELF ABOVE
(in a 2-oven Aga)
Baking fish, biscuits and cakes

THE SIMMERING OVEN

This oven has a minimum of three cooking positions: the floor, the grid shelf on the floor of the oven, and the middle runners which take the cold plain shelf and the Aga roasting tins, as well as the grid shelf. In addition, the 2-oven Aga has a further 2 sets of runners. The temperature of the oven can vary, but is generally around 100°C (212°F), within an ideal range for slow, gentle cooking. Almost all dishes need to be started off at a higher temperature (on one of the hot plates on top of the Aga or in one of the other ovens), then they should be transferred to the simmering oven to complete cooking.

The main uses of this oven are as follows:

■ ROOT VEGETABLES Place your chosen vegetables in a saucepan, cover with cold water, put the lid on the pan and bring to the boil on the boiling plate. Cook for 3-5 minutes, then drain off all the water. Salt vegetables lightly, cover the pan with a lid and transfer to the simmering oven to steam until tender, about 20-30 minutes. Potatoes, in particular, benefit from being cooked in this way: they will be soft through to the centre without falling apart.

■ STOCKS Bring stocks to the boil in a covered pan on the boiling plate, then transfer to the floor of the simmering oven. By cooking in this way, you will be able to make flavoursome, jellied stocks, without any of the unpleasant cooking smells usually associated with boiling stocks.

■ CASSEROLES These cook superbly in the gentle heat of this oven. First bring to a simmer on one of the hot plates, then place in the simmering oven to cook slowly. To speed up cooking, you can place the casserole on the grid shelf on the floor of the roasting oven for 15-20 minutes of each hour.

■ MERINGUES Perfect light, crisp meringues can be cooked entirely in the simmering oven; the floor is the ideal position.

■ PORRIDGE can be cooked overnight in this oven.

■ CAKES With a 2-oven Aga, the simmering oven is often used to complete the cooking of cakes which have been part-baked in the roasting oven. Large rich fruit cakes (such as wedding or Christmas cakes) can be cooked overnight on the grid shelf on the floor of the simmering oven without being started off elsewhere – to delicious effect.

■ KEEPING FOODS HOT/REHEATING The temperature of the simmering oven is perfect for keeping foods warm, without spoiling.

■ RESTING MEAT If you have a 2-oven Aga, the simmering oven is most useful for resting roasted poultry and joints of meat.

THE FOUR-OVEN AGA BAKING OVEN

This is situated below the roasting oven and has the same number of runners and corresponding versatile cooking positions. The temperature in the middle of this oven averages 180°C (350°F) – ideal for many baking purposes.

■ The top of the oven is used for baking biscuits, small cakes, roulades, etc.

■ The middle is used for sandwich cakes, crumbles, poaching and baking fish.

■ The bottom of the oven with the grid shelf in position is used for casseroles, deep cakes, and poaching ham.

THE FOUR-OVEN AGA WARMING OVEN

This is maintained at approximately 70°C (160°F) and is very temperate.

■ It is the ideal place to warm plates and serving dishes, and to keep foods warm without spoiling, including delicate sauces.

■ Allow roasts to rest in this oven for 20 minutes before carving.

■ Meringues and porridge can be cooked overnight in this oven.

THE BOILING PLATE

The main function of this hot plate is to bring foods up to a fast boil, before continuing to cook elsewhere in, or on the Aga. It is also used for quick frying, stir-frying, cooking green vegetables and making toast (with the special Aga toaster).

THE SIMMERING PLATE

This is used for bringing foods up to a gentle simmer; slow-frying, including sweating vegetables; foods which require gentle cooking with constant attention, such as delicate sauces.

■ The hot plate also doubles up as an excellent griddle: simply lightly oil or butter the clean surface and cook drop scones, crumpets, tortillas, nan bread and poppadoms etc, directly on it.

THE FOUR-OVEN AGA WARMING PLATE

This is a useful additional warm surface – ideal for holding dishes taken out of one of the ovens, and warming the teapot. Some Aga cookers may have their warming plate replaced by an electric or gas hob.

■ It is also suitable for melting chocolate, butter, etc.

■ Bread dough can be risen on this hot plate: place the bowl on a folded towel to avoid direct contact.

■ Note that the area at the back of an Aga is also a good source of warmth.

AGA EQUIPMENT

The following items are supplied with your Aga:

GRID SHELF This has non-tilt runners, so it can be drawn out to the full extent without danger of tipping.

COLD PLAIN SHELF This is used as a shelf, a full-size baking sheet, and to lower the temperature in the roasting oven (see page 8). When not in use, the cold plain shelf should be stored outside the cooker. A second one of these is most useful.

AGA ROASTING TINS These have many uses and two are supplied: the full-size tin and a half-size roasting tin, both of which can be hung from the runners in the ovens. Apart from the obvious functions, the roasting tins can be used for grilling, with the rack in position; traybakes, such as flapjacks; bain-maries, for custards etc. The large roasting tin can also be used as an alternative cold shelf (see page 8).

THE AGA TOASTER This is used to toast bread, crumpets, etc of any thickness on the boiling plate.

Other items of equipment which you will find useful:

SPLATTER GUARD This is most useful for covering pans during frying, to protect the Aga surface.

THE AGA GRILL PAN This ridged cast-iron non-stick pan is excellent for cooking steaks, chops, etc. It is first preheated on the floor of the roasting oven for 5-10 minutes, then used on the boiling plate. (A similar ovenproof ridged cast-iron skillet can be used.)

THE AGA CAKE BAKER A non-essential item, but one that you will find most useful if you are a 2-oven Aga owner and often bake large cakes that take longer than

45 minutes to cook, such as Madeira, rich fruit cakes, etc. It can also be used as a large pan for stocks, or large scale entertaining.

PANS AND COOKWARE

Although it isn't essential to buy a whole new range of pots and pans when you become an Aga owner, it is important to make sure that the bases of your existing pans are perfectly flat, to ensure good contact with the hot plate. Good quality pans with thick ground bases which conduct heat well should really be used. (Ask the Aga Shop or Cooker Centre in your area for advice on the suitability of your pans.)

■ All of your saucepans should be suitable for use in the simmering oven (with handles and lids heat resistant to the temperature range of this oven), as well as on the hot plates. For the recipes in this book, it is assumed that this is the case.

■ Ovenproof is used in these recipes to denote that the pan (or casserole) must be suitable for use in the roasting oven.

■ Hard anodised aluminium, stainless steel and cast-iron pans are the most suitable choices. Aga have their own ranges of cookware in these materials, so you may prefer to choose from these if you are buying new cookware. The pans are designed with flat lids, so that they can be stacked on top of each other to save space in the oven, as well as when being stored, if required.

■ Cast-iron cookware is particularly efficient to use with an Aga, and is most attractive. You may, however, find that the very large pans are heavy to lift in and out of the ovens.

If you are buying new pans, consider the following basic selection:

■ 4 saucepans, ranging from 2-4 litre (3½-7 pint) capacity
■ 1 large 25-30 cm (10-12 inch) ovenproof frying pan
■ 1 omelette pan (can also be used as a crêpe pan)
■ 2-3 casseroles, ranging from 2-4 litre (3½-7 pint) capacity – suitable for use on the hot plates)
■ The Aga grill pan (or other ridged skillet)
Note: The large 11 litre (20 pint) pan is useful for making preserves and cooking for crowds.

CLEANING THE AGA

This is an easy task because most of the cooking takes place in the ovens and you therefore have very little grease to contend.

■ The hot plates, roasting oven and 4-oven Aga baking oven are largely self-cleaning. Anything which is spilt will carbonise and can be brushed away easily with the wire brush provided.

■ The other areas of the cooker do not become as dirty, due to the type of cooking they are used for. Simply wipe down with warm soapy water, then polish with a soft, dry cloth.

■ Clean the enamel and chrome areas regularly with a cream cleaner then spray with silicone polish so they wipe clean easily.

■ Wipe away any spills as soon as they occur. This is particularly important for spilled milk, fruit juice, preserves and other acidic foods which might otherwise damage the enamel with prolonged contact.

SPRING CLEANING YOUR AGA

Aim to give your Aga a thorough clean to coincide with its recommended regular service:

■ Carefully lift off the oven doors and lay, enamel-side down, on a cloth. Clean the inside of the doors with a cream cleanser, or soap-filled wire pad if necessary. Wipe over the seal but do not allow it to become wet.

■ Clean the chrome shelves and the inside of the hot plate covers with a cream cleanser. Brush out the ovens.

■ Clean the rest of the enamel and chrome areas with a cream cleaner and, polish with a soft, dry cloth.

THE AGA ISN'T JUST A COOKER...

Your Aga will make your kitchen an efficient drying and airing room.

■ An old-fashioned clothes airer can be suspended from a high kitchen ceiling to provide plenty of additional drying space. Traditional cast-iron and pine ones are available, and these are an attractive feature in any kitchen, without any running costs. You may even find that your tumble dryer becomes obsolete!

■ Herbs, flowers and petals for pot pourri can be hung near the cooker to dry in the gentle warmth.

■ On a bitterly cold night, you may wish to leave the kitchen door ajar. You will find that the warmth from the Aga will take the chill off the house.

SOUPS

Parsnip Soup with Parmesan Crisps

PREPARATION TIME:
30 MINUTES

COOKING TIME:
I HOUR

FREEZING:
COMPLETE TO THE
END OF STEP 3,
THEN COOL, PACK
AND FREEZE. THAW
AT COOL ROOM
TEMPERATURE
OVERNIGHT.
COMPLETE THE
RECIPE.

355 CALS PER
SERVING

MAKES 2 LITRES
(3½ PINTS)

Parsnip soup always has a glorious texture but needs a hot and spicy ingredient to create a really interesting flavour. Here the paprika and spicy chorizo make a change from the more familiar curried parsnip soup.

40 g (1½ oz) butter
150 g (5 oz) onion, roughly chopped
225 g (8 oz) floury potatoes, such as King Edward's, peeled and chopped
400 g (14 oz) parsnips, peeled and chopped
20 ml (4 level tsp) paprika, plus extra to dust
1.1 litres (2 pints) fresh chicken or vegetable stock
450 ml (¾ pint) milk

60 ml (4 tbsp) double cream
salt and freshly ground black pepper
65 g (2½ oz) sliced chorizo sausage, cut into fine strips

FOR THE PARMESAN CRISPS
I large parsnip, weighing about 75 g (3 oz), peeled
vegetable oil for frying
45 ml (3 level tbsp) grated Parmesan cheese

1 Melt the butter in a large heavy-based saucepan. Add the onion and cook on the SIMMERING PLATE for 5 minutes or until soft. Add the potatoes, parsnips and paprika, mix well and cook gently, stirring occasionally, for about 2 minutes, then transfer to the SIMMERING OVEN for 15 minutes or until the vegetables have begun to soften.

2 Add the stock, milk, cream and seasoning. Bring to the boil and return to the SIMMERING OVEN for 30 minutes or until the vegetables are very soft. Add 50 g (2 oz) of the chorizo.

3 Allow the soup to cool a little, then place in a blender or food processor; process until smooth. The soup can be thinned with additional stock or milk, if wished. Correct the seasoning and return to the saucepan.

4 To prepare the Parmesan Crisps, using a vegetable peeler (the wide swivel ones are best for this), peel off long strips of parsnip until there is nothing left to peel. The strips should be as wide as possible.

5 In a large saucepan or deep-sided frying pan, pour in the oil to a depth of 2.5 cm (1 in) and heat to a moderate temperature on the BOILING PLATE. Shallow-fry the parsnip strips in batches until they're light golden and crisp. Drain on kitchen paper and sprinkle lightly with salt. Arrange the strips in six little piles on a baking sheet, then sprinkle with half the Parmesan cheese and the remaining chorizo. Set aside.

6 Cook Parmesan Crisps on the grid shelf on the floor of the ROASTING OVEN for 2-3 minutes or until the cheese begins to melt. Don't let the crisps become too brown or they will taste bitter. Meanwhile, reheat the soup. Serve topped with the Parmesan Crisps, sprinkled with remaining Parmesan cheese and dusted with paprika.

COOK'S TIP
To prepare ahead, complete to the end of step 5 up to one day in advance. Cool, cover and chill soup; chill the crisps, uncovered. To use, complete the recipe.

Tomato and Harissa Soup with Coriander Cream

PREPARATION TIME:
20 MINUTES

COOKING TIME:
30 MINUTES

FREEZING:
COMPLETE TO THE
END OF STEP 2,
THEN COOL, PACK
AND FREEZE. THAW
AT COOL ROOM
TEMPERATURE
OVERNIGHT.
REHEAT THE SOUP
AND COMPLETE
THE RECIPE.

215-170 CALS PER
SERVING

MAKES 2.8 LITRES
(5 PINTS);
SERVES 8-10

This is a delicious hot and spicy winter soup with a fragrant whipped cream topping. Harissa is a chilli paste often used in North African cooking.

90 ml (6 tbsp) oil
450 g (1 lb) onion, finely chopped
4 garlic cloves, crushed
20 ml (4 level tsp) ground cumin
10 ml (2 level tsp) harissa
30 ml (2 level tbsp) tomato paste
2 x 400 g cans chopped plum tomatoes in tomato juice
2.5 cm (1 in) fresh ginger, grated
10 ml (2 level tsp) caster sugar

2 litres (3⅓ pints) light vegetable or chicken stock
salt and freshly ground black pepper
200 ml (7 fl oz) double cream
90 ml (6 level tbsp) roughly chopped fresh coriander
coriander sprigs and crushed black pepper, to garnish
warm naan bread, to accompany

1 Heat the oil in a saucepan and cook the onion gently on the SIMMERING PLATE for 5 minutes or until soft but not coloured. Add the garlic and cumin, cook for 30 seconds, then add the harissa and tomato paste and fry for 1 minute. Add the tomatoes, ginger, sugar and stock. Season and bring to the boil, then cook gently in the SIMMERING OVEN for 20 minutes.

2 Allow the mixture to cool a little. Place in a blender and process until smooth. Sieve, then return the soup to the pan. Bring to the boil and season again.

3 Lightly whip the cream, then season and fold in coriander. To serve, spoon the cream on top of the soup, garnish and accompany with warm naan bread.

COOK'S TIP
To prepare ahead, complete to the end of step 2, then cool, cover and chill for up to two days. To use, reheat the soup and complete the recipe.

Spiced Beef and Noodle Soup

PREPARATION TIME:
10 MINUTES

COOKING TIME:
10 MINUTES

FREEZING:
UNSUITABLE

190 CALS PER
SERVING

SERVES 4

This hearty soup takes its influence from fragrant Asian flavours. If you cannot find lemon grass, add grated lemon rind and juice to taste.

30 ml (2 tbsp) oil
225 g (8 oz) fillet steak, cut into thin strips
1.1 litres (2¼ pints) beef stock
30 ml (2 tbsp) Thai fish sauce
15 g (½ oz) dried porcini or shiitake mushrooms, broken into pieces and soaked in 150 ml (¼ pint) boiling water for 15 minutes
1 large red chilli, de-seeded and finely chopped
1 stick lemon grass, trimmed and thinly sliced

2.5 cm (1 in) piece root ginger, peeled and finely chopped
6 spring onions, halved lengthways and cut into 2.5 cm (1 in) lengths
1 garlic clove, crushed
1.25 ml (¼ level tsp) caster sugar
50 g (2 oz) medium egg noodles
125 g (4 oz) spinach leaves, roughly chopped
60 ml (4 level tbsp) chopped fresh coriander
freshly ground black pepper

1 Heat the oil in a large saucepan on the BOILING PLATE, brown the meat in two batches and set aside. Pour the stock into the pan with the Thai fish sauce, mushrooms and their soaking liquor, chilli, lemon grass, ginger, spring onions, garlic and sugar. Bring to the boil.

2 Break the noodles up slightly and add to the pan, then stir gently until they begin to separate. Cook in the SIMMERING OVEN for 4-5 minutes or until the noodles are just tender.

3 Stir in the spinach, coriander and steak and bring to the boil. Adjust the seasoning, adding a little more Thai fish sauce if necessary. Serve in warmed bowls.

Jerusalem Artichoke Soup

PREPARATION TIME:
15 MINUTES

COOKING TIME:
1½ HOURS

FREEZING: SUITABLE

370 CALS PER
SERVING

SERVES 6

Jerusalem artichokes now come in an easy-to-peel shape – the knobbly, awkward vegetable of the past is now as easy to tackle as a carrot!

175 g (6 oz) onions
50 g (2 oz) celery
900 g (2 lb) Jerusalem artichokes
125 g (4 oz) carrots
125 g (4 oz) butter
1 garlic clove

300 ml (½ pint) dry white wine
1 sachet bouquet garni
salt and freshly ground black pepper
142 ml (5 fl oz) carton double cream
thyme sprigs, to garnish
French bread and goat's cheese, to serve

1 Chop onions and celery; peel and chop the artichokes and carrots. Melt the butter in a large saucepan, add onions and crushed garlic; cook on the SIMMERING PLATE for 2 minutes. Add the remaining vegetables and cook in the SIMMERING OVEN for 20 minutes.

2 Add the wine, bring to the boil on the BOILING PLATE and simmer until reduced by half. Add 1.1 litres (2 pints) water and the bouquet garni. Return to the boil, then cook in the SIMMERING OVEN for about 1 hour or until the vegetables are soft.

3 Cool slightly. Remove the bouquet garni and blend the soup in a liquidiser until smooth.

4 To serve, reheat gently in a pan, season and add half the cream. Spoon into bowls and drizzle with remaining cream. Serve with sliced French bread spread with goat's cheese and cooked on a baking tray on the top shelf of the ROASTING OVEN for 5-7 minutes until just golden. Garnish with thyme.

Chicken Soup with Garlic and Parmesan Croûtons

PREPARATION TIME:
30 MINUTES

COOKING TIME:
ABOUT 2½ HOURS

FREEZING: SUITABLE
(SOUP ONLY)

385 CALS PER
SERVING

SERVES 6

A wonderfully warming, spicy soup to make in advance and then reheat for a hearty lunch after a cold winter walk.

1 small chicken, about 1 kg (2 lb), cut into pieces	**75 g (3 oz) butter**
300 ml (½ pint) dry white wine	**2 garlic cloves, crushed**
a few peppercorns	**4 thick slices white bread**
1-2 red chillies	**45 ml (3 level tbsp) freshly grated Parmesan**
2 bay leaves	**75 g (3 oz) dried pasta shapes**
2 rosemary sprigs	**1 cos lettuce, finely shredded**
1 celery stalk, roughly chopped	**30 ml (2 level tbsp) chopped freshly parsley**
4 carrots	**salt and freshly ground black pepper**
3 onions	

1 Put the chicken pieces in a saucepan in which they fit snugly. Add the wine, peppercorns, chillies, bay leaves, rosemary and celery. Roughly chop 3 carrots; quarter 2 onions. Add to the pan with about 900 ml (1½ pints) cold water to almost cover the chicken. Bring to the boil, then cover and transfer to the SIMMERING OVEN for 2 hours.

2 Meanwhile, mix together 50 g (2 oz) softened butter and one garlic clove in a small bowl. Remove crusts from the bread, spread with the garlic butter and sprinkle with Parmesan. Cut into squares; place on a lightly greased baking sheet, spacing them a little apart. Bake on the grid shelf on the floor of the ROASTING OVEN for 5-7 minutes until just golden, then crispen in the SIMMERING OVEN for 10-15 minutes.

3 Leave the chicken to cool slightly, then transfer the chicken to a plate and strain the stock. When cool enough to handle, remove the chicken from the bones and tear into bite-size pieces; set aside.

4 Return the stock to the pan. Bring back to the boil, add the pasta and cook on the floor of the SIMMERING OVEN for 5 minutes.

5 Meanwhile, cut remaining carrot into fine matchsticks; chop remaining onion.

6 Melt 25 g (1 oz) butter in a small pan. Add the onion and the remaining garlic clove; cook on the SIMMERING PLATE for 5 minutes until softened. Add the carrot and cook for 2 minutes. Add to the stock and pasta; cook for 5 minutes. Stir in the chicken, lettuce and parsley. Heat gently, stirring, until lettuce has wilted. Season to taste.

7 Serve the chicken soup accompanied by the hot garlic and Parmesan croûtons.

Roasted Onion and Coconut Soup

PREPARATION TIME:
25 MINUTES

COOKING TIME:
1 HOUR 40
MINUTES

FREEZING:
UNSUITABLE

420 CALS PER
SERVING

SERVES 6

The unusual combination of roasted onions, red chillies and spices makes this a lovely party soup for winter entertaining.

4 large onions, about 1.1 kg (2½ lb), peeled and halved

10 ml (2 tsp) olive oil

3 large red chillies

6 garlic cloves, unpeeled

52.5 ml (½ level tsp) cumin seeds

900 ml (1½ pints) vegetable or chicken stock

2 stems of lemon grass

3 kaffir lime leaves

salt and freshly ground black pepper

2 x 400 ml cans coconut milk

FOR THE JAMAICAN SALSA

1 small banana (optional)

250 g (8 oz) plum tomatoes, quartered, de-seeded and finely chopped

1 green chilli, de-seeded and finely chopped

finely grated rind and juice of a lime

30 ml (2 level tbsp) chopped fresh coriander

coriander, finely sliced red chilli and coconut milk, to serve

1 Place the onions in a roasting tin and drizzle with oil. Cook on the floor of the ROASTING OVEN for 20-30 minutes or until brown. Add chillies, garlic and cumin seeds, cover with foil and cook on the bottom runners of the ROASTING OVEN for 40 minutes or until onions are soft. Leave to cool.

2 Peel, halve and de-seed the chillies; discard seeds. Squeeze the pulp from garlic and discard the skins. Process the chillies, garlic and onions until smooth. Transfer the onion purée to a pan, add stock, lemon grass and lime leaves. Season and bring slowly to the boil, cover and cook gently in the SIMMERING OVEN for 30 minutes.

3 For the salsa, chop the banana (if using) into small pieces. Mix with the plum tomatoes, green chilli, lime rind and juice and coriander.

4 Remove the lemon grass and lime leaves from the soup and discard. Stir in the coconut milk and heat gently. Serve soup with a spoonful of salsa, garnished with coriander, sliced chilli and a drizzle of coconut milk.

Pasta and Chickpea Soup with Pesto

PREPARATION TIME:
25 MINUTES

COOKING TIME:
ABOUT 1 HOUR

FREEZING:
UNSUITABLE

370 CALS PER
SERVING

SERVES 6

Pasta and chickpeas provide excellent contrasting textures in this robust soup. You can use borlotti beans instead of chickpeas or replace half the stock with an equal quantity of tomato juice if you wish.

45 ml (3 tbsp) olive oil

1 onion, chopped

2 garlic cloves, finely chopped

1 small leek, sliced

15 ml (1 level tsp) chopped fresh rosemary

397 g (14 oz) can chickpeas

1.2 litres (2 pints) vegetable stock

4 ripe tomatoes, skinned and chopped

1 courgette, diced

125 g (4 oz) shelled peas

125 g (4 oz) French beans

125 g (4 oz) shelled broad beans

50 g (2 oz) dried pastina (small soup pasta)

30 ml (2 tbsp) chopped fresh parsley

salt and freshly ground black pepper

ready-made pesto

freshly grated pecorino or Parmesan, to serve

1 Heat the oil in a large saucepan, add the onion, garlic, leek and rosemary and fry on the SIMMERING PLATE for 5-6 minutes or until softened but not coloured. Add the chickpeas with their liquid, the stock and tomatoes. Bring to the boil, cover and simmer on the floor of the SIMMERING OVEN for 40 minutes.

2 Add the courgette, peas, halved French beans and the shelled broad beans. Return to the boil, then cook on the SIMMERING PLATE for 10 minutes. Add pasta and parsley and cook in the SIMMERING OVEN for 6-8 minutes until al dente. Season to taste.

3 Serve topped with a spoonful of pesto and a sprinkling of cheese.

Quick Mussel
and Smoked Haddock Chowder

PREPARATION TIME:
5 MINUTES

COOKING TIME:
10 MINUTES

FREEZING:
UNSUITABLE

375 CALORIES PER
SERVING

SERVES 4

Prepared very easily with vacuum-packed mussels, this robust and aromatic soup makes a most satisfying lunch on a cold day.

1 large onion, diced
1 large carrot, diced
30 ml (2 tbsp) virgin olive oil
300 g (11 oz) Finnan haddock on the bone or 200 g (7 oz) smoked haddock fillet
600 ml (1 pint) milk
400 g can flageolet beans, drained and rinsed

4 tomatoes, chopped
500 g (1 lb 2 oz) vacuum packet of cooked mussels in garlic butter
salt and freshly ground black pepper
60 ml (4 tbsp) parsley, chopped, or snipped chives
hot, crusty bread, to serve

1 Place the onion, carrot and olive oil in a large saucepan on the SIMMERING PLATE and lay the haddock on top, skin side up. Cover with a lid and cook for 5 minutes, until the vegetables are pale golden and the skin and bones separate from the fish. Uncover the pan and set aside to cool for 1-2 minutes, then lift off and discard the skin and bones.

2 Lightly flake the fish, add the milk to the saucepan and bring to the boil on the BOILING PLATE. Add the drained beans and the tomatoes, plus the entire contents of the packet of mussels. Bring to a fast boil for 1-2 minutes, season to taste, then sprinkle with the herbs and serve with hot, crusty bread.

COOK'S TIPS
To prepare ahead, complete to the end of step 1, cool and chill for up to 24 hours. To use, complete the recipe.

Vacuum-packed mussels are widely available and take all the hassle out of making this soup. Use an empty pair of shells as 'tweezers' to pick the mussels out of their shells.

QUICK MUSSEL AND
SMOKED HADDOCK
CHOWDER

Tuscan Bean Soup with Toasted Garlic

PREPARATION TIME:
20 MINUTES, PLUS
OVERNIGHT
SOAKING

COOKING TIME:
ABOUT 2 HOURS

FREEZING:
SUITABLE

330 CALS PER
SERVING

SERVES 6

A substantial white bean soup from Tuscany. Sliced garlic is fried in olive oil until golden, then poured over the soup at the last moment. It is often served as a main course ladled over toasted country bread. If the soup is thicker than you like, thin it down with a little extra water or stock.

225 g (8 oz) dried white haricot or cannellini beans, soaked overnight in cold water
4 garlic cloves, peeled

150 ml (¼ pint) olive oil
salt and freshly ground black pepper
15-30 ml (1-2 tbsp) chopped fresh parsley (optional)

1 Drain the beans and place in a flameproof casserole. Cover with cold water to a depth of 5 cm (2 in) above the beans. Bring to the boil, cover tightly and bake in the SIMMERING OVEN for about 2 hours or until tender (see Cook's Tip). Keep them in their cooking liquid.

2 Meanwhile, finely chop half the garlic and thinly slice the remainder. Heat half the olive oil in a frying pan, add the chopped garlic and fry gently on the SIMMERING PLATE until soft and golden.

3 Transfer half of the beans and liquid to a food processor or blender and process until smooth. Add this purée to the beans in the casserole and stir well.

4 Cook gently on the SIMMERING PLATE for 10 minutes. Taste and season well with salt and pepper. Pour into a warmed tureen or individual soup bowls.

5 Heat the remaining olive oil in the frying pan on the BOILING PLATE and fry the sliced garlic until golden. Meanwhile, pour the soup into a warmed tureen or individual bowls. Spoon the garlic over the soup and serve at once, sprinkled with chopped parsley if preferred.

COOK'S TIP
The cooking time depends on the freshness of the beans. Older beans will take longer to cook. Begin testing them after 1½ hours.

Broccoli and Goat's Cheese Soup

PREPARATION TIME:
10 MINUTES

COOKING TIME:
20 MINUTES

FREEZING: OMIT
THE GARLIC AND
MAKE THE SOUP TO
STEP 4; FREEZE.
THAW THE SOUP
AND RETURN TO
THE BOIL; ROAST
THE GARLIC.

150 CALORIES PER
SERVING

SERVES 6

This is a delicious green soup. Double the quantity of goat's cheese if you prefer a stronger taste, or substitute a soft garlic cheese such as Boursin for a really garlicky flavour. This soup is also good served with croûtons.

700 g (1½ lb) broccoli
50 g (2 oz) butter
2 medium onions, chopped
1 litre (1¾ pints) vegetable, chicken or turkey stock

1 head of garlic, separated into cloves (see Cook's Tips)
15 ml (1 tbsp) olive oil
150 g (5 oz) goat's cheese
salt and freshly ground black pepper

1 Break the broccoli into small florets. Peel the thick skin off the stout stalks and discard. Chop up the stalks.

2 Melt the butter in a saucepan on the SIMMERING PLATE, add the onion, then cover the pan and cook for 4-5 minutes until translucent. Add half the stock, bring to the boil on the BOILING PLATE. Add the broccoli and return to the boil, then cover and transfer to the SIMMERING OVEN for 15-20 minutes or until the broccoli is tender.

3 Toss the cloves of garlic in the oil and tip into a roasting tin. Roast on the second runners of the ROASTING OVEN for 15 minutes until soft when squeezed.

4 Cool the soup slight, then add the goat's cheese and purée in a food processor (see Cook's Tips). Return the soup to the pan and add the remaining stock. Bring the soup to the boil on the BOILING PLATE and season to taste.

5 Squeeze the garlic out of its skin and scatter over the soup.

COOK'S TIPS

The roasted garlic is optional but quite delicious.

Always purée soups in a food processor with a minimum amount of liquid for efficiency. If using a blender, more liquid is required. You can leave the soup slightly chunky if you wish.

Cheesy Leek Soup

PREPARATION TIME:
15 MINUTES

COOKING TIME:
40 MINUTES

FREEZING:
UNSUITABLE

375 CALS PER
SERVING

MAKES 2 LITRES;
SERVES 6

This hearty soup can be made in minutes, using up any leftover hard cheese. At any time of the year, but especially at Christmas, it's a good idea to have plenty of garnishes in the storecupboard, like the Oven-baked Pesto Croûtons (see below), for livening up soups and salads or for topping steamed green vegetables, such as broccoli, courgettes and beans.

700 g (1½ lb) trimmed leeks
225 g (8 oz) onions
225 g (8 oz) Stilton or Gruyère cheese
50 g (2 oz) butter
15 ml (1 level tbsp) plain flour
1.4 litres (2½ pints) turkey or chicken stock (see Aga Tip)

142 ml (5 fl oz) carton double cream
10 ml (2 level tsp) grainy mustard
salt and freshly ground black pepper
Oven-baked-Pesto Croûtons, to accompany (see below)
shavings of Stilton, to garnish (see Cook's Tips)

1 Roughly chop the leeks and finely chop the onions. Cut the cheese into small dice.
2 Melt the butter in a large saucepan, add the onion and cook on the SIMMERING PLATE for 5 minutes or until soft. Add the leeks, cover the pan and cook on the BOILING PLATE for 5 minutes, stirring from time to time.
3 Add the flour and mix until smooth, stirring continuously, then add the stock. Bring to the boil, then transfer to the floor of the SIMMERING OVEN for 15 minutes.
4 Stir in the cream and mustard. Add the cheese in batches, allowing it to melt between each addition. Season well with salt and pepper and serve in warmed soup bowls. Accompany with Oven-baked Pesto Croûtons and garnish with shavings of Stilton.

COOK'S TIPS

To prepare ahead, complete the recipe. Cool the soup quickly, cover and refrigerate. To use, warm the soup through gently in a saucepan and heat the croûtons in the SIMMERING OVEN for 10-15 minutes.

To make Stilton shavings, chill a small wedge of Stilton then, using a 'swivel' vegetable peeler, shave off thin slivers. Store in a single layer on a baking sheet in the fridge until ready to use.

AGA TIP

To make stock from a cooked carcass, break it into pieces and place in a large pan with cut-up root vegetables to add flavour. Cover with cold water, bring slowly to the boil, skim and add 5 ml (1 level tsp) black peppercorns and two bay leaves. Cook in the SIMMERING OVEN, covered, overnight, then strain and cool quickly. Store, covered, for up to two days in the fridge.

Oven-baked Pesto Croûtons

Cut four slices of day-old bread into 2.5 cm (1 in) cubes. Toss the cubes in 45-60 ml (3-4 level tbsp) ready-made pesto mixed with 15 ml (1 tbsp) olive oil in a polythene bag. Tip into a small roasting tin lined with foil. Cook on the grid shelf on the floor of the ROASTING OVEN for about 8 minutes until golden, then transfer to the SIMMERING OVEN for 10-15 minutes until crisp. Store in an airtight container for up to two days.

FISH AND SHELLFISH

Creamy Fish Gratin with Soufflé Topping

PREPARATION TIME:
30 MINUTES

COOKING TIME:
1 HOUR 20
MINUTES

FREEZING:
COMPLETE THE
RECIPE TO THE END
OF STEP 2; COOL,
WRAP AND FREEZE.
THAW, COMPLETE
THE RECIPE,
COOKING FOR
1 HOUR 50
MINUTES.

630 CALS PER
SERVING

SERVES 6

In this dish, a creamy sauce made with fish stock covers flakes of salmon, monkfish, scallops and prawns. As a cheaper alternative, try cod, haddock, smoked fish or shelled mussels. The soufflé topping is also superb spooned over roasted vegetables and cooked for 50 minutes. If you can't find curly kale, use broccoli, spring greens or spinach.

150 g (5 oz) butter
1 medium leek, roughly chopped
300 ml (½ pint) fish stock (see Cook's Tips)
300 ml (½ pint) vermouth
60 ml (4 tbsp) Pernod (see Cook's Tips)
350 g (12 oz) each monkfish and salmon fillet, cut into large pieces
225 g (8 oz) raw prawns, peeled and de-veined
225 g (8 oz) raw scallops, halved
2 medium onions, chopped
100 g (3½ oz) plain flour

142 ml (5 fl oz) carton double cream
salt and freshly ground black pepper
450 ml (¾ pint) milk
75 g (3 oz) each Parmesan and Gruyère cheese, grated
15 ml (1 level tbsp) Dijon mustard
4 large eggs, separated
15 g (½ oz) coarse breadcrumbs
700 g (1½ lb) curly kale, trimmed of any tough stalks
fresh dill sprigs, to garnish

1 Melt 25 g (1 oz) butter. Add the leeks and cook, stirring, on the BOILING PLATE for 2-3 minutes or until golden. Pour in stock, vermouth and Pernod; bring to the boil. Add monkfish and salmon; simmer for 2-3 minutes. Add prawns and scallops; simmer for another 3 minutes. Place fish and leeks in a 2.3 litre (4 pint) deep ovenproof dish, reserving the liquor.

2 Add 50 g (2 oz) butter and the onions to the pan; cook for 10 minutes or until soft and golden. Stir in 50 g (2 oz) flour; cook for another 1 minute. Pour in reserved poaching liquor and the cream, whisking to prevent lumps forming, then bring to the boil and bubble hard on the BOILING PLATE for 5-6 minutes; season, then pour the hot sauce over the fish. Set aside while you make the topping.

3 For the soufflé, melt 50 g (2 oz) butter in a large pan, add remaining flour and cook, stirring for 1 minute. Pour in the milk and, whisking continuously, bring the mixture to the boil; season. Stir in 125 g (4 oz) grated cheeses and the mustard. Cover the pan tightly to prevent a skin forming; cool slightly; stir in the egg yolks. Season well.

4 Whisk whites to a soft peak. Fold into the sauce. Spoon the soufflé topping over the fish; sprinkle with remaining cheeses and the breadcrumbs.

5 Cook on the grid shelf on the floor of the ROASTING OVEN for 50-55 minutes or until the soufflé has risen and the fish is piping hot (see Cook's Tips). Place the cold plain shelf above the soufflé if it browns before it is cooked.

6 Just before the end of the cooking time, cook the kale in boiling and salted water for 1-2 minutes. Drain, toss in remaining butter and season. Serve with the gratin, garnished with dill.

COOK'S TIPS
If you have any ouzo or Pastis lurking at the back of your cupboard, use it instead of Pernod.

CREAMY FISH GRATIN WITH SOUFFLÉ TOPPING

To test if the gratin is cooked, insert a skewer into the fish mixture. Leave for 30 seconds. The skewer should be hot to the touch.

As a variation, omit the soufflé topping and serve the fish mixture in a shallow pie dish topped with puff pastry, cooked in the ROASTING OVEN for 15-20 minutes.

The young, the elderly, pregnant women and those suffering from immune-deficiency diseases should not eat raw or lightly cooked eggs, to avoid the risk of salmonella.

Cod Fillet with a Herb Crust and Roast Leeks

PREPARATION TIME:
10 MINUTES

COOKING TIME:
20 MINUTES

FREEZING:
UNSUITABLE

340 CALS PER
SERVING

SERVES 4

This is a wonderfully quick and easy recipe. You can use other fish such as salmon or monkfish to ring the changes.

450 g (1 lb) leeks
15 ml (1 tbsp) olive oil
50 g (2 oz) fresh breadcrumbs
1 pot of fresh parsley (leaves and stems), chopped
1 pot of fresh coriander (leaves and stems), chopped
1 garlic clove, finely chopped

finely grated rind of ½ lemon
50 g (2 oz) butter
salt and freshly ground black pepper
4 x 175 g (6 oz) thick cod fillets, skin removed
90 ml (6 tbsp) white wine
15 ml (1 level tbsp) chopped fresh parsley for the sauce

1 Trim most of the green part from the leeks and discard. Cut the white part diagonally into 2.5 cm (1 in) lengths. Toss in the oil, season and place in a small roasting tin.

2 Mix together the breadcrumbs, parsley, coriander, garlic and lemon rind. Melt 25 g (1 oz) of the butter, stir into breadcrumb mixture and season.

3 Place the cod fillets in a lightly buttered large ovenproof dish. Spread the herb and breadcrumb mixture on top, covering the surface of the fish.

4 Roast the leeks for 15-20 minutes on the second runners of the ROASTING OVEN until just tender. Bake the fish for 8-10 minutes in the ROASTING OVEN until the fish is firm and just cooked.

5 Spoon any juices from the fish into a small pan with the wine and place on the BOILING PLATE to reduce slightly. Meanwhile, return the fish to the SIMMERING OVEN to complete cooking, adding the leeks to the dish when ready. Remove the sauce from the heat and whisk in the butter. Stir in the parsley and serve the sauce immediately with the fish and roasted leeks.

COOK'S TIP
To prepare ahead, complete to the end of step 3. Cover and chill for up to 6 hours. To use, complete the recipe.

Spiced Red Mullet

PREPARATION TIME:
5 MINUTES, PLUS
10 MINUTES
SOAKING

COOKING TIME:
20 MINUTES

FREEZING:
UNSUITABLE

415 CALS PER
SERVING

SERVES 4

These sweet and spicy Moroccan flavours complement the red mullet perfectly.

4 x 125 g (4 oz) red mullet fillets, scaled and small bones removed
salt and freshly ground black pepper
5 ml (1 level tsp) cumin seeds
75 ml (5 tbsp) olive oil
225 g (8 oz) onion, halved and cut into petals

2 garlic cloves, crushed
150 g (5 oz) couscous
50 g (2 oz) raisins
150 ml (¼ pint) orange juice
flat-leafed parsley, to garnish

1 With a sharp knife, slash the skin side of the red mullet fillets two or three times. Season and press on the cumin seeds, then set aside.

2 Heat 45 ml (3 tbsp) oil in a large frying pan and fry the onion on the BOILING PLATE for 3 minutes or until brown and soft. Add the garlic and fry for 1 minute, then remove and set aside. Meanwhile, soak the couscous according to the packet instructions, cover and place in the SIMMERING OVEN. Wipe out the pan and heat 30 ml (2 tbsp) oil. Fry the fish for about 3 minutes on each side. Remove and keep warm in the SIMMERING OVEN.

3 Add the raisins and orange juice to the pan, bring to the boil and bubble for 2-3 minutes or until lightly syrupy. Fork the onion through the soaked couscous and season. Serve the red mullet with the couscous and orange sauce, garnished with parsley.

AGA TIP

Pre-soaking couscous allows it to cook more quickly. It is usually steamed for 20-25 minutes, but this oven cooking method is far more suitable for the Aga as it conserves heat. The couscous is also less likely to become lumpy.

Fettucine with Spicy Seafood Sauce

PREPARATION TIME:
10 MINUTES

COOKING TIME:
40 MINUTES

FREEZING:
UNSUITABLE

345 CALS PER
SERVING

SERVES 4

This delicious Italian dish is one you can indulge in without piling on the pounds.

I red onion
I red pepper
I red chilli
15 ml (1 tbsp) olive oil
I fat clove garlic
2.5 ml (½ level tsp) ground coriander
2.5 ml (½ level tsp) ground cumin
15 ml (1 level tbsp) sun-dried tomato paste

150 ml (5 fl oz) red wine
2 x 397 g cans chopped tomatoes
salt and freshly ground black pepper
350 g (12 oz) cooked prawns
175 g (6 oz) dried tagliatelle or 350 g (12 oz) fresh
chopped fresh parsley, to garnish

1 Slice the onion. De-seed and finely chop the pepper and chilli. To make the sauce, heat the oil in a large, non-stick saucepan. Add the onion, pepper, chilli and crushed garlic. Cover and cook on the SIMMERING PLATE for about 7 minutes or until the onion begins to soften. Add the spices and tomato paste; cook for 1-2 minutes.

2 Pour in the wine and bring to the boil, then bubble to reduce by half. Add the tomatoes then seasoning and cook, uncovered, on the grid shelf on the floor of the ROASTING OVEN for about 30 minutes or until the sauce is reduced and thickened. Add the prawns and heat through for 1-2 minutes only. Season to taste.

3 Bring the pasta to the boil in a pan of salted water, then transfer to the SIMMERING OVEN until just tender. Drain well.

4 Stir the sauce through the pasta to serve. Garnish with chopped fresh parsley.

AGA TIP

Cooking pasta in the SIMMERING OVEN ensures it does not boil over and create a mess.

PASTA WITH SMOKED HADDOCK AND SPINACH

FISH TAGINE WITH COUSCOUS

Pasta with Smoked Haddock and Spinach

Pasta dishes are all-time family favourites. This one combines a really tasty fish and one of the healthiest vegetables to give a nutritious meal in a moment.

PREPARATION TIME:
10 MINUTES

COOKING TIME:
ABOUT 15 MINUTES

FREEZING:
UNSUITABLE

370 CALS PER
SERVING

SERVES 4

225 g (8 oz) pasta shapes
450 g (1 lb) smoked haddock, skinned
freshly ground black pepper
15 g (½ oz) butter
450 g (1 lb) baby spinach
142 ml (5 fl oz) carton soured cream

30 ml (2 level tbsp) fresh chives, snipped
15 ml (1 level tbsp) lemon juice
salt
pinch of nutmeg
lemon wedges, to serve

1 Bring the pasta to the boil in a large pan of water, then transfer to the SIMMERING OVEN for the time given on to the packet instructions. Season the haddock with black pepper, then slice diagonally into 4 cm (1½ in) pieces.
2 Meanwhile, melt the butter in a large frying pan, add the haddock and cook on the SIMMERING PLATE for about 4-5 minutes.
3 Drain the pasta. Place the spinach in the pan and cook on the SIMMERING PLATE for 1-2 minutes or until just wilted. Return the pasta to the pan, then stir in the soured cream, chives, lemon juice, salt and nutmeg and stir well. Gently stir the haddock into the pasta and serve immediately with lemon wedges.

Fish Tagine with Couscous

PREPARATION TIME:
30 MINUTES

COOKING TIME:
1 HOUR 30 MINUTES

FREEZING:
UNSUITABLE

569-420 CALS PER
SERVING

SERVES 6-8

A supper dish full of the aromatic, spicy flavours characteristic of North Africa. The word 'tagine' refers to the clay dish in which the stew is cooked.

**FOR THE HARISSA CHILLI PASTE
(SEE COOK'S TIPS)**
3 large red chillies
2 large garlic cloves, peeled
15 ml (1 level tbsp) ground coriander
30 ml (2 level tbsp) cumin seeds
large pinch saffron threads
grated rind and juice of 1 lemon
30 ml (2 tbsp) olive oil

FOR THE TAGINE
1.1 kg (2½ lb) firm fish fillets, such as monkfish or cod, skinned and cut into large chunks
450 g (1 lb) aubergines, cubed
120 ml (8 tbsp) olive oil, plus extra for drizzling

900 g (2 lb) onions, roughly chopped
400 g can chopped plum tomatoes
500 g carton passata (see Cook's Tips)
200 ml (7 fl oz) fish stock (see Cook's Tips)
125 g (4 oz) pitted green olives
salt and freshly ground black pepper
30 ml (2 level tbsp) chopped fresh coriander
30 ml (2 level tbsp) chopped fresh flat-leaf parsley
coriander leaves, to garnish

FOR THE COUSCOUS
350 g (12 oz) couscous
60 ml (4 level tbsp) chopped fresh mint

1 To make chilli paste, place the chillies on a baking sheet and roast in the middle of the ROASTING OVEN for 10 minutes. Cool, peel and de-seed the chillies. Place in a processor with the next six ingredients. Pulse to a fine paste.

2 To make the tagine, place the fish in a bowl with 30 ml (2 level tbsp) chilli paste. Toss the fish in the paste, then cover the bowl and chill. Leave to marinate while you make the sauce.

3 Halve the aubergine, score it with the point of a knife, sprinkle with salt and leave for 20 minutes. Squeeze out the juices, drizzle with oil and place cut side down in a roasting tin. Cook on the floor of the ROASTING OVEN for 20-25 minutes until golden underneath.

4 Heat 45 ml (3 tbsp) of the olive oil in a heatproof casserole and cook the onions on the BOILING PLATE for 10 minutes until golden brown. Add remaining chilli paste and cook for a further 5 minutes. Chop the aubergines and add to the onions, then mix in chopped tomatoes, passata and stock. Bring to the boil, then simmer in the SIMMERING OVEN for 30 minutes.

5 Add the marinated fish to the casserole and then the green olives, spoon some of the sauce over the fish. Season, cover and cook on the grid shelf in the ROASTING OVEN for a further 15-20 minutes. The fish should be white rather than opaque when cooked. Season to taste.

6 Place the couscous in a bowl. Pour 450 ml (¾ pint) boiling water over, cover and leave to soak, according to packet instructions, in the SIMMERING OVEN. Season, fork in the mint and drizzle with olive oil. Stir the coriander and parsley into the tagine, garnish and serve immediately with the warm couscous.

COOK'S TIPS
This recipe uses traditional home-made harissa chilli paste, but you could substitute ready-made instead. Passata is sieved tomatoes. If you can't find it, use another can of chopped tomatoes.

Some supermarkets sell fresh fish stock, but it's simple to make. Place 450 g (1 lb) fish bones, such as sole or cod, in a large pan with a medium onion, quartered, a bouquet garni, 5 ml (1 level tsp) peppercorns, 1 litre (1¾ pints) water and a glass of white wine. Bring slowly to the boil; simmer on the SIMMERING PLATE for 20-30 minutes, strain and use as required. (Store, covered, in a fridge for up to two days; in a freezer for up to three months.) You may also use fish stock cubes.

To prepare ahead, complete the recipe to the end of step 4. Quickly cool the sauce. Cover and chill the sauce and fish separately for up to 24 hours. To use, bring the sauce to the boil and bubble for 3-4 minutes. Complete the recipe from step 5. The fish may be spicier if marinated overnight.

Prawn and Lemon Risotto

PREPARATION TIME:
15 MINUTES

COOKING TIME:
40 MINUTES

FREEZING:
UNSUITABLE

370 CALS PER
SERVING

SERVES 4

This satisfying dish is very low on calories but is bound to fill you up.

**225 g (8 oz) sugar-snap peas, sliced
diagonally**
**175 g (6 oz) baby courgettes, sliced
diagonally**
salt and freshly ground black pepper
30 ml (2 tbsp) olive oil
1 onion, finely chopped
**1.25 ml (¼ level tsp) saffron strands
(optional)**
225 g (8 oz) arborio (risotto) rice

1 garlic clove, crushed
**225 g (8 oz) brown-cap mushrooms,
quartered**
juice and rind of 1 lemon
**750 ml (1¼ pints) hot fish, chicken or
vegetable stock**
300 g (11 oz) cooked, peeled prawns
45 ml (3 level tbsp) finely chopped chives
**spring onion curls (see Cook's Tips) and
grated lemon rind, to garnish**

1 Place the sugar-snap peas and courgettes in a pan of boiling salted water, then bring to the boil. Cook for 1-2 minutes on the BOILING PLATE, then drain and plunge into ice-cold water.

2 Heat the olive oil in a medium, non-stick saucepan, then add the onion and saffron strands, if using. Cook on the SIMMERING PLATE for 2-3 minutes or until soft. Add the rice, garlic and mushrooms and cook, stirring for 1-2 minutes; season.

3 Add the grated lemon rind and about one-third of the stock (see Cook's Tips). Bring to the boil, cover and transfer to the SIMMERING OVEN for 5 minutes until most of the liquid has been absorbed. Add another one-third of the stock, then repeat the process.

4 Add the remaining stock. Cook as before or until the rice is tender and most of the stock has been absorbed. Add the prawns, drained vegetables, 15-30 ml (1-2 tbsp) lemon juice and the chives, then heat in the SIMMERING OVEN for 3-4 minutes. Garnish with spring onion curls and grated lemon rind to serve.

COOK'S TIPS
To make spring onion curls, thinly slice the onions lengthways, soak in ice-cold water for 30 minutes, then drain.

Adding the stock gradually to the rice gives the risotto its creamy texture.

Puff-Topped Seafood

PREPARATION TIME:
20 MINUTES

COOKING TIME:
15 MINUTES

FREEZING:
UNSUITABLE

570 CALS PER
SERVING

SERVES 4

You can use any variety of mixed fish and shellfish for this quick and easy dish.

**225 g (8 oz) mixed raw seafood, such as
squid rings and prawns (see Aga Tip)**
**125 g (4 oz) salmon fillet, cut into small
cubes**
125 g (4 oz) cooked, shelled mussels
30 ml (2 tbsp) double cream
salt and freshly ground black pepper

flour, for dusting
375 g (12 oz) ready-rolled puff pastry
**40 g (1½ oz) herb and garlic butter (see
Cook's Tips)**
1 large beaten egg to glaze

1 Mix the seafood, salmon and mussels with the cream and season. On a lightly floured worksurface, roll out the ready-rolled pastry a little more thinly. Using the top of a 450 ml (¾ pint) ovenproof bowl as a guide, cut out four circles at least 5 mm (¼ in) bigger all round.

2 Divide the seafood between four 450 ml (¾ pint) ovenproof bowls and top with the herb and garlic butter. Brush the rim of each bowl and 5 mm (¼ in) down the outside with beaten egg. Place a pastry circle on top of each bowl and press it down the sides. Make a steam hole in the centre and glaze the pastry with beaten egg.

3 Bake in the middle of the ROASTING OVEN for 12-15 minutes until the pastry is well risen and golden. Serve immediately.

COOK'S TIPS
To prepare ahead, complete up to the end of step 2, 3-4 hours in advance. Chill. To use, complete the recipe.

For home-made garlic butter, beat 40 g (1 ½ oz) softened butter with two crushed garlic cloves and 15 ml (1 level tbsp) chopped fresh herbs, such as parsley or chives.

AGA TIP
Packs of frozen mixed seafood are an excellent standby to keep in the freezer and, like the pastry, take only one hour to thaw when placed near the warmth of the Aga.

Provençal Fish Fillets

PREPARATION TIME:
20 MINUTES

COOKING TIME:
15 MINUTES

FREEZING:
UNSUITABLE

425 CALS PER
SERVING

SERVES 4

Fast, fresh and very good for you, fish dishes such as this one are the ideal food to cook when you are in rather a hurry.

225 g (8 oz) shallots	100 ml (4 fl oz) oil
50 g (2 oz) butter	100 ml (4 fl oz) medium dry white wine
5 ml (1 level tsp) caster sugar	300 ml (½ pint) fish stock
375 g (12 oz) young leeks, finely sliced on the diagonal	125 g (4 oz) cherry tomatoes, halved or quartered
salt and freshly ground black pepper	75 g (3 oz) pitted black olives
4 x 125 g (4 oz) fish fillets, such as plaice, skinned	flat-leafed parsley and slices of lemon, to garnish

1 Place the shallots in a pan of water, bring to the boil and cook on the BOILING PLATE for 5 minutes. Drain and plunge into cold water. Trim the ends, peel off skins and dry well.
2 Heat 25 g (1 oz) butter in a frying pan, add the shallots and sugar and cook on the SIMMERING PLATE for 5 minutes or until golden. Add the leeks and cook for 4-5 minutes until just soft. Set aside.
3 Season the fish with salt and pepper. Heat the oil and remaining butter in the pan. Fry the fish on the BOILING PLATE for 3 minutes on each side or until golden (see Cook's Tip). Remove and keep warm in the SIMMERING OVEN.
4 Pour the wine into the pan, bring to the boil and bubble on the BOILING PLATE until the liquid is reduced by half. Add the stock, return to the boil and bubble for 10 minutes or until syrupy. Add the tomatoes and olives and bubble for 1 minute, then return the shallots and leeks to the pan to warm through; season. Garnish with parsley and slices of lemon and serve.

COOK'S TIP
The fish is easier to fry if it is lightly dusted with plain flour, but the fish won't look as golden. Cooking over a high heat means the juices do not escape from the fish.

POULTRY & GAME

Chicken and Champ with Cherry Tomato Dressing

PREPARATION TIME:
10 MINUTES, PLUS
15 MINUTES
INFUSING

COOKING TIME:
40 MINUTES

FREEZING:
UNSUITABLE

550 CALS PER
SERVING

SERVES 4

The combination of champ (mashed potato made with onion-flavoured milk), chicken and the cherry tomato dressing makes this a great recipe for all the family.

3 garlic cloves, crushed
15 ml (1 level tbsp) caster sugar
45 ml (3 tbsp) balsamic vinegar
125 g (4 oz) cherry tomatoes, halved
salt and freshly ground black pepper
125 g (4 oz) spring onions, finely sliced

50 g (2 oz) butter
150 ml (¼ pint) milk
900 g (2 lb) large potatoes
4 chicken legs or breasts, with skin on
30 ml (2 tbsp) olive oil

1 In a bowl, whisk together the garlic, sugar and balsamic vinegar. Stir in the tomatoes and seasoning; set aside.

2 Place the spring onions, butter and milk in a small pan, bring to boil on the BOILING PLATE, then cover and place at the front of the SIMMERING OVEN for 15 minutes to infuse. Cut potatoes into even-sized pieces and place in a pan of salted water. Bring to a fast boil on the BOILING PLATE, then pour away all but 1 cm (½ in) of the water. Cover the pan and cook the potatoes at the back of the SIMMERING OVEN until tender. Drain, dry and mash. Beat in the flavoured hot milk mixture and season. Keep warm.

3 Season the chicken. Heat the oil in a large heavy-based frying pan, add the chicken and cook skin-side down on the BOILING PLATE for 6-7 minutes. Turn over and cook for a further 6-7 minutes or until golden. Transfer to the SIMMERING PLATE until they are cooked right through to the centre. Add the tomato mixture; bubble for 2-3 minutes (see Cook's Tips).

4 To serve, arrange the chicken breasts on top of the champ, then spoon the tomatoes and juices over.

COOK'S TIPS
To prepare ahead, complete the recipe to the end of step 2 up to 6 hours ahead; cover and chill the dressing and champ separately. To use, reheat the champ and complete the recipe.

If the tomato juices reduce too much, add a little water to the pan.

Chicken Casserole with Herb Dumplings

PREPARATION TIME:
50 MINUTES

COOKING TIME:
2½ HOURS

FREEZING:
SUITABLE,
WITHOUT THE
DUMPLINGS

295 CALS PER
SERVING

SERVES 6

Excellent for winter lunches, this casserole is similar to the French 'Pot au Feu' dishes, falling somewhere between a very satisfying soup and a main dish.

1.4 kg (3 lb) oven-ready chicken
225 g (8 oz) onions, roughly chopped
I medium carrot, roughly chopped
50 g (2 oz) celery, roughly chopped
I bay leaf
salt and freshly ground black pepper
15 ml (I tbsp) olive oil
900 g (2 lb) leeks, trimmed and thickly sliced

125 g (4 oz) self-raising flour
2.5 ml (½ level tsp) baking powder
50 g (2 oz) butter
15 ml (I level tsp) each chopped flat-leafed parsley and fresh thyme
125 g (4 oz) ready-to-eat pitted prunes
chopped fresh chives, to garnish
cooked baby carrots, to serve

1 Place the chicken in a pan. Add the onions, carrot, celery, bay leaf and 5 ml (I level tsp) salt. Add I litre (1¾ pints) cold water, bring to the boil, then cover and place on the floor of the SIMMERING OVEN for 2 hours or until the chicken is cooked.

2 Meanwhile, heat the oil and cook the leeks on the BOILING PLATE for 5-6 minutes or until lightly golden. Add to the casserole for the last 20 minutes of the cooking time.

3 Lift the chicken out of the pan and discard the skin and bones, roughly shred the meat and return to the saucepan with the stock.

4 Sift the flour, baking powder and a pinch of salt into a bowl. Rub in butter, then stir in the herbs and 60 ml (4 tbsp) water to make a soft dough, shape into twelve 2.5 cm (I in) balls. Place on a baking sheet lined with greaseproof paper and cook on the grid shelf on the floor of the ROASTING OVEN for 12-15 minutes or until golden.

5 Bring the casserole to the boil, season well, then add the prunes and simmer gently for 5 minutes. Garnish with chives and serve hot with the dumplings and carrots.

COOK'S TIPS
To prepare ahead, complete to the end of step 3, cool quickly and chill overnight. To use, complete the recipe.

For a thicker casserole, in step 5, after simmering the prunes mix 30 ml (2 tbsp) olive oil and 45 ml (3 tbsp) flour to a paste. Stir briskly into the casserole, return to the boil, garnish with the herbs and serve.

Chicken and Leek Pilaff

PREPARATION TIME:
15 MINUTES

COOKING TIME:
55 MINUTES

FREEZING:
UNSUITABLE

685 CALS PER
SERVING

SERVES 4

Ready-boned chicken thighs make this a very quick, economical and tasty supper dish.

45 ml (3 tbsp) vegetable oil
350 g (12 oz) skinless chicken thighs, cut into I cm (½ in) strips
225 g (8 oz) streaky bacon, cut into strips
4 medium-sized leeks, about 450 g (I lb), washed and thinly sliced
175 g (6 oz) small mushrooms, cut into quarters
5 ml (I level tsp) ground cumin

2.5 ml (½ level tsp) cayenne
30 ml (2 level tbsp) tomato paste
225 g (8 oz) easy-cook long grain rice
400 g can plum tomatoes, chopped
600-750 ml (1-1¼ pints) chicken stock
salt and freshly ground black pepper
30 ml (2 level tbsp) chopped fresh chives, plus fresh chives and fried leeks, to garnish

1 Heat the oil in a large deep frying pan or flameproof casserole. Add the chicken, season with black pepper and cook on the BOILING PLATE for 1-2 minutes. Add the bacon, and cook for 5 minutes. Add the leeks and mushrooms and continue to cook for another 5 minutes.

2 Stir in the spices and tomato paste and cook for 3-4 minutes, stirring frequently. Add the rice and cook, stirring, for 1 minute or until it turns opaque. Stir in the tomatoes, stock and seasoning. Bring to the boil, cover and cook in the SIMMERING OVEN for 30-35 minutes or until the rice is tender. (The amount of stock required depends on the absorbency of the rice you're using.) Add the chopped chives and more seasoning if necessary. Garnish with chives and leeks and serve.

Roast Chicken with Spiced Orange Sauce

PREPARATION TIME: 20 MINUTES, PLUS SOAKING TIME

COOKING TIME: 1 HOUR

FREEZING: UNSUITABLE

460 CALS PER SERVING

SERVES 6

This interesting yet easy to make Turkish recipe provides an excellent combination of spices and fruit.

45 ml (3 level tbsp) dried currants

juice of 4 large oranges, about 300 ml (½ pint) in total

salt and freshly ground black pepper

6 chicken portions, with skin, 1.1 kg (2½ lb) total weight

25 g (1 oz) butter

15 ml (1 tbsp) olive oil

225 g (8 oz) red onions, sliced into large petals

6 whole garlic cloves

15 ml (1 level tbsp) coriander seeds, roughly crushed

2 large red chillies, split and seeds removed

15 ml (1 level tbsp) honey

2 cinnamon sticks

50 g (2 oz) whole blanched almonds, toasted

2 small thin-skinned oranges, roughly chopped

450 ml (¾ pint) chicken stock

1 bunch fresh mint, tied

Minted Yoghurt, to accompany (see Cook's Tips)

1 Soak the currants in half the orange juice in a covered dish in the SIMMERING OVEN for 30-45 minutes. Season the chicken skin. Heat half the butter and oil in a shallow casserole on the BOILING PLATE; brown the chicken, adding remaining butter and oil as necessary (see Cook's Tips). Remove and set aside.

2 Add onions, garlic and coriander to the pan. Cook, stirring, on the SIMMERING PLATE for 5-7 minutes or until onions are lightly browned and soft. Add chillies, honey, cinnamon sticks, almonds, currants and soaking liquor, remaining orange juice, chopped oranges, stock and mint.

3 Bring to the boil, place chicken on top and cook, uncovered, on the grid shelf on the floor of the ROASTING OVEN for 30-40 minutes or until tender. Remove chicken and keep warm in the SIMMERING OVEN. Discard the mint, bring pan juices to the boil on the BOILING PLATE and bubble for 5 minutes or until syrupy. Adjust seasoning.

4 Serve chicken with the sauce and Minted Yogurt (see Cook's Tips).

COOK'S TIPS

To prepare ahead, complete the recipe to end of step 3 up to one day ahead, then cool, cover and chill. To use, return to the ROASTING OVEN for 10-15 minutes.

Browning the chicken in batches on both sides releases the fat from beneath the skin, leaving it appetisingly brown and crisp. Browning the meat will also help to give a more tender result to the finished dish.

For the Minted Yogurt accompaniment, combine 30 ml (2 level tbsp) chopped fresh mint and 200 ml (7 fl oz) Greek yogurt. Season well with salt and freshly ground black pepper to taste and garnish with fresh thyme or mint sprigs to serve. This can also be used to accompany any barbecued meats or fish.

Crisp Chicken Liver Risotto

PREPARATION TIME:
15 MINUTES

COOKING TIME:
40 MINUTES

FREEZING:
UNSUITABLE

885 CALS PER
SERVING

SERVES 4

The Aga is perfect for making a rich, creamy risotto with no fear of it sticking to the pan. The texture is beautifully contrasted with the crisp liver, bacon and salami. Follow Italian tradition and serve with a large bowl of salad.

225 g (8 oz) fresh chicken livers
50 g (2 oz) Italian salami, sliced
225 g (8 oz) streaky bacon rashers, thinly sliced
100 g (3½ oz) butter
225 g (8 oz) onions, roughly chopped
375 g (12 oz) risotto (arborio) rice
30 ml (2 level tbsp) tomato paste

1 litre (1¾ pints) chicken or vegetable stock
200 ml (7 fl oz) white wine
30 ml (2 level tbsp) finely chopped fresh rosemary
freshly grated Parmesan cheese, to serve
salt and freshly ground black pepper
rosemary sprigs, to garnish

1 Halve the chicken livers if very large. Place the salami and bacon in an even layer in a large roasting tin. Cook on the middle runners of the ROASTING OVEN for 15-20 minutes or until crisp and brown, then drain on kitchen paper.

2 Meanwhile, melt 25 g (1 oz) butter in a large pan, add the livers and fry briskly for 2-3 minutes on the BOILING PLATE. Drain and set aside, then wipe out the pan. Add the remaining butter to the pan and cook the onions for 5-7 minutes until soft. Stir in the rice and tomato paste and cook for 1 minute. Bring the stock and wine to the boil together and pour 2 ladlefuls of hot liquid into the rice. Stir vigorously for 30 seconds, then cover the pan and leave in the SIMMERING OVEN for 4-5 minutes. Add another 2 ladlefuls of liquid, boil and stir vigorously as before. Repeat this process until all the liquid is added – the risotto will become thick and creamy and the rice tender. Add more stock if the risotto looks dry (the amount needed may vary depending on the rice's absorbency).

3 To serve, discard any juices from the chicken livers, then add to the risotto with the chopped rosemary. Parmesan cheese, crisp salami, bacon and seasoning. Stir for 1 minute over the heat, then garnish with rosemary sprigs to serve immediately.

COOK'S TIP
You can also use duck, goose or turkey livers when they are available.

Chicken Breasts with Courgette and Herb Stuffing

PREPARATION TIME:
45 MINUTES, PLUS
10 MINUTES
STANDING

COOKING TIME:
40 MINUTES

FREEZING:
UNSUITABLE

395 CALS PER
SERVING

SERVES 6

Simple fresh ingredients can create inspired recipes. This particular chicken dish originates from Ireland's County Cork.

225 g (8 oz) courgettes, coarsely grated
sea salt and freshly ground black pepper
25 g (1 oz) butter
1 small onion, finely chopped
50 g (2 oz) cream cheese
50 g (2 oz) fresh breadcrumbs
1 large egg
25 g (1 oz) Parmesan cheese, grated

30 ml (2 level tbsp) chopped fresh herbs
6 chicken breasts, with skin
30 ml (2 tbsp) olive oil
100 ml (4 fl oz) white wine
450 ml (¾ pint) fresh chicken stock
fresh thyme and rosemary sprigs
tarragon and marjoram sprigs, to garnish
broccoli florets, to accompany

1 In a colander, sprinkle the courgettes with 5 ml (1 level tsp) salt, mix and leave to stand for 10 minutes. Rinse and pat dry. Melt the butter in a saucepan on the SIMMERING PLATE, add the onion and cook until soft; cool.

2 Whizz the courgettes, onion, cream cheese, 25 g (1 oz) breadcrumbs, egg, cheese and chopped herbs in a food processor. If the stuffing is a little too wet, add some more breadcrumbs; season.

3 Cut a pocket in each breast. Spoon in the stuffing and secure with a cocktail stick.

4 Heat the oil in a large roasting tin. Brown the chicken, skin side down, for 2-3 minutes on the BOILING PLATE, then turn and seal for 1 minute. Set aside. Pour wine into the tin, bring to the boil and scrape the sediment from the base of the tin. Add 150 ml (¼ pint) stock, thyme and rosemary; season. Bring to the boil.

5 Return chicken to the roasting tin, skin side up in a single layer. Cook on the bottom runners of the ROASTING OVEN for 15-20 minutes or until the juices run clear.

6 Slice the chicken and keep warm. Skim any fat from the liquid in the casserole, add the remaining stock, bring to the boil on the BOILING PLATE and bubble for 10 minutes or until syrupy. Spoon over the chicken, garnish with tarragon and marjoram and serve with steamed broccoli florets.

COOK'S TIP
To prepare ahead, complete the recipe to the end of step 3, wrap and chill overnight. To use, complete the recipe.

Chicken Roasted in a Lemon Vinaigrette

PREPARATION TIME:
10 MINUTES

COOKING TIME:
40 MINUTES

FREEZING:
UNSUITABLE

360 CALS PER
SERVING

SERVES 6

This is an excellent recipe to prepare ahead, ready to pop into the oven. The roasted lemon and shallots and the subtle flavour of balsamic vinegar give the dish a modern touch. This is good served with mashed potato to mop up the lemony sauce.

2 lemons
175 g (6 oz) shallots or onions
30 ml (2 tbsp) balsamic vinegar
30 ml (2 tbsp) sherry vinegar
60 ml (4 tbsp) runny honey

150 ml (5 fl oz) olive oil
6 chicken supremes or 12 boneless thighs, with skin
salt and freshly ground black pepper

1 Grate the rind and squeeze the juice from one lemon, then set aside. Thinly slice the remaining lemon, then peel and thickly slice the shallots. Scatter the lemon slices and shallots over the base of a small roasting tin.

2 Whisk together the grated lemon rind and juice, vinegars, honey and oil in a bowl. Place the chicken in the roasting tin, season generously and pour the lemon vinaigrette over.

3 Cook on the bottom runners of the ROASTING OVEN, basting regularly, for 35 minutes or until the chicken is golden and cooked through. Remove the chicken to a serving dish and keep warm in the SIMMERING OVEN. Place the roasting tin with juices on the SIMMERING PLATE. Bring to the boil and bubble for 2-3 minutes or until syrupy; spoon over the chicken.

COOK'S TIP
To prepare ahead, complete to end of step 2 up to one day ahead; refrigerate, covered, in a non-metallic dish as it is such an acidic mixture. Transfer the chicken to the roasting tin before cooking. To use, complete the recipe as from step 3.

Chicken and Artichoke Pie

PREPARATION TIME:
20 MINUTES

COOKING TIME:
45 MINUTES

FREEZING: SUITABLE

320 CALS PER
SERVING

SERVES 4

Lightly topped with a few scrunched up sheets of filo pastry, this pie is as delightful to look at as it is to eat.

3 skinless chicken breasts, about 350 g (12 oz)
150 ml (¼ pint) dry white wine
225 g (8 oz) reduced low-fat soft cheese with garlic and herbs
400 g can artichoke hearts in water (see Cook's Tips)

salt and freshly ground black pepper
4 sheets filo pastry, about 40 g (1½ oz)
olive oil
5 ml (1 level tsp) sesame seeds
fresh thyme, to garnish

1 Bring the chicken and wine to the boil in a pan on the BOILING PLATE. Cover, transfer to the SIMMERING PLATE and simmer for 10 minutes. Set chicken aside. Add the cheese to the wine and mix until smooth. Bring to the boil; simmer until thickened.

2 Cut the chicken into bite-sized pieces. Drain and quarter the artichokes; add to sauce with the chicken. Season and mix well. Place the mixture in a shallow ovenproof dish.

3 Brush the pastry lightly with oil, scrunch slightly and place on top of the chicken. Sprinkle with sesame seeds.

4 Cook on the grid shelf on the floor of the ROASTING OVEN for 30-35 minutes or until crisp. Check after 20 minutes and if the pastry is sufficiently brown, place the cold plain shelf above the pie, or transfer to the BAKING OVEN. Serve garnished with thyme.

COOK'S TIPS
To prepare ahead, complete to the end of step 2, cool quickly, then chill overnight. To use, complete the recipe.

When using filo pastry, thaw it in the fridge, then unroll, leaving the sheets stacked together to prevent them drying and becoming brittle.

If you wish, replace the artichoke hearts with 225 g (8 oz) brown cap mushrooms, cooked in a little water, seasoning and lemon juice.

This dish can be easily adapted to use up leftover cold turkey. Just boil the wine and cheese together, cool and then add the turkey and artichokes.

Guinea Fowl with Madeira and Spiced Oranges

PREPARATION TIME:
30 MINUTES

COOKING TIME:
2-2½ HOURS

FREEZING:
COMPLETE THE
RECIPE. COOL,
THEN PACK AND
FREEZE. THAW AT
COOL ROOM
TEMPERATURE
OVERNIGHT.
REHEAT AS IN
COOK'S TIPS.

600 CALS PER
SERVING

SERVES 6

Guinea fowl has a much meatier flavour than chicken and is the ideal meat to partner the spiced oranges. Vacuum-packed chestnuts are the easiest to use.

15 ml (1 tbsp) oil
25 g (1 oz) butter
6-8 guinea fowl joints or corn-fed chicken joints, 2 kg (4½ lb) total weight
225 g (8 oz) shallots or button onions, peeled, with the root end trimmed
225 g (8 oz) streaky bacon, cut into thin strips or lardons
4 tangerines, such as honey, halved, and the juice squeezed from one
50 g (2 oz) kumquats, halved
2.5 cm (1 in) piece fresh root ginger, peeled and coarsely grated

2 garlic cloves, crushed
30 ml (2 level tbsp) plain flour
300 ml (½ pint) Madeira
600 ml (1 pint) fresh chicken stock
1 cinnamon stick
45 ml (3 level tbsp) redcurrant jelly
200 g (7 oz) vacuum-packed chestnuts (optional)
chopped flat-leafed parsley, to garnish
couscous, to accompany

1 Heat the oil and butter in a deep flameproof casserole on the BOILING PLATE (see Cook's Tips). Add the guinea fowl or chicken joints in batches and cook until brown on the skin side before turning and browning on the other side. Remove with a slotted spoon and set aside. Add the shallots or button onions, bacon or lardons, halved tangerines and kumquats to the pan and cook, stirring, until brown. Stir in the ginger and garlic and cook for 1 minute.

2 Stir in flour, Madeira and stock. Return the joints to the casserole, then add the cinnamon stick, tangerine juice and redcurrant jelly.

3 Bring to the boil; cover and cook on the floor of the SIMMERING OVEN for 1½-1¾ hours or until tender. (Cooking time depends on thickness of the joints, not their weight, so return to the oven if necessary.)

4 Discard cinnamon stick. Lift guinea fowl out of the sauce onto a serving dish, cover with foil and return to the SIMMERING OVEN to keep warm. In a saucepan, bring the sauce to the boil, add chestnuts, if using, and bubble for 5-10 minutes on the SIMMERING PLATE or until reduced and syrupy. Pour over the guinea fowl, garnish and serve with couscous.

COOK'S TIPS
To prepare ahead, complete recipe. Cool, then cover and chill for up to one day. To use, place the guinea fowl and sauce in a flameproof casserole and reheat in the SIMMERING OVEN for 1 hour or until hot to the centre, then transfer to the ROASTING OVEN for 5-10 minutes.

If you don't have a large enough casserole, brown the guinea fowl, bacon and vegetables in a large frying pan and continue the recipe using a large roasting tin covered with foil.

Duck Breasts with Cinnamon Plum Sauce

PREPARATION TIME:
45 MINUTES, PLUS
AT LEAST 1 HOUR
MARINATING

COOKING TIME:
1 HOUR 10 MINUTES

FREEZING:
UNSUITABLE

SERVES 6

560 CALS PER
SERVING

This impressive dish is ideal for special occasion entertaining.

450 g (1 lb) red plums
2 small onions
duck breast fillets, about 1 kg (2¼ lb) total weight (see Cook's tips)
salt and freshly ground black pepper
3.75 ml (¾ level tsp) ground cinnamon
vegetable oil
300 ml (½ pint) red wine

25 g (1 oz) butter
2.5 ml (½ level tsp) caster sugar
20 ml (4 level tsp) redcurrant jelly
juice of 2 medium oranges
15 ml (1 tbsp) red wine vinegar
300 ml (½ pint) chicken stock
caramelised plum slices (see Cook's Tips) and thyme sprigs, to garnish

1 Reserve two plums for the garnish; halve and stone the others, then roughly chop; finely chop the onions. Using a sharp knife, remove the silvery membrane from the fleshy side of the duck breasts. Season with salt and pepper and sprinkle with 2.5 ml (½ level tsp) ground cinnamon. Turn over the duck breasts, score the skin side (to release its fat during cooking), rub with a little oil and sprinkle with salt. Place the duck, skin-side up, in a shallow, non-metallic dish and pour 150 ml (¼ pint) wine around. Leave uncovered in the fridge for at least 1 hour to marinate.

2 Heat the butter in a wide saucepan and cook the onions on the SIMMERING PLATE for 3-4 minutes. Add plums, sugar, redcurrant jelly, orange juice, red wine vinegar, stock, marinade from the duck and the remaining ground cinnamon and red wine. Bring to the boil and simmer in the SIMMERING OVEN for 15-20 minutes or until very soft and well reduced. Cool a little, then pour into a food processor and process until smooth; sieve and return to the clean saucepan.

3 Preheat a heavy non-stick frying pan and fry the duck breasts skin-side down, in batches, on the SIMMERING PLATE for 10-15 minutes until the fat runs and the skin is dark brown and crisp. Turn the breasts over and cook for a further 3-4 minutes (see Cook's Tips).

4 Using a slotted spoon, transfer the duck breasts, skin-side up, to a warmed serving dish. Cover loosely with foil and leave in the SIMMERING OVEN for 15 minutes so the flesh becomes evenly 'rosy'. Bring the plum sauce to the boil and bubble for 2-3 minutes.

5 To serve, slice the duck thickly, spoon the Cinnamon Plum Sauce around and garnish with caramelised plum slices and thyme sprigs.

COOK'S TIPS
If you can't find magret, use English duck breasts, each weighing about 75 g (6 oz). Whether you're using magrets or English duck breasts, allow an extra 5 minutes cooking time if you like your duck breasts cooked medium.

To caramelise plums, slice the two reserved plums and toss them in a bag containing 30 ml (2 tbsp) granulated sugar. Brush pieces of foil with duck fat. Lay the plums on the foil and place on the SIMMERING PLATE. Cook uncovered for 1-2 minutes until brown, then turn over and cook for a further minute.

Duck and Juniper Cassoulet

PREPARATION TIME:
1 HOUR, PLUS
OVERNIGHT
MARINATING

COOKING TIME:
ABOUT 3 HOURS

FREEZING:
COMPLETE RECIPE
AND FREEZE. THAW
AT ROOM
TEMPERATURE
OVERNIGHT; COOK
IN THE ROASTING
OVEN FOR 1 HOUR-
1 HOUR 10
MINUTES.

950 CALS PER
SERVING

SERVES 6

Cooked gently for a long time, this is worth the wait, especially on a chilly day. As with most stews, it's best made the day before so the flavours can develop.

6 juniper berries, crushed
6 duck legs, about 1.4 kg (3 lb) total weight
4 bay leaves
105 ml (7 tbsp) oil
9 garlic cloves, crushed
sea salt and freshly ground black pepper
450 g (1 lb) Toulouse sausages or any garlicky sausage
175 g (6 oz) whole piece of streaky bacon, rind removed and roughly chopped
700 g (1½ lb) tomatoes, preferably plum, peeled, quartered and de-seeded
30 ml (2 level tbsp) chopped fresh thyme, plus 3 sprigs

350 g (12 oz) each onions, carrots and celery, peeled and roughly chopped
1 bottle white wine
900 ml (1½ pints) chicken stock, preferably home-made (see Cook's Tips)
30 ml (2 level tbsp) tomato paste
420 g can each white haricot beans and cannellini beans, drained and rinsed
2 sprigs fresh rosemary or 5 ml (1 level tsp) dried
225 g (8 oz) coarse rustic breadcrumbs
sea salt for sprinkling and rosemary sprigs, to garnish

1 Rub the juniper berries over the duck legs, then scatter the bay leaves on top and pour 60 ml (4 tbsp) oil over. Stir in six of the crushed garlic cloves, then season with sea salt and black pepper. Cover and marinate overnight in the fridge.

2 Place the marinated duck legs in a roasting tin with the oil and seasonings from the marinade. Cook on the top runners of the ROASTING OVEN for 15 minutes. Cut the sausages in half and add to the duck with the bacon. Cook for a further 30 minutes. Set aside, spooning off and reserving the fat.

3 Combine the tomatoes and chopped thyme in a large bowl. Toss the onions, carrots and celery in the remaining oil and cook in another roasting tin on the floor of the ROASTING OVEN for 30 minutes or until golden. Add the tomatoes and chopped thyme, then cook for a further 15 minutes and season.

4 Add the white wine to the vegetables, bring to the boil on the BOILING PLATE, then return to the floor of the ROASTING OVEN for 20 minutes. Add the stock and tomato purée to the vegetables, reduce on the SIMMERING PLATE for 5-10 minutes, then stir in the beans. Spoon into a 2.8 litre (5 pint) casserole dish. Season to taste.

5 Tuck the duck legs into the beans, vegetables and sauce. Scatter the sausages and bacon over, then add sprigs of thyme and rosemary. Combine the remaining garlic and reserved fat with the breadcrumbs.

6 Sprinkle breadcrumbs over the cassoulet and cover.

■■ Cook for 1½ hours in the SIMMERING OVEN, then uncover and cook for 45 minutes on the grid shelf on the floor of the ROASTING OVEN or until the topping is crisp and the duck tender.

■■■■ Cook for 1 hour in the BAKING OVEN, then uncover and cook for a further hour or until the topping is crisp and the duck tender.
Garnish with salt and rosemary.

COOK'S TIPS
To make your own stock, place 1.6 kg (3½ lb) chicken, duck or turkey bones in a large saucepan with 225 g (8 oz) each carrots, celery and leeks. Pour in enough cold water to cover, add a bouquet garni and 5 ml (1 level tsp) peppercorns. Cook in the SIMMERING OVEN overnight, then strain. Cool quickly, pour into ice cube trays, freeze and store in plastic bags in the freezer for up to three months.

To prepare ahead, complete recipe, cool quickly, cover and chill. From chilled, cook on the grid shelf on the floor of the ROASTING OVEN with the cold plain shelf above or in the middle of the BAKING OVEN for 45 minutes or until heated through and bubbling.

Game Pie with Rosemary and Juniper Crust

PREPARATION TIME:
I HOUR

COOKING TIME:
2½-5 HOURS, PLUS
I HOUR

FREEZING:
COMPLETE STEP 8
AND FREEZE. THAW
FOR 12 HOURS IN
THE FRIDGE, THEN
STAND FOR I HOUR
AT ROOM
TEMPERATURE
BEFORE BAKING AS
IN STEP 9.

685-585 CALS PER
SERVING

SERVES 12-14

Juniper, rosemary and game make a perfect combination, and once you have made this delicious pastry crust, you will wonder why pastry is sometimes so boring. This pie is ideal for feeding a crowd for lunch.

4 dressed pheasant
15 ml (I tbsp) oil
200 g (7 oz) smoked streaky bacon, roughly chopped
12 medium onions, chopped
500 ml (¾ pint) robust red wine
75 g (2½ oz) game dripping or butter
300 g (12 oz) mushrooms, wiped and quartered
75 g (5 tbsp) flour
salt and freshly ground black pepper

FOR THE PASTRY
350 g (12 oz) plain flour
175 g (6 oz) butter
25 g (I oz) white vegetable fat
30 ml (2 tbsp) juniper berries, crushed
15 ml (I tbsp) dry English mustard
30 ml (2 tbsp) fresh rosemary, chopped
5 ml (I tsp) salt

I Pluck any remaining feathers from the pheasant. Heat the oil in a large pan on the BOILING PLATE. Brown the pheasant on all sides, two at a time. Lift them out and set aside when they are a good colour.

2 Add the bacon and onion to the pan and cook briskly on the BOILING PLATE until coloured, then pour on the wine and 500 ml (¾ pint) water. Return the pheasant to the pan, bring to the boil, cover and transfer to the SIMMERING OVEN for 2-4 hours until tender – this will depend on the age of the birds (see Cook's Tips).

3 Pour the contents of the pan into a small roasting tin and strain the juices back into the large pan. Allow the birds to cool sufficiently to handle with ease. Skim any game dripping from the surface of the stock and reserve.

4 Strip the meat from the birds. Place the meat back in the roasting tin with onions and bacon. Place the bones and skin in the pan of game stock. Bring the stock to the boil on the BOILING PLATE, then cover and transfer to the ROASTING OVEN for 20 minutes or the SIMMERING OVEN for I hour. Strain stock, measure and make up to I litre (1¾ pints) with water.

5 Heat the dripping or butter in a separate saucepan, add mushrooms and fry on the BOILING PLATE without stirring until golden on one side, shake the pan and allow to colour again.

6 Remove the pan from the heat. Stir the flour into the mushrooms, then pour in the measured stock. Bring to the boil, then simmer for 3-5 minutes. Season to taste, then pour over the meat. Cover with foil and leave to cool.

7 To make the pastry, combine all the ingredients in a food processor and process to the texture of large crumbs. If making by hand, rub the fat into the flour and stir in the remaining ingredients. Gather into a ball.

8 Roll out the pastry to fit the top of the roasting tin plus 1.5 cm (¾ in) all around. Trim off the edge. Moisten the top edge of the roasting tin with water and stick the cut-off strips of pastry around the tin edge. Moisten this pastry, then top with the large sheet of pastry. Trim any edges and pinch to flute the border.

9 Brush with beaten egg and bake on the grid shelf on the floor of the ROASTING OVEN for 30 minutes, turning halfway through the cooking time to ensure even colouring. Transfer to the SIMMERING OVEN for ½-I hour before serving, so the pie is very hot and the flavours mingle.

COOK'S TIPS
To prepare ahead, complete the pie to the end of step 8 and chill for 24 hours. To use, bake as in step 9.

Two 2 kg (4½ lb) chickens may be used instead of the pheasant.

GAME PIE WITH
ROSEMARY AND
JUNIPER CRUST

Venison and Cranberry Daube

PREPARATION TIME:
1 HOUR, PLUS
MARINATING

COOKING TIME:
ABOUT 2 HOURS 30
MINUTES

FREEZING:
COMPLETE STEP 5.
COOL QUICKLY,
PACK AND FREEZE.
THAW OVERNIGHT
AT COOL ROOM
TEMPERATURE.
PLACE THE
CASSEROLE ON THE
GRID SHELF ON THE
FLOOR OF THE
ROASTING OVEN
FOR 30-40 MINUTES
UNTIL PIPING HOT.
COMPLETE STEP 6.

490 CALS PER
SERVING

SERVES 6

Marinating overnight and long, slow cooking ensure that the venison is melt-in-the-mouth tender as well as giving the final dish its distinctive flavour.

1 kg (2¼ lb) stewing venison (see Cook's Tips)

FOR THE MARINADE
1 medium onion
1 medium carrot
stick of celery
5 ml (1 level tsp) black peppercorns
2 oranges
4 garlic cloves
15 ml (1 level tsp) dried thyme
75 ml (3 fl oz) olive oil

FOR THE DAUBE
450 g (1 lb) shallots or button onions
30 ml (2 tbsp) oil
75 g (3 oz) butter
45 ml (3 level tbsp) flour
100 ml (4 fl oz) red wine vinegar
30 ml (2 level tbsp) redcurrant jelly
300 ml (½ pint) port
300 ml (½ pint) beef stock (see Cook's Tips)
salt and freshly ground black pepper
1 fresh bay leaf, plus extra to garnish
125 g (4 oz) dried cranberries
roasted root vegetables, to accompany

1 Cut venison into 4 cm (1½ in) cubes. For the marinade, roughly dice the onion, carrot and celery. Roughly crush the peppercorns. Finely grate the rind and squeeze the juice of the oranges; reserve the juice. Place venison in a bowl with the vegetables, rind, peppercorns, crushed garlic, thyme and olive oil. Cover; refrigerate overnight.

2 Heat the oil in a large flameproof casserole, add 25 g (1 oz) butter and the shallots and fry on the SIMMERING PLATE until golden. Set to one side. Brown the venison in small batches in the same casserole on the BOILING PLATE. Cover the pan with a splatterguard to protect yourself and the cookertop. No further fat should be required. Set to one side when browned.

3 Add the marinade vegetables to the pan with the remaining butter and cook until shrivelled. Add the flour and cook, stirring continuously, for 2-3 minutes until brown. Add the vinegar, redcurrant jelly, port, stock and reserved marinade; bring to the boil and bubble for 1-2 minutes.

4 Return the venison and any venison bones to the pan. Season and add one bay leaf. Bring to simmering point and cover tightly.

▓▓ Cook on the grid shelf on the floor of the ROASTING OVEN for 25 minutes.

▓▓▓▓ Cook on the grid shelf on the floor of the BAKING OVEN for 30 minutes.

5 Add reserved shallots, orange juice and cranberries. Transfer to the SIMMERING OVEN for 2½-3 hours or until very tender (see Cook's Tips).

6 Remove the casserole from the oven and adjust seasoning if necessary. Discard the bay leaf and any bones. Garnish with fresh bay leaves and serve accompanied by roasted root vegetables.

COOK'S TIPS

To prepare ahead, prepare to the end of step 5. Cool and chill overnight, then reheat as in the freezing instructions.

Buy a whole piece of venison, either shoulder or haunch, so you can cut it into generous cubes. Reserve any bones to add to the casserole for extra flavour.

To remove skin from the shallots, pour over boiling water to cover and leave for 5-10 minutes. Drain and remove the skin (it should peel away easily). To prevent shallots from falling apart, just trim the root end rather than removing it completely.

Be prepared to be adaptable with the amount of cooking time required, as this will depend on the cut of venison, whether it is farmed or wild, and for how long it has been hung. It is wise, therefore, to cook in advance and reheat.

Pheasant with Cider and Apples

PREPARATION TIME:
50 MINUTES

COOKING TIME:
2½ HOURS

FREEZING:
UNSUITABLE

675-510 CALS PER
SERVING

SERVES 6-8

Usually pheasants are hung to improve flavour and tenderise the meat, but this can vary from bird to bird; generally, the older the pheasant, the longer the cooking time. If you prefer, you can ask your butcher to cut the pheasant into portions for you.

225 g (8 oz) onions
275 g (10 oz) celery
4 eating apples, eg Granny Smith
15 ml (1 tbsp) lemon juice
15 ml (1 level tbsp) dried juniper berries
2.5 cm (1 in) piece fresh root ginger
2 pheasants, each weighing about 700 g (1½ lb)
salt and freshly ground black pepper
30 ml (2 level tbsp) flour, plus extra for dusting

50 g (2 oz) butter
4 streaky bacon rashers
300 ml (½ pint) chicken stock
2 x 440 ml cans dry cider
142 ml (5 fl oz) carton double cream
fried apple wedges, thyme sprigs and juniper berries, to garnish
Potato 'Spiders' to serve (see below)

1 Chop the onions and celery. Quarter, core and cut the apples into large pieces, then toss in the lemon juice. Lightly crush the juniper berries. Peel and finely chop the ginger.

2 Cut each pheasant into four portions, then season and dust lightly with flour. Melt the butter in a large, flameproof casserole and brown the pheasant pieces in batches on the BOILING PLATE until deep golden brown. Remove and keep warm.

3 Place the bacon rashers in the casserole and cook on the BOILING PLATE for 2-3 minutes or until golden. Add the onions, celery, apples, juniper and ginger. Cook for 4-5 minutes. Stir the 30 ml (2 level tbsp) flour into the vegetables and cook for a further 2 minutes, then add the stock and cider and bring to the boil.

4 Return the pheasant to the casserole and cover.
■■ Cook on the floor of the SIMMERING OVEN for 1½-2 hours or until tender.
■■■■ Cook on the grid shelf on the floor of the BAKING OVEN for 45 minutes-1 hour or until tender.

5 Lift the pheasant out of the sauce and keep it warm in the SIMMERING OVEN. Strain the sauce through a sieve and return it to the casserole with the cream. Bring to the boil and bubble on the SIMMERING PLATE for 10-15 minutes or until syrupy. Return the pheasant to the sauce and season.

6 To serve, garnish the pheasant with fried apple wedges, thyme sprigs and juniper berries and accompany with Potato 'Spiders' (see below).

COOK'S TIP
To prepare ahead, complete to the end of step 5, cool quickly, cover and chill for up to two days. To use, reheat in the BAKING OVEN for 20-25 minutes or in the SIMMERING OVEN for 40-45 minutes.

Potato 'Spiders'

Peel and cut 700 g (1½ lb) floury baking potatoes into long, very thin sticks, then dry well in a clean tea-towel. Fry in clumps in 4 cm (1½ in) hot oil in a deep pan on the BOILING PLATE. Drain the 'Spiders' well on absorbent kitchen paper and season to taste.

MEAT DISHES

Roast Pork with Apple and Saffron Chutney

PREPARATION TIME:
20 MINUTES, PLUS
COOLING

COOKING TIME:
1 HOUR 30 MINUTES,
PLUS 20 MINUTES
RESTING

FREEZING:
UNSUITABLE

530 CALS PER
SERVING

SERVES 8

Traditional roast pork is given a lift with apple and saffron chutney, making it an ideal dish for a Sunday lunch with a difference.

30 g (1¼ oz) butter
75 g (3 oz) caster sugar
2 large Cox's orange pippin apples, 350 g (12 oz), peeled, cored and roughly diced
75 ml (5 tbsp) cider vinegar
pinch of saffron threads
100 g (3½ oz) dried cranberries
50 g (2 oz) sultanas

350 g (12 oz) pumpkin, peeled and diced
½ red chilli, de-seeded and finely chopped
2.3 kg (5 lb) loin pork, boned, skin finely scored (choose a thin, narrow joint)
salt
chopped flat-leafed parsley and saffron threads, to garnish

1 To make the chutney, melt the butter and sugar in a heavy-based saucepan on the SIMMERING PLATE until golden. Add the next seven ingredients and cook, stirring, on the BOILING PLATE until caramelised. Add 30 ml (2 tbsp) water and cook in the SIMMERING OVEN for 5-8 minutes. Set the chutney aside to cool.

2 Slit the pork lengthways, almost through the muscle, and open out. Place two-thirds of the chutney down the middle and roll up. Tie joint at intervals with string, but not too tightly. Reserve the leftover chutney.

3 Place the pork in a roasting tin and sprinkle the skin generously with salt, then cook on the bottom runners of the ROASTING OVEN for 1¼ hours. Add the reserved chutney to the roasting tin for last 10 minutes of cooking time, then remove pork from oven, cover loosely and rest in the SIMMERING OVEN for 20 minutes. Slice the pork thickly and garnish with parsley and saffron threads.

COOK'S TIP

To prepare ahead, complete the recipe to end of step 2. Cover and chill separately for up to 24 hours ahead. To use, remove pork from fridge 30 minutes before cooking, then complete recipe.

Sweet and Sour Spiced Pork

PREPARATION TIME:
30 MINUTES, PLUS
15 MINUTES
CHILLING

COOKING TIME:
50 MINUTES

FREEZING:
UNSUITABLE

490 CALS PER
SERVING

SERVES 4

Succulent, full of flavour and with less fat than chicken, pork is the perfect meat for family suppers and informal dinner parties. Inspired by classic Chinese cookery, this combination of chilli, ginger and plum sauce is delicious.

2 garlic cloves
1.1 kg (2½ lb) boneless loin of pork, rind removed
1 large red chilli
2.5 cm (1 in) piece root ginger
150 ml (¼ pint) plum sauce (see Cook's Tips)

15 ml (1 tbsp) dark soy sauce
5 ml (1 level tsp) Chinese five-spice powder
30 ml (2 tbsp) oil
½ cucumber, 5 spring onions and 1 red chilli, to garnish

1 Thinly slice the garlic; trim the fat side of the loin of pork and lightly bat out (see Cook's Tips). Turn the loin over and, using a small sharp knife, make deep slits in the meat then insert the slices of garlic. De-seed and finely chop the chilli; peel and finely chop the ginger. Place in a bowl with 15 ml (1 tbsp) water, plum sauce, soy sauce and Chinese five-spice powder.

2 Heat the oil in a small roasting tin on the BOILING PLATE and brown the meat, fat side down, for 5 minutes. Turn over and brown the other side for 2-3 minutes. Brush the surface of the pork with a little of the plum sauce mixture. Cook on the grid shelf on the floor of the ROASTING OVEN for about 40 minutes. Baste the pork occasionally, brushing with some of the plum sauce mixture (see Cook's Tips) until the fat has caramelised and the pork is cooked.

3 For the garnish, cut the cucumber in half lengthways, remove the seeds with a teaspoon and discard, then cut the flesh into thin matchsticks. Cut the trimmed spring onions into similar-sized thin strips. De-seed the red chilli and cut into very fine matchsticks. Place the cucumber and onion in a large bowl of ice-cold water for about 15 minutes until the spring onions begin to curl. Drain and dry well.

4 Lift the pork from the roasting tin, cover loosely with foil and place in the SIMMERING OVEN to keep warm. Tilt the roasting tin and skim off fat. Add the remaining plum sauce mixture to the juices in the roasting tin, bring to the boil on the SIMMERING PLATE and simmer for 1-2 minutes.

5 To serve, thickly slice the pork, spoon the sauce around it and garnish with the cucumber spring onions and chilli.

COOK'S TIPS
To prepare ahead, up to one day ahead, complete to the end of step 1; cover and chill the pork and plum sauce mixture separately. Prepare the cucumber and spring onion together as in step 3, cover and chill. To use, remove the pork from the fridge 30 minutes before cooking to bring it back to room temperature – this ensures that the cooking time is accurate. Complete the recipe.

Cover the pork with a sheet of greaseproof paper and flatten with a rolling pin to a thickness of about 6.5 cm (2½ in) – any more and the pork will take longer to cook.

Take care not to brush too much plum sauce on the pork in the roasting tin as it may burn the base.

Pork Steaks with Sage and Apple

PREPARATION TIME:
5 MINUTES

COOKING TIME:
10 MINUTES

FREEZING:
UNSUITABLE

380 CALS PER
SERVING

SERVES 4

This recipe is loosely based on the traditional Italian dish of saltimbocca, which includes veal, prosciutto (Parma ham), sage and white wine. It is good served with an accompaniment of curly kale and buttered parsnips.

4 pork shoulder steaks, about 150 g (5 oz) each
4 thin slices Parma ham or pancetta, about 50 g (2 oz), (see Cook's Tips)
6 fresh sage leaves
freshly ground black pepper

15 ml (1 tbsp) oil, if necessary
150 ml (¼ pint) pure, unsweetened apple juice (see Cook's Tips)
50 g (2 oz) chilled butter, diced
squeeze of lemon juice

1 Halve any large steaks. Lay a slice of Parma ham or pancetta on top with a sage leaf, then secure to the meat with a wooden cocktail stick. Season with pepper.

2 Heat the oil in a shallow frying pan or non-stick frying pan (don't add oil if using non-stick) and fry the pork steaks on the BOILING PLATE for about 3-4 minutes on each side until they are golden brown.

3 Pour in apple juice – it will sizzle and start to evaporate immediately. Scrape the bottom of the pan to loosen any crusty bits and let the liquid bubble until reduced by half. Lift the pork out on to a warm dish.

4 Return the frying pan to the BOILING PLATE, add the butter and swirl it around. When it has melted into the pan juices, add some lemon juice and pour this sauce over the pork steaks before serving.

COOK'S TIPS
Thinly sliced pancetta is an Italian bacon with a great flavour and is well worth trying. Once found only in delis, it's now much more widely available – you'll find it beside the pre-packed hams in supermarkets.

Pure unsweetened apple juice makes a great substitute for white wine in many recipes if you don't wish to use alcohol. Choose a juice with a sharp, clean flavour.

Pork and Spinach Pots with a Brioche Crust

PREPARATION TIME:
20 MINUTES

COOKING TIME:
50 MINUTES

FREEZING:
COMPLETE TO END
OF STEP 6 AND
FREEZE. THAW AT
ROOM
TEMPERATURE AND
BAKE ON THE GRID
SHELF OF THE
ROASTING OVEN
FOR 20 MINUTES
UNTIL PIPING HOT
AND GOLDEN
BROWN.

435 CALS PER
SERVING

SERVES 4

This is a good comfort dish for wintry weather! Try to buy the best-quality mince you can find for a richer, fuller flavour.

50 g (2 oz) ready-to-eat dried apricots
125 g (4 oz) onions
15 ml (1 tbsp) oil
2 garlic cloves
450 g (1 lb) minced pork
5 ml (1 level tsp) ground cinnamon
10 ml (2 level tsp) ground coriander
45 ml (3 tbsp) Worcestershire sauce
300 ml (½ pint) tomato juice
1 beef stock cube
15 ml (1 level tbsp) sun-dried tomato paste

salt and freshly ground black pepper
50 g (2 oz) slice of brioche loaf or roll
50 g (2 oz) Emmenthal or Gruyère cheese
30 ml (2 level tbsp) chopped fresh chives
300 g (11 oz) frozen leaf spinach, thawed
15 g (½ oz) butter
30 ml (2 tbsp) double cream
grating of nutmeg
thyme sprigs and crushed black peppercorns, to garnish

1 Finely chop the dried apricots; roughly chop the onions.

2 Heat the oil in a medium-sized covered saucepan or flameproof casserole with the onion and

48

crushed garlic on the SIMMERING PLATE for 3-4 minutes or until beginning to soften. Uncover, add the mince, transfer to the BOILING PLATE and cook for 5 minutes, stirring continuously, or until the mince is golden brown.

3 Add the ground cinnamon and coriander, then cook the mixture for 1 minute. Add the chopped apricots, Worcestershire sauce, tomato juice, stock cube, sun-dried tomato paste, 150 ml (¼ pint) water and plenty of seasoning to taste. Bring to the boil, cover and transfer to the SIMMERING OVEN for 1 hour.

4 Meanwhile, roughly break the brioche up into coarse crumbs. Coarsely grate the cheese and mix with the brioche, chives and plenty of seasoning.

5 Squeeze as much liquid as you can from the spinach. Heat the butter in a shallow saucepan on the BOILING PLATE, add the spinach and stir with the cream until hot and wilted. Season to taste with salt and pepper and a good grating of nutmeg.

6 Divide the spinach among four 200 ml (7 fl oz) capacity ovenproof dishes, spoon the pork mixture over and roughly sprinkle with the brioche crumb mixture.

7 Place on a baking sheet and cook on the grid shelf on the floor of the ROASTING OVEN for 10 minutes or until golden brown. Garnish with thyme sprigs and crushed black pepper.

COOK'S TIP

To prepare up to one day ahead, complete to the end of step 6, cover and chill. To use, complete the recipe, allowing an extra 10 minutes cooking time.

Mustard and Peppered Beef Stroganoff

A great dish if you're suddenly faced with unexpected guests. If you can't find shiitake mushrooms, use brown-cap or flat mushrooms instead.

PREPARATION TIME:
10 MINUTES

COOKING TIME:
15 MINUTES

FREEZING: SUITABLE

575 CALS PER SERVING

SERVES 4

350 g (12 oz) rump steak, cut into thick strips
freshly ground black pepper
15 ml (1 level tbsp) mustard seeds, roughly ground
125 g (4 oz) unsalted butter
225 g (8 oz) shiitake mushrooms, quartered if large
60 ml (4 tbsp) brandy

200 ml carton crème fraîche
5 ml (1 tsp) anchovy essence
30 ml (2 level tbsp) wholegrain mustard
30 ml (2 level tbsp) chopped fresh tarragon
pasta shapes, such as fiorelli, to serve
roughly chopped chives, to garnish

1 Toss the steak strips in ground black pepper and mustard seeds. Heat 75 g (3 oz) butter in a heavy-based frying pan on the BOILING PLATE until hot and sizzling, then cook the strips in three batches, each for 1-2 minutes. Remove from pan and keep warm in the SIMMERING OVEN.

2 Heat the remaining butter and cook the mushrooms on the SIMMERING PLATE for 2-3 minutes. Add the brandy and bubble for 1 minute, then add the crème fraîche and bubble until syrupy. Stir in the anchovy essence, wholegrain mustard and tarragon. Season with black pepper.

3 Return the beef to the sauce and bring to the boil just before serving. Bring the pasta to the boil in a large pan of boiling salted water, then cover and transfer to the SIMMERING OVEN for the time given on the packet instructions. Serve with the beef, garnished with chives.

Anchovy and Caper Tapenade Roast Beef

PREPARATION TIME:
10 MINUTES

COOKING TIME:
35-40 MINUTES,
PLUS AT LEAST 10
MINUTES RESTING

FREEZING:
UNSUITABLE

380 CALS PER
SERVING

SERVES 4

The pungent flavours of the anchovy tapenade melt into the meat, giving a deliciously different taste. Serve this beef with sauce as a traditional roast or with golden baked polenta and a rocket salad. Spoon any leftover tapenade on to grilled tomatoes or stir into pasta with Parmesan cheese.

50 g (2 oz) can anchovy fillets, drained
30 ml (2 level tbsp) capers
15 ml (1 level tbsp) Dijon mustard
60 ml (4 level tbsp) roughly chopped parsley
about 15 fresh mint leaves
2 garlic cloves
15 ml (1 tbsp) balsamic vinegar

45 ml (3 tbsp) extra-virgin olive oil
900 g (2 lb) rolled topside beef
15 ml (1 level tbsp) plain flour
600 ml (1 pint) beef stock
150 ml (¼ pint) red wine
salt and freshly ground black pepper

1 Finely chop the anchovies in a food processor with the capers, mustard, herbs, garlic and vinegar. With the motor running, add 15 ml (1 tbsp) olive oil until combined.

2 Untie the topside and trim away any excess fat. Make a deep cut along the length of the beef to create a pocket. Spread half the anchovy mixture inside the cut. Fold the meat back over and tie at intervals with string.

3 Heat remaining oil in a small roasting tin on the BOILING PLATE and brown the meat well on all sides. Cook on the top runners of the ROASTING OVEN for 25 minutes for medium-rare (see Aga Tips).

4 Spread a little of the remaining anchovy mixture over the meat and return to the oven for 5-10 minutes. Remove from the dish and leave to rest for at least 10 minutes (see Aga Tips).

5 Blend the flour into the pan juices and cook on the SIMMERING PLATE for 1 minute, stirring. Remove from the heat and whisk in the stock and wine (see Cook's Tips). Transfer to the BOILING PLATE and cook briskly to reduce by half. Adjust the seasoning, remembering that anchovies are salty so don't add too much salt. Slice the beef thickly and serve.

COOK'S TIPS
To prepare ahead, complete the recipe to the end of step 2; cover and chill overnight. To use, complete the recipe.

Whisk any anchovy mixture that may fall off the beef into the gravy.

AGA TIPS
For medium beef, cook for 30 minutes; for well done, cook for 35-40 minutes.

Resting meat in the gentle heat of the SIMMERING OVEN allows the fibres to relax and ensures it's tender and easy to slice.

Meatballs with Olive and Pesto Pasta

PREPARATION TIME:
15 MINUTES

COOKING TIME:
30 MINUTES

FREEZING:
UNSUITABLE

715 CALS PER
SERVING

SERVES 4

Really good meatballs made with minced meat and plenty of flavourings, such as garlic, herbs and spices, are delicious with pasta. An easy way to make meatballs is to buy a packet of premium-quality sausages (now available in butchers and supermarkets), then skin them and roll the filling into balls.

450 g (1 lb) premium-quality coarse pork sausages
30 ml (2 tbsp) olive oil
350 g (12 oz) red onion, sliced
225 g (8 oz) dried pappardelle noodles
salt and freshly ground black pepper

125 g (4 oz) black olives (see Cook's Tips)
30 ml (2 level tbsp) chopped fresh parsley or chives (or a mix of both)
30 ml (2 level tbsp) pesto sauce
snipped and whole chives, to garnish

1 Slit the sausages from top to bottom with a sharp knife then peel off the skin. Break each sausage in half and roll each piece into a ball then flatten slightly with floured hands.

2 Place the meatballs at one end of a large roasting tin and place the onions at the other. Drizzle the onions with oil and toss. Place the tin on the floor of the ROASTING OVEN with the meatballs towards the back where it is hottest. Bake for 12-15 minutes until the meatballs are golden underneath. Turn the meatballs over, toss the onions and return to the oven, again with the meatballs towards the back, for a further 12-15 minutes. Pour off the surplus fat immediately.

3 To cook the pasta, bring a large pan of salted water to the boil. Add the pasta and return to the boil, uncovered. Transfer to the SIMMERING OVEN for the time recommended on the packet instructions. Drain and return to the pan. Stir the olives, herbs and pesto into the pasta, heat for 1 minute, then add the meatballs and onions and any juices that have collected in the tin. Season with pepper. To avoid breaking up the meatballs, shake the pan gently over the heat rather than stirring. Serve at once, garnished with chives.

COOK'S TIPS
To prepare ahead, complete to the end of step 2, cool quickly, cover and chill overnight. To use, complete the recipe.

Look out for Niçoise olives which are much smaller than the more familiar varieties but have a wonderful flavour. To release the olives' natural juices, put them in a polythene bag and lightly crush them with a rolling pan.

A squeeze of lemon juice sprinkled over the finished dish will sharpen the flavours if the pesto sauce is very salty.

Beef Jambalaya

PREPARATION TIME:
10 MINUTES

COOKING TIME:
30 MINUTES

FREEZING:
UNSUITABLE

615 CALS PER
SERVING

SERVES 4

Jambalaya is a traditional Cajun dish, similar to paella but with more spice. It's great with a crisp, green salad and a sharp lemon dressing. If you like your food really hot and spicy, add Tabasco sauce to taste at the end of step 4. Alternatively, allow your guests to add their own.

275 g (10 oz) fillet steak
20 ml (4 level tsp) mild chilli powder
salt and freshly ground black pepper
2 celery sticks
2 red peppers
oil
140 g (4½ oz) pack chorizo sausage, sliced and cut into strips, or 125 g (4 oz) cubed
1 medium onion, roughly chopped
2 garlic cloves, crushed

275 g (10 oz) long-grain white rice
15 ml (1 level tbsp) tomato paste
15 ml (1 level tbsp) ground ginger
10 ml (2 level tsp) Cajun seasoning (see Cook's Tips)
600 ml (1 pint) beef stock
8 large cooked prawns, shelled
salad leaves such as lamb's lettuce, to serve

1 Mix the sliced steak with 5 ml (1 level tsp) each mild chilli powder and ground black pepper. Cut the celery and peppers into thin 5 cm (2 in) strips.

2 Heat 15 ml (1 tbsp) oil in a large frying pan on the BOILING PLATE and cook the chorizo until golden. Add the celery and peppers to the pan and cook until just beginning to soften and brown. Remove from the pan and set aside. Add 30 ml (2 tbsp) oil to the pan and fry the steak in batches; set aside and keep warm in the SIMMERING OVEN.

3 Add a little more oil to the pan if necessary and cook the onions. Add the garlic, rice, tomato paste, remaining chilli powder, ground ginger and Cajun seasoning, then cook for 2 minutes until the rice turns translucent. Stir in the stock, season with salt and bring to the boil. Cover and transfer to the SIMMERING OVEN for about 20 minutes until the rice is tender and most of the liquid absorbed (add a little more water during cooking if necessary).

4 Add the reserved steak, chorizo, peppers, celery and prawns. Heat gently on the SIMMERING PLATE, stirring, until piping hot. Adjust the seasoning (see Cook's Tips) and serve with salad leaves.

COOK'S TIPS
Cajun seasoning can be found in the spice section of most supermarkets.

If you find the dish too spicy, serve it accompanied with a little soured cream as this will take away some of the heat.

Slow-Braised Beef

PREPARATION TIME:
15 MINUTES

COOKING TIME:
5-7 HOURS

FREEZING:
COMPLETE TO THE
END OF THE
RECIPE, COOL
QUICKLY, COVER
AND FREEZE FOR
UP TO SIX
MONTHS. TO USE,
THAW, THEN
REHEAT AS IN
COOK'S TIPS.

335 CALS PER
SERVING

SERVES 4

The anchovies in this dish melt away, leaving a rich flavour with little gravy. This dish takes just 15 minutes to prepare, and can be made ahead and reheated the next day – the Aga provides the ideal slow cooking to create the meltingly tender beef. This is excellent served with buttery mashed potato.

45 ml (3 tbsp) olive oil or the anchovy oil

700 g (1½ lb) piece braising steak cut into small 'steaks'

350 g (12 oz) onion, thickly sliced

25 g (1 oz) can anchovy fillets in oil, drained and chopped

30 ml (2 level tbsp) capers, chopped (see Cook's Tips)

30 ml (2 level tbsp) chopped fresh parsley

15 ml (1 level tbsp) chopped fresh thyme, plus extra sprigs to garnish

5 ml (1 level tsp) ready-made English mustard

1 Heat the oil in a flameproof casserole on the SIMMERING PLATE and brown the meat well a few pieces at a time. When the last of the meat has been browned, stir in 60 ml (4 tbsp) cold water to loosen any sediment from the bottom of the pan. Return all the meat to the casserole.

2 Add the onion, anchovies, capers, herbs and mustard to the casserole. Mix together until thoroughly combined.

3 Crumple a sheet of greaseproof paper, then wet it. Open out and press down over the surface of the meat. Cover the casserole tightly and if there is a steam vent in the lid, plug it with a paste of flour and water. Cook on the floor of the SIMMERING OVEN for 5-7 hours or until the beef is meltingly tender. Check the casserole occasionally and add water if it looks dry. Garnish with thyme and serve.

COOK'S TIPS

To prepare ahead, complete to the end of the recipe, cool quickly, cover and chill. To use, reheat by adding 50 ml (2 fl oz) water and place over a medium heat for 12-15 minutes or until piping hot.

Capers now come in more than one form. Don't use the salted variety for this recipe but opt for capers in vinegar.

Beef and Beer Stew with Parsnip Purée

PREPARATION TIME:
25 MINUTES

COOKING TIME:
ABOUT 1 HOUR 45
MINUTES

FREEZING:
SUITABLE, EXCEPT
PARSNIP PURÉE

500 CALS PER
SERVING

SERVES 6

This wonderfully dark, glossy stew is enriched with good strong beer and a hint of treacle. A creamy parsnip purée is the perfect robust accompaniment to soak up the delicious flavoursome juices. Serve with jacket potatoes too if you like, and sautéed cabbage or another green vegetable.

1.1 kg (2½ lb) chuck or blade beef

30 ml (2 tbsp) plain flour

salt and freshly ground black pepper

3 large onions

4 celery sticks

several thyme sprigs

2 bay leaves

450 g (1 lb) turnips

50 g (2 oz) beef dripping or lard

300 ml (½ pint) strong beef stock

450 ml (¾ pint) strong beer

45 ml (3 tbsp) black treacle

celery leaves, to garnish

FOR THE PARSNIP PURÉE

900 g (2 lb) parsnips

45 ml (3 tbsp) double cream

1 Cut the meat into large chunks, discarding excess fat. Season the flour with salt and pepper and use to coat the meat. Peel and thinly slice the onions. Cut two 5 cm (2 in) lengths of celery.

Tie in bundles with the thyme and bay leaves. Cut the remaining celery into chunks. Peel the turnips and cut into large chunks.

2 Heat half the dripping or lard in a large flameproof casserole on the BOILING PLATE. When the pan is very hot, add a third of the meat and fry, turning, until browned. Remove with a slotted spoon and fry the remainder in two batches; remove.

3 Add the onions and celery to the pan and fry until softened. Return the meat to the pan and add the herb bundles. Stir in the stock, beer and treacle, then add the turnips. Bring just to the boil, cover with a lid and transfer to the SIMMERING OVEN. Cook for 3-4 hours or until the meat and vegetables are tender. Remove the meat and boil the sauce to reduce and thicken on the floor of the ROASTING OVEN. Season to taste.

4 Peel the parsnips and cut into 7.5 cm (3 in) lengths; cut lengthways into even-sized pieces. Put the parsnips into a saucepan and cover with water. Bring to the boil, drain off all but 5 mm (¼ in) water, cover and cook on the floor of the SIMMERING OVEN for 20-30 minutes until completely tender.

5 Transfer to the BOILING PLATE and boil, uncovered, to reduce the liquid. Add the cream and seasoning and mash well until completely smooth.

6 Divide the stew between warmed serving plates and add spoonfuls of the parsnip purée. Garnish with celery leaves.

Chilli Beef with Salsa

PREPARATION TIME:
25 MINUTES

COOKING TIME:
40 MINUTES

FREEZING:
COMPLETE STEP 3.
THAW AT ROOM
TEMPERATURE.
ALLOW AN EXTRA
5-10 MINUTES
COOKING TIME IN
STEP 5 TO ENSURE
THE WHOLE DISH IS
PIPING HOT.

565 CALS PER
SERVING

SERVES 4

Chilli is a great supper dish. You could also serve it in taco shells with lettuce and soured cream.

1 large ripe avocado, peeled and chopped
175 g (6 oz) cherry tomatoes, quartered
4 spring onions, finely sliced
15 ml (1 tbsp) olive oil
10 ml (2 tbsp) white wine vinegar
1 garlic clove, crushed
15 ml (1 level tbsp) chopped fresh coriander
30 ml (2 tbsp) olive oil
225 g (8 oz) red onions, roughly chopped
1 large red chilli, de-seeded and finely chopped

1 garlic clove, crushed
5 ml (1 level tsp) ground cumin
450 g (1 lb) lean minced beef
400 g can chopped tomatoes
15 ml (1 level tbsp) tomato paste
450 ml (¾ pint) beef or vegetable stock
400 g can pinto beans, drained
salt and freshly ground black pepper
tortilla chips and grated Cheddar cheese, to serve

1 Place the first seven ingredients in a bowl, mix together and chill (see Cook's Tip).

2 Pour 15 ml (1 tbsp) oil into a broad based, lidded ovenproof pan, add the onions, cover and cook on the SIMMERING PLATE for 4-5 minutes or until soft but not coloured. Add garlic, chilli and cumin, cook for 1 minute, then set aside.

3 Transfer the pan to the BOILING PLATE, add the remaining oil and mince; cook for 5-6 minutes, stirring regularly. Add the onion mixture, tomatoes, tomato paste and stock. Bring to the boil and place uncovered on the floor of the ROASTING OVEN for 15 minutes. Add the pinto beans and cook for a further 15 minutes; season.

4 Pile the chilli into a serving dish with a handful of tortilla chips and sprinkle some cheese over the top.

5 Place the dish on the highest shelf level possible in the ROASTING OVEN, pushing the dish to the back of the oven where it is hottest, for 7-12 minutes or until bubbling. Spoon salsa over and serve.

COOK'S TIP
To save time, use a bought salsa, adding chopped avocado and fresh coriander.

Herb-Scented Lamb with Balsamic Dressing

PREPARATION TIME:
20 MINUTES

COOKING TIME:
35 MINUTES

FREEZING:
UNSUITABLE

365 CALS PER
SERVING

SERVES 4

Lamb fillets make a perfect roast for two or four people. Cooked very quickly with no waste, they soon become a firm favourite. The roast herbs are meant for flavouring and garnish – they are not to be eaten as the twigs will stick between your teeth! This recipe is good served with potato purée.

about 50 g (2 oz) each thyme and rosemary sprigs
3 best-end fillets of lamb, about 800 g (1¾ lb) total weight (see Cook's Tips)
freshly ground black pepper
6 whole unpeeled garlic cloves
150 ml (¼ pint) olive oil

150 g (5 oz) spring onions, thinly sliced
225 g (8 oz) cherry tomatoes
45 ml (3 tbsp) balsamic vinegar
300 ml (½ pint) lamb or chicken stock
15 ml (1 level tbsp) chopped fresh thyme

1 Place two or three sprigs of rosemary and thyme on a board, put one lamb fillet over them, season with pepper, then top with a further two to three herb sprigs. Tie the herbs and lamb into a bundle with string, secured at about 4 cm (1½ in) intervals. Repeat the process with the remaining lamb and herbs.

2 Place the lamb in a roasting tin with the garlic cloves. Drizzle with 60 ml (4 tbsp) olive oil and season with pepper.

3 Cook on the bottom runners of the ROASTING OVEN for about 20 minutes for medium-rare (see Aga Tip). Remove the lamb from the roasting tin and place covered with foil in the SIMMERING OVEN while you prepare the dressing. Reserve the pan juices and garlic cloves and set aside.

4 For the dressing, heat the remaining oil in the roasting pan, then add the reserved garlic cloves, along with the spring onions and tomatoes. Gently fry for 5 minutes, then lift out and set aside. Pour in the balsamic vinegar and bubble on the BOILING PLATE to reduce by half. Add the stock and reserved pan juices, bring to the boil and continue bubbling for 5-10 minutes. Add the chopped fresh thyme and return the garlic cloves, spring onions and tomatoes to the tin.

5 To serve, cut the string, cut the meat into thick slices and use the herbs for garnish. Serve drizzled with the warm onion and tomatoes in balsamic dressing.

COOK'S TIPS
To prepare ahead, complete to the end of step 2 up to one day in advance. Cover and chill. Complete the recipe.

To save time, ask your butcher to trim the lamb fillets, removing the silvery membrane. If you buy the fillets untrimmed, do this yourself.

AGA TIP
The cooking times given here are for lamb that is medium-rare. If you prefer medium-cooked lamb, cook for a further 5 minutes; for well done, cook for a further 10 minutes.

Roast Leg of Lamb with Herby Onion Sauce

PREPARATION TIME:
40 MINUTES

COOKING TIME:
ABOUT 1 ½ HOURS,
PLUS RESTING

FREEZING:
UNSUITABLE

810 CALS PER
SERVING

SERVES 8

Onion sauce is the traditional accompaniment for mutton, but this updated version is delicious with lamb roasted with garlic, shallots and new potatoes.

FOR THE HERBY ONION SAUCE
700 g (1 ½ lb) large onions
salt and freshly ground black pepper
20 g (¾ oz) butter
10 ml (2 level tsp) mixed dried herbs
20 g (¾ oz) flour
300 ml (10 fl oz) milk
30 ml (2 tbsp) double cream
45 ml (3 level tbsp) fresh mixed herbs,
such as fresh parsley, tarragon and chives

FOR THE ROAST LEG OF LAMB
2 garlic bulbs
450 g (1 lb) new potatoes
450 g (1 lb) shallots
2.7 kg (6 lb) leg of lamb (see Cook's Tip)
sprigs of rosemary and mint
30 ml (2 tbsp) oil
freshly ground black pepper
broccoli and carrots, to accompany

1 To make the sauce, chop the onions, then place in a pan with 150 ml (5 fl oz) salted water. Bring to the boil for 2 minutes on the BOILING PLATE, then cover and place in the SIMMERING OVEN for 15-20 minutes or until soft. Drain well, reserving the cooking liquid and making it up to 150 ml (5 fl oz) with water if it has reduced.

2 Melt the butter in a heavy-based saucepan, add the dried herbs and cook for 1-2 minutes on the SIMMERING PLATE. Add the flour and cook gently for 1 minute, stirring. Off the heat, stir in the milk and reserved cooking liquid. Bring to the boil slowly and continue to cook, stirring all the time, until the sauce comes to the boil and thickens. Add the cooked onions, cover the pan and return to the SIMMERING OVEN for 5 minutes; season to taste. Cover and set aside.

3 For the lamb, thinly slice 2 garlic cloves. Wash and halve the potatoes. Peel the shallots. Make cuts in the skin of the lamb and insert herb sprigs and garlic slices into each cut. Rub the lamb with oil and season well with black pepper.

4 Place on a wire rack over a roasting tin and cook on the third runners of the ROASTING OVEN for about 15 minutes per 450 g (1 lb) for medium-rare, 20 minutes for medium and 25 minutes for well-done. Baste every 20 minutes. After the lamb has been in the oven for 20 minutes, place the potatoes and shallots in the tin with 150 ml (5 fl oz) water. After the lamb has been in the oven for 40 minutes, add the remaining garlic bulbs to the tin.

5 When lamb is cooked, all the liquid should have evaporated and the vegetables should be glazed by the juices. Cover the lamb with foil; rest for 15 minutes in the SIMMERING OVEN before carving.

6 Re-heat the sauce on the SIMMERING PLATE, stir in the cream and add the chopped fresh mixed herbs. Serve the lamb and vegetables with the sauce plus broccoli and carrots.

COOK'S TIP
Ask the butcher to remove the pelvic bone from the leg of lamb as this will make carving much easier.

Spaghetti with Lamb Ragu

PREPARATION TIME:
25 MINUTES

COOKING TIME:
2½-3 HOURS

740-495 CALS PER
SERVING

FREEZING: SUITABLE
AFTER STEP 4

SERVES 4-6

A good ragu needs long, slow cooking and is ideal for the Aga. The sauce is reduced to a flavoursome concentrate and the meat becomes meltingly tender. Tossed with perfectly cooked spaghetti and freshly grated Parmesan cheese, this is real Italian comfort food which is hard to beat.

1 onion
2 garlic cloves
10 ml (2 level tsp) fennel seeds
2 carrots
2 celery stalks
45 ml (3 tbsp) extra-virgin olive oil
350 g (12 oz) minced lamb
200 ml (7 fl oz) red wine
45 ml (3 tbsp) chopped fresh oregano

1 rosemary sprig
½ cinnamon stick
397 g (14 oz) can chopped tomatoes
salt and freshly ground black pepper
400 g (14 oz) dried spaghetti, fettucine or long fusilli
75 ml (5 tbsp) freshly grated Parmesan cheese

1 Peel and finely chop the onion and garlic. Lightly crush the fennel seeds. Finely slice the carrots and celery.

2 Place the oil in a saucepan. Add the onion and garlic and cook on the BOILING PLATE for 1-2 minutes until softened but not browned. Add the fennel seeds and cook for 1 minute, then add the carrot and celery and cook, stirring, for 1-2 minutes.

3 Add the lamb to the pan and cook for about 7 minutes, breaking up the pieces with a wooden spoon, until browned. Stir in the wine and let it bubble for 4-5 minutes until the liquid has reduced by about half.

4 Add the oregano, rosemary sprig and cinnamon to the pan with the canned tomatoes and their juice. Bring to the boil and season lightly with salt and pepper. Cook, uncovered, on the floor of the SIMMERING OVEN for 2½-3 hours, stirring occasionally until the lamb is meltingly tender and the oil separates from the sauce (see Aga Tip). Remove and discard the cinnamon and rosemary. Spoon off the oil, soaking up any excess with kitchen paper. Adjust the seasoning to taste.

5 Just before serving, cook the spaghetti in a large pan of boiling salted water. Bring to the boil on the BOILING PLATE, then cover and transfer to the SIMMERING OVEN until 'al dente' or according to packet instructions. Drain thoroughly.

6 To serve, toss the ragu with the pasta and about half of the grated Parmesan. Serve at once, sprinkled with the remaining Parmesan.

COOK'S TIPS
The sauce tastes even better if it is prepared ahead, allowed to cool and left to stand for a while. Remove any fat from the surface and reheat thoroughly before serving.

For the classic Spaghetti alla Bolognese substitute lean minced beef for the lamb. Replace the rosemary with a few sprigs of fresh thyme.

AGA TIP
If you wish, you can cover the ragu and cook for an additional ½-1 hour.

Lamb and Chestnuts en Croûte

PREPARATION TIME:
30 MINUTES, PLUS
CHILLING

COOKING TIME:
1 HOUR

FREEZING:
COMPLETE TO END
OF STEP 6. WRAP
AND FREEZE. THAW
OVERNIGHT AT
COOL ROOM
TEMPERATURE AND
COMPLETE STEP 7.

560 CALS PER
SERVING

SERVES 8

Wrapping the lamb fillets in spinach and ham seals in the moisture, keeping the meat tender and ensuring that the pastry stays crisp.

2 racks of lamb, trimmed, each 350 g (12 oz)
75 g (3 oz) shallots or onions
225 g (8 oz) mixed mushrooms
100 g (3½ oz) cooked, vacuum-packed chestnuts
100 g (3½ oz) washed and prepared spinach
50 g (2 oz) butter
3 garlic cloves
45 ml (3 tbsp) balsamic vinegar

5 ml (1 level tsp) chopped fresh thyme
142 ml (5 fl oz) carton double cream
salt and freshly ground black pepper
4 thin slices cooked ham
500 g packet puff pastry
1 egg
Thyme and Port Gravy (see right), mashed sweet potatoes and broccoli, to serve

1 Cut meat from bones in one piece; save bones for gravy. Chop shallots, mushrooms and chestnuts. Plunge spinach in boiling water for 2 seconds. Drain, refresh with cold water and dry.

2 Melt butter in a large pan. Add shallots, and cook, stirring, on the BOILING PLATE for 2-3 minutes. Add mushrooms; cook for 3-4 minutes. Stir in crushed garlic and vinegar; cook for 1 minute. Add chestnuts, thyme and cream. Boil for 10 minutes or until reduced to a sticky glaze. Season; cool.

3 On cling film, place two ham slices to form a rectangle 20 × 15 cm (8 × 6 in). Cover with a layer of spinach. Season lamb; place in the middle. Spread with half the mushroom mixture. Wrap tightly, 'sealing' with cling film. Repeat with other fillet. Chill.

4 Roll out 125 g (4 oz) of the pastry to 30 × 20 cm (12 × 8 in) to make the pastry base. Place on a baking sheet and prick well; chill for 30 minutes. Cook on the bottom runners of the ROASTING OVEN for 6 minutes, then turn the tray around for even colouring and bake for a further 6 minutes or until golden and crisp. Cool; cut into two rectangles 20 × 15 cm (8 × 6 in).

5 Remove cling film from fillets; place one on each piece of pastry. Trim pastry to size.

6 Thinly roll out remaining pastry to 56 × 23 cm (22 × 9 in). Cut into two, 28 × 23 cm (11 × 9 in). Brush with beaten egg; wrap around lamb (egg-side down). Trim, leaving 2.5 cm (1 in) to tuck under the cooked pastry base. Brush with egg; decorate with trimmings. Cover lightly with cling film; chill for at least 1 hour. Brush again with egg.

7 Cook on the second runners of the ROASTING OVEN, turning the tray round after 12 minutes for even colouring. Cook for a total of 20-30 minutes (medium-rare); 30-35 minutes (well-done) — lamb should be pink in the centre. Lower the tray if the pastry is becoming too dark. Stand for 5 minutes before serving with gravy, mashed sweet potatoes and broccoli.

LAMB AND CHESTNUTS
EN CROÛTE

Thyme and Port Gravy

PREPARATION TIME:
10 MINUTES

COOKING TIME:
1 HOUR 30
MINUTES

FREEZING: COOL,
COVER AND
FREEZE. THAW
OVERNIGHT AT
COOL ROOM
TEMPERATURE.
BRING TO BOIL;
SIMMER FOR 1-2
MINUTES.

85 CALS PER
SERVING

SERVES 8

50 g (2 oz) each leek, onion, carrot and celery
30 ml (2 tbsp) oil
lamb bones (see recipe left, step 1)
300 ml (½ pint) red wine

1.7 litres (3 pints) chicken stock
5 ml (1 level tsp) chopped fresh thyme
150 ml (¼ pint) port
5 ml (1 level tsp) redcurrant jelly
salt and freshly ground black pepper

1 Chop vegetables. Place the bones and vegetables in a small roasting tin, toss in the oil and place on the top runners of the ROASTING OVEN for 30 minutes or until well browned.

2 Add wine; return to the oven for 7 minutes until the wine is reduced by half. Add stock and thyme, bring to boil and cook, uncovered, for ¾-1 hour on the floor of the ROASTING OVEN; strain; return to rinsed pan.

3 Add port and jelly. Boil stock briskly for 20-30 minutes or until syrupy – there should be about 450 ml (¾ pint). Season.

COOK'S TIP

To prepare ahead, complete to end of step 3, cool quickly; chill for up to five days. To use, bring to boil; simmer for 1-2 minutes.

Lamb and Bamboo Shoot Red Curry

PREPARATION TIME:
10 MINUTES

COOKING TIME:
20-50 MINUTES

FREEZING:
UNSUITABLE

325 CALS PER
SERVING

SERVES 4

Red curry paste is used to flavour this curry. For a much hotter version, use green curry paste instead. Serve with rice or noodles.

1 large onion
2 garlic cloves
450 g (1 lb) lean boneless lamb
30 ml (2 tbsp) sunflower oil
30 ml (2 level tbsp) Thai red curry paste
150 ml (¼ pint) lamb or beef stock
30 ml (2 tbsp) Thai fish sauce

10 ml (2 level tsp) soft brown sugar
200 g (7 oz) can bamboo shoots, drained
1 red pepper
30 ml (2 level tbsp) chopped fresh mint
15 ml (1 level tbsp) chopped fresh basil
25 g (1 oz) raw peanuts, toasted
basil leaves, to garnish

1 Peel the onion and cut into wedges; peel and finely chop the garlic; cut the lamb into 3 cm (1¼ in) cubes.

2 Heat the oil in a large frying pan, add the onion and garlic and fry on the SIMMERING PLATE for 5 minutes.

3 Transfer to the BOILING PLATE. Add the lamb and the curry paste and stir fry for 5 minutes (see Aga Tip). Add the stock, fish sauce and sugar. Bring to the boil.

▨▨ Place on the floor of the SIMMERING OVEN and cook for 40-50 minutes.

▨▨▨▨ Place on the floor of the BAKING OVEN and cook for 20 minutes.

4 Meanwhile, slice the bamboo shoots into strips; de-seed and slice the red pepper. Stir into the curry with the herbs and cook, uncovered, for a further 10 minutes. Stir in the peanuts and serve at once, garnished with basil.

AGA TIP

Use a splatterguard when stir frying the lamb to protect the Aga cookertop.

Cannelloni with Roasted Garlic

PREPARATION TIME: 40 MINUTES

COOKING TIME: ABOUT 1 HOUR

FREEZING: FREEZE AT THE END OF STEP 7. THAW IN FRIDGE OVERNIGHT OR COOK FROM FROZEN, ADDING AN EXTRA 10 MINUTES IF CHILLED OR AN EXTRA 20-30 IF FROZEN, THEN UNCOVER TO ALLOW TO BROWN.

470 CALS PER SERVING

SERVES 6

Don't be put off by the number of garlic cloves! Roasted whole garlic has a mild, sweet flavour.

20 unpeeled garlic cloves
30 ml (2 tbsp) extra-virgin olive oil
15 g (½ oz) dried porcini mushrooms
5 shallots or button onions, finely chopped
700 g (1½ lb) lean minced meat
175 ml (6 fl oz) red wine
30 ml (2 level tbsp) chopped fresh thyme

salt and freshly ground black pepper
about 12 lasagne sheets (see Cook's Tips)
142 ml (5 fl oz) carton single cream
30 ml (2 level tbsp) sun-dried tomato paste
butter, for greasing
75 g (3 oz) Gruyère cheese, finely grated

1 Put the unpeeled but separated garlic cloves in a small roasting tin with 15 ml (1 tbsp) oil. Toss to coat garlic in oil and bake on the grid shelf on the floor of the ROASTING OVEN for 10-15 minutes or until soft. Leave to cool.

2 Meanwhile, put the porcini in a bowl; cover with 150 ml (¼ pint) boiling water and place in the SIMMERING OVEN to soak for 20 minutes. Drain, reserving liquor. Rinse to remove any grit; chop finely.

3 Heat remaining oil in a pan. Add the shallots, cover and cook on the SIMMERING PLATE for 3 minutes until soft. Transfer to the BOILING PLATE and stir in the meat. Cook, stirring frequently, until browned. Add wine, mushrooms with liquor, and thyme. Cook on the floor of the ROASTING OVEN for 15-20 minutes or until the liquid has almost evaporated (the mixture should be quite moist).

4 Skin the garlic cloves and mash them, using a fork, to a rough paste. Stir into the meat mixture, season and set aside.

5 Cook the lasagne in a large roasting tin of boiling, salted water on the floor of the SIMMERING OVEN for 10-15 minutes until 'al dente' (see Aga Tip). Drain, rinse with cold water and drain again.

6 Lay the lasagne sheets flat. Spoon meat mixture along one long edge; roll up to enclose the filling. Cut the tubes in half and arrange a layer of filled tubes in the base of a buttered, shallow baking dish or small roasting tin.

7 In a small bowl, mix together cream and sun-dried tomato paste. Season with pepper. Spoon half the tomato cream over the filled tubes and sprinkle with half the cheese. Arrange the remaining tubes on top and cover with remaining tomato cream and cheese.

8 Cover dish with foil and bake in the ROASTING OVEN for 10-20 minutes. Uncover and bake for a further 10 minutes or until lightly browned and bubbling. Serve at once.

COOK'S TIPS

To prepare ahead, complete to the end of step 7. Chill and bake for an extra 5-10 minutes at step 8, then uncover and allow to brown.

To save time, you can buy ready-to-use cannelloni tubes instead of using lasagne.

AGA TIP

To cook lasagne sheets, place one layer of pasta sheets in a roasting tin, cover with a layer of foil, then add a second layer of pasta sheets. The foil will prevent the pasta sheets sticking together. Pour over a kettle of boiling water and, using a spoon, press the pasta down to submerge.

Tomato, Artichoke and Prosciutto Pizza

PREPARATION TIME:
30 MINUTES, PLUS
RISING

COOKING TIME:
15-20 MINUTES

FREEZING:
UNSUITABLE

665 CALS PER
SERVING

SERVES 4

A large sumptuous crisp pizza topped with chunky vegetables and sweet prosciutto which cooks to a delicious crispness. The artichokes and plum tomatoes give the pizza juiciness, the latter keeping their shape in the short cooking time.

FOR THE PIZZA DOUGH
15 g (½ oz) fresh yeast, 15 ml (1 tbsp) dried active baking yeast, or 1 sachet easy-blend yeast
pinch of sugar
250 ml (8 fl oz) warm water
350 g (12 oz) strong plain white flour
30 ml (2 tbsp) olive oil
2.5 ml (½ tsp) salt

FOR THE TOPPING
4 ripe plum tomatoes
8 artichoke hearts in oil, drained
4 large garlic cloves
150 g (5 oz) mozzarella cheese
45 ml (3 tbsp) sun-dried tomato paste
6 slices prosciutto
olive oil, for drizzling
45 ml (3 tbsp) freshly grated Parmesan cheese
oregano or basil leaves, to garnish

1 To make the pizza dough, in a bowl, cream the fresh yeast with the sugar, then whisk in the warm water. Leave for 10 minutes until frothy. For other yeasts, use according to the packet instructions.

2 Sift the flour into a large bowl and make a well in the centre. Pour in the yeast mixture, olive oil and salt. Mix together with a round-bladed knife, then using your hands until the dough comes together.

3 Tip out onto a floured surface. With clean, dry hands, knead the dough for 10 minutes until smooth, elastic and quite soft (or for 2 minutes in a food processor). If too soft to handle, knead in a little more flour.

4 Place in a clean oiled bowl, cover with a damp tea-towel and leave to rise for about 1 hour until doubled in size.

5 Cut each tomato into six wedges. Halve or quarter the artichoke hearts. Peel and finely slice the garlic. Slice the mozzarella.

6 Knock back the dough and roll out, or stretch with your fingers, to a 30 cm (12 in) circle on the floured plain shelf.

7 Spread the sun-dried tomato paste over the pizza base. Arrange half the mozzarella slices on the base. Scatter over the tomatoes, artichoke hearts and garlic. Scrunch up the prosciutto and drape over the pizza. Scatter over the remaining mozzarella and drizzle with oil. Sprinkle with the Parmesan. Bake for 10 minutes on the floor of the ROASTING OVEN until golden and sizzling. Serve immediately, sprinkled with oregano or basil leaves.

COOK'S TIPS
To make two smaller pizzas, halve the dough and roll out two 20 cm (8 in) circles.

For a vegetarian pizza, replace the ham with grilled aubergine slices.

Rigatoni Baked with Spicy Sausage

PREPARATION TIME:
15-20 MINUTES

COOKING TIME:
30-35 MINUTES

FREEZING:
UNSUITABLE

1000-670 CALS PER
SERVING

SERVES 4-6

You can use any good quality spicy sausages for this recipe, but – if at all possible – buy Italian-style uncooked sausages 'loose' from a good butcher or delicatessen, rather than pre-packed ones. Prepare the sauce in advance if you wish, but don't toss with the pasta until ready for the oven, otherwise the pasta will become soggy.

45 ml (3 tbsp) extra-virgin olive oil
350 g (12 oz) uncooked spicy sausage
1 onion
2 garlic cloves
12 black olives
5 sun-dried tomatoes
90 ml (3 fl oz) dry white wine
30 ml (2 tbsp) chopped fresh oregano
15 ml (1 tbsp) chopped fresh parsley

2 x 397 g (14 oz) cans plum tomatoes
salt and freshly ground black pepper
400 g (14 oz) dried rigatoni
15 g (½ oz) butter
175 g (6 oz) mozzarella cheese (preferably smoked), diced
50 g (2 oz) Parmesan cheese, in one piece
oregano sprigs, to garnish

1 Heat 15 ml (1 tbsp) of the oil in a large frying pan on the BOILING PLATE, then add the sausage, cut into lengths to fit the pan, if necessary. Fry for 2-3 minutes, turning frequently, until lightly browned. Transfer to a plate and cut into slices. Set aside.

2 Peel and chop the onion and garlic. Slice the olives from their stones; dice the sun-dried tomatoes. Add the remaining oil to the frying pan. Stir in the onion and garlic and cook on the SIMMERING PLATE for 5 minutes, until softened but not browned. Return the sliced sausage to the pan and add the wine and herbs. Transfer to the BOILING PLATE and cook for 3-4 minutes until about two-thirds of the wine has evaporated.

3 Stir in the canned tomatoes and their juice, breaking them up with a wooden spoon. Add the sun-dried tomatoes and olives. Cook, uncovered, on the grid shelf on the floor of the ROASTING OVEN for 15-20 minutes until the tomatoes are pulp-like; do not reduce the sauce too much. Season to taste.

4 Cook the rigatoni in a large pan of boiling salted water in the SIMMERING OVEN until almost 'al dente', or for about 2 minutes less time than packet instructions. Drain thoroughly.

5 Butter a baking dish large enough to hold the pasta and sauce. Transfer the pasta to the dish and toss with sauce. Scatter the mozzarella over the rigatoni. Using a potato peeler 'shave' the Parmesan cheese over the top.

6 Bake near the top of the ROASTING OVEN for about 15 minutes, until piping hot. Serve at once, garnished with oregano sprigs.

COOK'S TIPS
To prepare ahead, complete the sauce to the end of step 3 up to 2 days ahead and chill. To use, complete and back, allowing an extra 5-10 minutes until the sauce is piping hot and the pasta cooked.

If you wish, use cooked sausages, such as chorizo, instead of raw ones. Omit stage 1. Simply slice the sausages and add at stage 2.

AGA TIP
Cooking pasta in the SIMMERING OVEN ensures it does not boil over.

Wine-Braised Sausages with Lentils

PREPARATION TIME:
10 MINUTES

COOKING TIME:
30-50 MINUTES

FREEZING:
UNSUITABLE

50 CALS PER
SERVING

SERVES 4

Most good butchers pride themselves on their own sausages recipes, and supermarkets premium brands are good too.

450 g (1 lb) good meaty sausages
oil, if necessary
2 red onions, finely chopped
6 baby red peppers, halved and de-seeded
or 2 large peppers, de-seeded and thickly sliced

150 ml (¼ pint) light stock
200 ml (7 fl oz) red wine
420 g can cooked green lentils
salt and freshly ground black pepper
chopped fresh parsley, to garnish

1 Brown the sausages in a large flameproof casserole on the BOILING PLATE for 4-5 minutes. If they don't produce enough fat and begin to stick, add 15 ml (1 tbsp) oil to the pan.

2 Add the onions to the pan and fry on the SIMMERING PLATE until soft – about 5 minutes. Stir in the peppers and fry until slightly browned.

3 Pour in the stock and red wine and bring to the boil. Rinse and drain the lentils, stir into the casserole, season and cover tightly, then simmer gently on the SIMMERING PLATE for about 15 minutes. Transfer to the SIMMERING OVEN for 30 minutes or place on the grid shelf on the floor of the ROASTING OVEN for 15 minutes or until most of the liquid has been absorbed and the peppers are quite soft. Garnish with parsley to serve.

COOK'S TIP
To prepare ahead, complete the recipe. Cool quickly, cover and chill overnight. To use, re-heat for 30 minutes in the SIMMERING OVEN or for 15 minutes in the ROASTING OVEN until piping hot.

WINE-BRAISED SAUSAGES WITH LENTILS

Potato and Celeriac Puffs

PREPARATION TIME:
45 MINUTES

COOKING TIME:
55 MINUTES

FREEZING:
UNSUITABLE

450 CALS PER
SERVING

SERVES 4

Delicious buttery potatoes topped with celeriac soufflés. This dish can either be served as a vegetarian main meal or to accompany cold meats such as ham or turkey.

FOR THE POTATO BASE
350 g (12 oz) waxy potatoes, peeled and sliced
40-50 g (1½-2 oz) butter
salt and freshly ground black pepper

FOR THE CELERIAC TOPPING
700 g (1½ lb) celeriac, peeled and cut into 2.5 cm (1 in) chunks
90 ml (6 tbsp) carton double cream

2 garlic cloves, crushed
1 bay leaf
pinch grated nutmeg
salt and freshly ground black pepper
3 medium eggs, separated
Tomato and Apple Chutney (see page 142), to serve
fresh chives, to garnish

1 To make the potato bases, place the sliced potatoes in a saucepan of cold salted water, bring to the boil on the BOILING PLATE, bubble for 1 minute and drain. Heat half the butter in a large non-stick frying pan on the BOILING PLATE and cook the potatoes in batches for 2-3 minutes or until golden brown on both sides, adding more butter when necessary. Cool slightly and arrange in layers in the bottom of six 6.5 cm (2½ in) metal rings (see Cook's Tips), placed on a baking sheet. Season between each layer and set aside.

2 To make the celeriac topping, place the celeriac chunks in a pan of boiling water. Boil for 2 minutes on the BOILING PLATE, then drain, returning the celeriac to the pan with the cream, garlic, bay leaf, nutmeg and seasoning. Bring to the boil, tossing the celeriac well in the cream, then place the pan in the SIMMERING OVEN for 20-25 minutes until tender. Transfer to the BOILING PLATE and cook briskly to reduce the liquid to about 30 ml (2 tbsp). Process the celeriac with the cooking liquid until smooth. Beat in the egg yolks. Whisk the egg whites until they form soft peaks and fold in the celeriac mixture.

3 Spoon the mixture on top of the potatoes, filling to the top of the rings. Cook on the grid shelf on the floor of the ROASTING OVEN for 20-25 minutes or until puffed and golden.

4 Remove the rings from the puffs, place a spoonful of the Tomato and Apple Chutney on top, then garnish with chives.

COOK'S TIPS
To prepare ahead, complete to the end of step 3. Cool, cover a chill for up to 4 hours. To use, place the puffs on a baking sheet.
■■ *Reheat on the grid shelf on the floor of the ROASTING OVEN for 7-10 minutes.*
■■■■ *Reheat on the grid shelf on the floor of the BAKING OVEN for 10-15 minutes.*

To make your own moulds, take six pieces of extra-thick foil, 15 x 33 cm (6 x 13 in), fold each four times to form a long strip, form each strip into a ring 6.5 cm (2½ in) in diameter, fold over the ends to secure.

Tuscan Bean Stew

PREPARATION TIME:
30 MINUTES

COOKING TIME:
50 MINUTES

FREEZING: SUITABLE

255 CALS PER
SERVING
(PLUS 40 CALS PER
PESTO CROÛTE)

SERVES 4

Beans are an excellent source of dietary fibre, which helps to reduce high blood cholesterol levels. Their other advantage, particularly if you have a hearty appetite, is that they are incredibly filling. Use a mixture of beans for this recipe.

30 ml (2 tbsp) olive oil
175 g (6 oz) red onions, finely chopped
4 garlic cloves, crushed
30 ml (2 level tbsp) sun-dried tomato paste
2.5 ml (½ level tsp) chilli powder (optional)
125 g (4 oz) carrots, sliced
75 g (3 oz) celery sticks, sliced
4 tomatoes, preferably plum, peeled, de-seeded and roughly chopped
2 thyme sprigs or a large pinch dried

2 bay leaves
salt and freshly ground black pepper
350 ml (¾ pint) vegetable stock
2 x 400 g cans beans, such as butter, flageolet, kidney or chickpeas, drained and rinsed
50 g (2 oz) French beans, trimmed and cut into short lengths
small thyme sprigs, to garnish
pesto croûtes, to serve (see Aga Tip)

1 In a non-stick pan, heat the oil on the SIMMERING PLATE, add the onions and cook for 6 minutes or until soft. Add garlic, tomato paste and chilli powder; cook for 1-2 minutes.
2 Add the next five ingredients and season. Pour in the stock, bring to the boil and transfer to the SIMMERING OVEN for 20-30 minutes or until soft.
3 Add the beans and French beans, then simmer for 5-10 minutes or until beans have heated through and the French beans are just tender. Serve hot, garnished with thyme and accompanied with pesto croûtes.

COOK'S TIP
To prepare ahead, complete to the end of step 2, cool quickly and chill overnight. To use, complete the recipe.

AGA TIP
To make pesto croûtes, slice French bread, drizzle with a little olive oil and spread with ready-made pesto. Bake in a roasting tin on the floor of the ROASTING OVEN for 7-10 minutes

Creamy Baked Potatoes with Mustard Seeds

PREPARATION TIME:
15-20 MINUTES

COOKING TIME:
1 HOUR 15
MINUTES

FREEZING:
COMPLETE STEP 2,
COOL QUICKLY,
WRAP AND FREEZE.
THAW AT COOL
ROOM
TEMPERATURE
OVERNIGHT. COOK
AS IN STEP 3 FOR
20-25 MINUTES OR
UNTIL HOT TO THE
CENTRE.

330 CALS PER
SERVING

SERVES 6

Baked potatoes make a very healthy meal and are easy to cook in the Aga. However, they can be a little boring, so try this variation.

6 baking potatoes, approximately 1.4 kg (3 lb)
30 ml (2 tbsp) sunflower oil
15 ml (1 level tbsp) coarse sea salt
4-5 large garlic cloves, unpeeled
50 g (2 oz) butter

90 ml (6 tbsp) crème fraîche
30 ml (2 level tbsp) mustard seeds, toasted and lightly crushed
salt and freshly ground black pepper
oregano sprigs, to garnish

1 Prick potato skins, rub with oil and sprinkle with salt. Cook in a roasting tin on the grid shelf on the floor of the ROASTING OVEN for 40 minutes. Add the garlic to the roasting tin and cook for a further 20 minutes.
2 Slice the tops off the potatoes, scoop the flesh into a warm bowl, squeeze the garlic out of the skin and add to the potato with the butter, crème fraîche and mustard seeds. Mash and season. Return mixture to the hollowed skins.
3 Cook in the ROASTING OVEN for a further 15 minutes or until golden brown. Garnish with oregano and serve.

Red Cabbage Timbales with Mushroom Stuffing

PREPARATION TIME:
I HOUR, PLUS
COOLING FOR
30 MINUTES

COOKING TIME:
I HOUR

FREEZING:
UNSUITABLE

400 CALS PER
SERVING

SERVES 6

This impressive dish is an ideal alternative to turkey for vegetarian guests at Christmas. If you make double the quantity of stuffing, half can be used to stuff the turkey for meat eaters.

FOR THE STUFFING
450 g (I lb) brown-cap mushrooms
75 g (3 oz) toasted, salted cashew nuts
200 g (7 oz) onions
50 g (2 oz) butter
90 ml (4 level tbsp) chopped flat-leafed parsley
125 g (4 oz) fresh breadcrumbs
2 large eggs, beaten
salt and freshly ground black pepper

FOR THE TIMBALES
I medium red cabbage, about 1.4 kg (3 lb)
375 g (12 oz) onions
40 g (I½ oz) butter
45 ml (3 tbsp) balsamic vinegar
salt and freshly ground black pepper

FOR THE SAUCE
60 ml (4 level tbsp) caster sugar
60 ml (4 tbsp) red wine vinegar
150 ml (¼ pint) red wine
15 ml (I tbsp) lemon juice
small thyme sprigs, to garnish (optional)

1 To make the stuffing, roughly chop the mushrooms and cashew nuts and finely chop onions.
2 Melt the butter in a frying pan on the BOILING PLATE, add the mushrooms and onions, stir once, then fry briskly without stirring until golden and until the moisture has evaporated. Mix in the chopped parsley, cashew nuts and breadcrumbs. Leave to cool, then stir in the beaten eggs and seasoning, mixing well. Cover and set aside.
3 To make the timbales, place the cabbage in a large pan of boiling water. Bring to the boil; simmer on the SIMMERING PLATE until outside leaves have softened enough to be eased away. Lift the cabbage out of the pan; set aside, reserving the water. Remove the three outer leaves and boil them for a further 3-4 minutes; place in a bowl of cold water. Quarter the reserved whole cabbage and remove the core. Take 700 g (I½ lb) and remove any heavy central vein from the leaves; discard. Shred the leaves very finely, cover and set aside.
4 Line six 150 ml (¼ pint) pudding moulds with microwave cling film. Drain the whole cabbage leaves and cut in half either side of the central vein. Discard the vein. Use the leaves to line the moulds. Fill with stuffing mixture and cover with foil.
5 Place in a large roasting tin; pour in enough warm water to come halfway up the sides of the moulds.
■■ Cook on the grid shelf on the floor of the ROASTING OVEN for 20-25 minutes or until just set to the centre.
■■■■ Cook on the second runners of the BAKING OVEN for 30-35 minutes or until just set to the centre.
6 Meanwhile, finely chop the onions. Melt the butter in a pan, add the onion and cook on the SIMMERING PLATE until soft. Mix in the reserved shredded cabbage, vinegar, salt and pepper. Cook, stirring for 2-3 minutes on the BOILING PLATE, then cover and transfer to the SIMMERING OVEN for 20-30 minutes or until beginning to soften.
7 To make the sauce, place sugar and red wine vinegar in a small pan. Cook on the SIMMERING PLATE until sugar has dissolved, bring to the boil and cook to a rich caramel. Pour in the wine, reduce by half, add lemon juice to taste and season. Cool.
8 Turn out the timbales, spoon shredded cabbage on top, drizzle red wine sauce over and garnish with thyme sprigs, if wished.

COOK'S TIP
To prepare ahead, complete to end of step 4 the day before, cover and chill. To use, complete the recipe.

Aubergine and Chickpea Pilaff

PREPARATION TIME:
10 MINUTES

COOKING TIME:
30 MINUTES, PLUS 5
MINUTES STANDING

FREEZING:
UNSUITABLE

290 CALS PER
SERVING

SERVES 6

This is perfect for a midweek supper dish. Serve with a large green salad for a really healthy meal.

I large aubergine
salt and freshly ground black pepper
60 ml (4 tbsp) olive oil
2 medium onions, chopped
25 g (I oz) butter

2.5 ml (½ level tsp) cumin seeds
175 g (6 oz) long-grain rice
600 ml (I pint) vegetable or chicken stock
400 g can chickpeas, drained and rinsed
225 g (8 oz) baby spinach

I Halve the aubergine, score the cut surface and sprinkle with salt. Leave for 10 minutes, then squeeze out the juices. Drizzle 30 ml (2 tbsp) olive oil over the cut surface, place cut side down in a small roasting tin and bake on the floor of the ROASTING OVEN for 20 minutes, until soft and golden underneath. Cut into dice. Heat the remaining oil in a flameproof casserole and cook the onions on the SIMMERING PLATE for 5 minutes or until golden and soft.

2 Add the butter, then stir in the cumin seeds and rice. Fry for 1-2 minutes, pour the stock over, season and bring to the boil. Reduce the heat, then simmer, uncovered, for 10-12 minutes on the floor of the ROASTING OVEN or until most of the liquid has evaporated and the rice is tender.

3 Remove the pan from the heat. Stir in the chickpeas, spinach and reserved, cooked aubergine. Cover with a tight-fitting lid and leave to stand for 5 minutes in the SIMMERING OVEN until the spinach is wilted and the chickpeas are heated through. Adjust the seasoning to taste. Fork through the rice grains to separate and make them fluffy before serving.

COOK'S TIP
To prepare a few hours ahead, cook the aubergine and onion as in step 1. To use, complete the recipe.

Broad Bean and Lemon Risotto

PREPARATION TIME:
25 MINUTES

COOKING TIME:
35 MINUTES

FREEZING:
UNSUITABLE

380 CALS PER
SERVING

SERVES 4

Broad beans, in common with other beans and pulses, are a good source of dietary fibre, particularly soluble fibre, which can help reduce high blood cholesterol levels. They also provide useful amounts of vitamin B1 and iron.

350 g (12 oz) frozen broad beans
salt and freshly ground black pepper
25 g (I oz) butter
I medium onion, finely chopped
200 g (7 oz) arborio rice

I litre (1¾ pints) hot vegetable stock
grated rind and juice of I lemon
75 g (3 oz) freshly grated Parmesan cheese
grated Parmesan cheese and lemon rind,
to garnish

I Cook the broad beans in a large pan of boiling salted water on the BOILING PLATE for 3-5 minutes or until just tender. Plunge into icy cold water to cool. Drain, peel off outer skin (optional) and set aside.

2 Melt the butter in large pan, add the onion and cook on the SIMMERING PLATE for 5 minutes or until beginning to soften. Add the rice and continue to cook, stirring, for 1-2 minutes. Pour in 2 ladlefuls of the hot stock and place in the SIMMERING OVEN for 5 minutes until the rice has absorbed most of the stock. Keep adding the stock in this way until the rice is tender but still has bite to it; this will take about 15-20 minutes. The risotto should look creamy and soft.

3 Add the broad beans, lemon rind and juice and warm through. Stir in the Parmesan and season to taste.

4 Serve the risotto immediately, garnished with grated Parmesan and lemon rind.

Thai Vegetable Curry

PREPARATION TIME:
15 MINUTES

COOKING TIME:
35 MINUTES

FREEZING: SUITABLE
(FOR THE CURRY)

435-290 CALS PER
SERVING

SERVES 4-6

When adding curry paste, cook spices thoroughly, otherwise the finished curry will taste raw. Curry pastes vary in heat depending on the brand.

30 ml (2 tbsp) vegetable oil
1 large onion, finely chopped
20 ml (4 level tsp) Thai green curry paste
600 ml (1 pint) vegetable stock
200 g (7 oz) washed new potatoes, cut in half
225 g (8 oz) easy-cook long grain rice
200 g (7 oz) courgettes, cut on the diagonal

200 g (7 oz) carrots, cut on the diagonal
150 g (5 oz) broccoli, divided into florets
125 g (4 oz) tomatoes, cut into quarters
150 g (5 oz) frozen spinach, thawed
300 ml (½ pint) coconut milk
coriander sprigs, to garnish (optional)

1 Heat the oil in a large frying pan. Add the onion and green curry paste, then cook for 4-5 minutes on the SIMMERING PLATE. Add the stock and potatoes, bring to the boil, then cover and transfer to the SIMMERING OVEN. Cook for 20 minutes or until the potatoes are just tender.

2 Meanwhile, cook the rice. Bring it to the boil in a large pan, cover and cook on the floor of the SIMMERING OVEN. Add courgettes, carrots and broccoli to the curry (see Cook's Tip). Cook for 3-4 minutes or until vegetables are tender. At the last minute add the tomatoes, spinach and coconut milk and heat through thoroughly. Serve the curry on a bed of rice and garnish with coriander.

COOK'S TIP
You can substitute any vegetables in season for the courgettes, carrots and broccoli.

Mushroom and Ricotta Cannelloni with Tomato Sauce

PREPARATION TIME:
15 MINUTES

COOKING TIME:
50 MINUTES

FREEZING: SUITABLE

240 CALS PER SERVING

SERVES 4

This cannelloni uses sheets of fresh lasagne. If you use dried instead, cook it according to the packet instructions but reduce the overall cooking time by 15 minutes. See page 62 for cooking instructions for the lasagne sheets.

15 g (½ oz) dried mushrooms
15 g (½ oz) butter, plus a little extra for greasing
225 g (8 oz) brown-cap mushrooms, finely chopped
250 g (9 oz) ricotta cheese
5 ml (1 tsp) anchovy essence

salt and freshly ground black pepper
4 sheets fresh lasagne, each measuring 11.5 x 16.5 cm (4½ x 6½ in)
2 x 300 ml tubs fresh tomato sauce
50 g (2 oz) Parmesan cheese shavings
black pepper and basil sprigs, to garnish

1 Wash the dried mushrooms, then pour 150 ml (¼ pint) boiling water over and leave in the SIMMERING OVEN for 15 minutes. Drain and finely chop. Lightly grease a large, shallow, ovenproof dish with butter.

2 Heat the butter in large frying pan, add the fresh and soaked dried mushrooms and cook on the SIMMERING PLATE for 10-15 minutes or until they are beginning to brown and any liquid has evaporated. Leave to cool.

3 Stir the ricotta cheese into the mushrooms, add the anchovy essence and seasoning, then mix until thoroughly combined.

4 Cook the lasagne according to the packet instructions, then halve widthways. Place about 45 ml (3 level tbsp) mushroom mixture along one edge of the lasagne, then roll up to enclose the filling. Repeat this process with the remaining lasagne. Arrange the filled pasta seam-side down in the prepared dish. Pour the tomato sauce over and sprinkle with the Parmesan cheese shavings. Cook on the grid shelf on the floor of the ROASTING OVEN for 30-35 minutes. Garnish with pepper and fresh basil sprigs to serve.

COOK'S TIPS
To prepare ahead, complete the recipe to end of step 4, cover and chill for up to 6 hours. To use, complete the recipe.

To make Parmesan shavings, use a swivel peeler to take ribbons off a block of fresh parmesan. The flavour is so much better than the packets of dry, ready grated cheese.

Tomato and Basil Tarte Tatin

PREPARATION TIME:
30 MINUTES, PLUS
30 MINUTES
CHILLING

COOKING TIME:
1 HOUR 25
MINUTES

FREEZING: THE
PASTRY CAN BE
FROZEN READY
ROLLED.

310 CALS PER
SERVING

SERVES 6

Many people are familiar with the traditional apple tarte tatin. This modern tomato version makes a delicious starter or lunch dish. The pastry is mouth-watering, but only turn the tart over when you are about to serve it so that the texture remains crisp.

120 ml (6 tbsp) olive oil
30 ml (2 level tbsp) tomato paste
400 g (14 oz) can chopped tomatoes
1 sprig fresh thyme or large pinch dried
salt and freshly ground black pepper
20 ml (4 level tsp) caster sugar
1.1 kg (2½ lb) plum tomatoes, halved lengthways
50 g (2 oz) ciabatta
2 garlic cloves, crushed

45 ml (3 level tbsp) roughly chopped fresh basil or thyme

FOR THE PASTRY
75 g (3 oz) chilled butter, cut into cubes
125 g (4 oz) plain flour, plus extra for dusting
60-75 ml (4-5 tbsp) soured cream
chervil sprigs and garlic-infused olive oil, to serve (see Cook's Tips)
crushed black peppercorns, to garnish

1 Heat a large ovenproof frying pan with 15 ml (1 tbsp) olive oil on the BOILING PLATE. When the oil is smoking, cook half the tomatoes, cut side down, until well browned. Repeat with the remaining tomatoes, then place the tomatoes in the SIMMERING OVEN for 5-10 minutes so they will fit snugly on the base. Arrange the tomatoes, cut-side down, in the base of a 25 cm (10 in) round non-stick cake tin (see Cook's Tips).

2 Heat 30 ml (2 tbsp) oil in a pan, add the tomato paste and cook, stirring, for 1 minute. Add the canned tomatoes, thyme, seasoning and 5 ml (1 level tsp) caster sugar. Bring to the boil, then simmer on the floor of the ROASTING OVEN for 15 minutes or until the sauce is reduced and very thick. Remove the thyme; cool.

3 Roughly chop the ciabatta. Process with the remaining 75 ml (3 tbsp) olive oil and the garlic to rough crumbs; season well and place in a small roasting tin. Cook on the second runners of the ROASTING OVEN for 5-10 minutes or until golden. Add the basil.

4 Next, make the pastry: place the butter and flour in a food processor. Pulse until the butter is roughly chopped, (you should still be able to see pieces), add the soured cream and pulse again until the mixture just comes together. Wrap and chill for at least 30 minutes.

5 Spread the seasoned tomato sauce over the tomatoes in the tin. Roll the pastry out on a lightly floured surface to a 25 cm (10 in) round, place on top of the tomatoes and trim the edges. Cut steam holes in the pastry.

6 Bake for 20-25 minutes on the third runners of the ROASTING OVEN, turning during cooking to ensure even colouring. Cool slightly before turning out.

7 Turn out the tart so it is tomato-side up, scatter over garlic and basil crumbs and cut into wedges. Garnish with chervil, drizzle with garlic oil and season with crushed peppercorns.

COOK'S TIPS
To prepare the day before, complete to end of step 4 but don't add basil to the crumbs. Cover and chill tomatoes, sauce, pastry, crumbs and basil separately. To use, complete the recipe.

For garlic-infused oil, place two thinly sliced garlic cloves in a pan with 90 ml (6 tbsp) olive oil. Warm gently in the SIMMERING OVEN until the garlic is golden; remove from heat and cool.

You can use an ovenproof frying pan with a removable metal handle and a 25 cm (10 in) base.

Make sure the tomato sauce is reduced and thick before you spoon it over the tomatoes in the tin. The rich pastry should be well chilled before you roll it out (step 5).

Wear rubber gloves when turning out the tart to protect your hands from hot juices and to get a better grip on the tin to lift it off.

Vegetarian Lasagne

PREPARATION TIME: ABOUT 1 HOUR

COOKING TIME: 40 MINUTES, TO BAKE

FREEZING: COMPLETE STEP 6 AND FREEZE. THAW AT ROOM TEMPERATURE FOR 3-4 HOURS, THEN COMPLETE THE RECIPE, ALLOWING AN EXTRA 5-7 MINUTES COOKING TIME.

685 CALS PER SERVING

SERVES 6

This vegetarian lasagne has a rich Mediterranean vegetable filling complemented by a set custard-like topping made from goat's cheese, eggs and cream. Use mild soft young goat's cheese – Chèvre Frais – which is usually sold in tubs. Alternatively you can use cream cheese or curd cheese instead.

4 red, orange or yellow peppers
2 medium aubergines
75 ml (5 tbsp) extra-virgin olive oil
2 onions, peeled
4 garlic cloves, peeled
45 ml (3 tbsp) chopped fresh oregano
75 ml (5 tbsp) red wine or water
90 ml (6 tbsp) sun-dried tomato paste
salt and freshly ground black pepper
12 sheets dried lasagne

FOR THE TOPPING
350 g (12 oz) fresh soft goat's cheese
2 eggs
150 ml (¼ pint) single cream
45 ml (3 tbsp) dry white breadcrumbs
30 ml (2 tbsp) freshly grated Parmesan cheese

1 Bake the peppers in a small roasting tin on the top runners of the ROASTING OVEN for 20-30 minutes until the skins are blackened and blistered all over. Place in a covered bowl and allow to cool slightly, then peel over a bowl to catch the juices. Chop the flesh, discarding the seeds, and set aside with the juices.

2 Meanwhile, halve and score the aubergines. Sprinkle liberally with salt. Leave for 20 minutes, to extract the bitter juices. Rinse, then drizzle the cut surface with half the oil. Place cut side down in a roasting tin and bake on the floor of the ROASTING OVEN for 20-25 minutes until golden underneath and soft. Cool.

3 Chop the onions; thinly slice the garlic. Heat the oil in a large saucepan on the SIMMERING PLATE. Add the onions and cook, stirring frequently, until soft and golden. Add the garlic and cook for a further minute. Add the wine and allow to bubble for 30 seconds, then stir in the aubergine, oregano, sun-dried tomato paste, peppers and seasoning. Mix well.

4 Pour a kettle of boiling water into a large roasting tin, add salt and float the sheets of lasagne in the tin. Cook in the SIMMERING OVEN for 10-15 minutes until 'al dente' or according to packet instructions. Drop the pasta sheets into a bowl of cold water with 30 ml (2 tbsp) oil added to prevent the sheets from sticking. Drain again and lay on a clean tea towel. (You may need to cook the pasta sheets in two batches.)

5 Oil a baking dish, measuring about 25 × 18 × 8 cm (10 × 7 × 3½ in), or a small roasting tin. Spread one third of the filling in the base and then cover with a layer of pasta, trimming to fit the dish as necessary. Add another third of the filling and cover with pasta as before. Cover with the last of the filling and arrange the remaining pasta sheets over the top.

6 To make the topping, place the goat's cheese in a bowl, add the eggs and beat well. Stir in the cream and seasoning. Pour over the lasagne and spread evenly. Sprinkle with the breadcrumbs and Parmesan.

7 ■■ Bake on the grid shelf on the floor of the ROASTING OVEN for 30-35 minutes, turning the tin round for the final 5 minutes to ensure even colouring.
■■■■ Bake on the second runners of the BAKING OVEN for 35-40 minutes, turning the tin round for the final 5 minutes to ensure even colouring.

COOK'S TIPS
To prepare ahead, complete to the end of step 6, then chill overnight. Allow an extra 5-7 minutes cooking time.

You can replace the goat's cheese topping with 350 g (12 oz) mozzarella, cut into slices.

ACCOMPANIMENTS

Winter Vegetable Roast

PREPARATION TIME:
20 MINUTES

COOKING TIME:
50 MINUTES

FREEZING:
UNSUITABLE

290 CALS PER
SERVING

Any seasonal root vegetables can be used in this recipe, but make sure you use a good mix of pale and colourful vegetables.

1.4 kg (3 lb) mixed root vegetables, such as carrots, sweet potato, parsnips, celeriac, turnips, squash or salsify, and pumpkin
150 g (5 oz) shallots, skin removed and root intact

60 ml (4 tbsp) olive oil
salt and freshly ground black pepper
150 g (5 oz) spicy sausages, such as merguez, twisted in half and cut in two
125 g (4 oz) vacuum-packed chestnuts

1 Peel and cut the vegetables into rough chunks, keeping the sweet potato and pumpkin in larger pieces as they cook more quickly. Cut the shallots in half lengthways if large. Place all the vegetables in a large roasting tin, drizzle with olive oil, season and toss well (see Cook's Tips).
2 Cook on the top runners of the ROASTING OVEN for 20 minutes, add the sausages and return to the oven for 15 minutes, stirring occasionally. Finally, add the chestnuts and cook on the middle runners for a further 10 minutes or until the vegetables are golden brown.

COOK'S TIPS
To prepare ahead, complete step 1, then cover and store in the fridge for up to one day. To use, complete the recipe.

Add salt to the vegetables only just before roasting as it draws liquid out of the vegetables, making successful roasting more difficult.

Pommes Anna

PREPARATION TIME:
15 MINUTES

COOKING TIME:
50 MINUTES

FREEZING:
UNSUITABLE

160 CALS PER
SERVING

SERVES 4

A classic French dish, this is a simple yet highly decorative way to serve potatoes.

4 large baking potatoes
50 g (2 oz) butter
salt and freshly ground black pepper

1 Peel the potatoes and slice very thinly by hand or on a mandolin. Melt the butter in a frying pan and fry the potato slices gently on the SIMMERING PLATE for 2-3 minutes until limp but not brown. Cover the pan and allow to cool slightly, then layer in 4 muffin tins, seasoning between each layer and pressing down firmly.
2 Cook on the floor of the ROASTING OVEN for 35-40 minutes or until cooked through and brown and crisp on top.
3 Using a round-bladed knife, ease the potatoes out of the tins and serve.

Buttered Carrots and Fennel

PREPARATION TIME:
5 MINUTES

COOKING TIME:
5 MINUTES

FREEZING:
UNSUITABLE

110-90 CALS PER
SERVING

SERVES 8-10

Lightly pre-cook these vegetables then toss in flavoured butter and lemon juice just before serving for the perfect texture and flavour.

1.4 kg (3 lb) young carrots
700 g (1½ lb) young fennel
salt

50 g (2 oz) butter
freshly ground black pepper
lemon juice to taste

1 Peel the carrots and halve (or quarter) the fennel lengthways. Place in a saucepan of salted water, bring to the boil on the BOILING PLATE and cook for 2-3 minutes. Drain and plunge into icy cold water; drain well.

2 When ready to serve, melt the butter in a saucepan on BOILING PLATE and cook until it is a nut brown colour, then add the drained carrots and fennel. Season with coarsely ground black pepper and toss for 1-2 minutes. Add a squeeze of lemon juice to taste, then serve.

77

Purée of Sweet Potatoes

PREPARATION TIME:
15 MINUTES

COOKING TIME:
25 MINUTES

FREEZING:
UNSUITABLE

185 CALS PER
SERVING

The sweet potato gives this smooth purée an almost nutty flavour. Be as bold as you like with the black pepper.

450 g (1 lb) orange-fleshed sweet potatoes, peeled and cut into large chunks (see Cook's Tips)

450 g (1 lb) old floury potatoes, peeled and cut into large chunks (see Cook's Tips)

salt and freshly ground black pepper

50 g (2 oz) butter

45 ml (3 level tbsp) chopped fresh thyme (optional)

1 Place the sweet potatoes and potatoes in a large saucepan. Cover with water and add salt. Bring to a fast boil on the BOILING PLATE for 2 minutes, then drain off all but 1 cm (½ in) of the water and transfer to the SIMMERING OVEN to cook in their steam for 20-30 minutes or until very tender. Drain and dry well.

2 Mash the potatoes until smooth. Beat in the butter, season well and stir in the fresh thyme if wished. Serve immediately.

COOK'S TIPS

To prepare ahead, peel the sweet potatoes and potatoes, cover with cold water and chill up to 8 hours ahead. To use, complete the recipe.

Be sure to peel the sweet potato deeply enough to expose the orange flesh or the resulting purée will be stringy.

If you have time, boil both types of potato whole in their skins and then peel. This will stop the potatoes absorbing water while they cook and give a lighter result. If sweet potato isn't available, try using butternut squash or even pumpkin, but cook separately from the potato.

Chiffonade of Sprouts

PREPARATION TIME:
5-7 MINUTES

COOKING TIME:
1-2 MINUTES

FREEZING:
UNSUITABLE

115-85 CALS PER
SERVING

SERVES 6-8

Cooked in a flash, this crunchy, pale green, nutty flavoured mound is far removed from the grey-green sodden lumps with that all-pervading smell that we remember from our schooldays.

1 kg (2¼ lb) sprouts (see Cook's Tips)

60 ml (4 tbsp) double cream or chicken stock

salt and freshly ground black pepper

freshly grated nutmeg

1 Trim the stalks of the sprouts and remove any yellowed outer leaves. Slice the sprouts very finely – this is best done in a food processor which will do it very quickly.

2 Pour the cream or stock into a wide based pan; season with salt, pepper and nutmeg. Tip the sprouts on top but do not toss. Cover with a lid.

3 Place the covered pan on the BOILING PLATE and allow to cook until you hear the liquid bubbling, then toss well and cook for another 30 seconds. Uncover and toss constantly until the sprouts are lightly wilted. Serve immediately.

COOK'S TIPS

If you wish to slice the sprouts in advance, store them tightly packed in a polythene bag in the fridge.

When preparing sprouts, never remove the outer green leaves. These are high in beta carotene and are a good protection against cancer. Only remove discoloured yellow leaves. Speckled weather marks on green leaves vanish during cooking.

Swede and Carrots with Mustard Seeds and Ginger

PREPARATION TIME:
20 MINUTES

COOKING TIME:
20 MINUTES

FREEZING:
UNSUITABLE

105 CALS PER
SERVING

SERVES 4

Swede has often been a much maligned vegetable, yet it has a distinctive flavour which is enhanced by herbs, spices and aromatic ingredients. Swede and carrots go well together, and the addition of mustard seeds and ginger makes the combination more exciting.

450 g (1 lb) swede
450 g (1 lb) carrots
2 pieces preserved stem ginger in syrup, drained, or 30 ml (2 tbsp) diced glacé ginger

25 g (1 oz) butter
5 ml (1 tsp) black mustard seeds
parsley or chervil sprigs, to garnish

1 Peel the swede and cut into small dice. Peel the carrots and slice thinly. Cook the vegetables in 75 ml (5 tbsp) salted water in a covered pan on the grid shelf of the ROASTING OVEN for 20 minutes until tender.

2 Meanwhile, finely chop the stem ginger. Melt the butter in a small heavy-based saucepan. Add the mustard seeds and heat gently on the SIMMERING PLATE until the seeds begin to pop. Add the chopped ginger and cook for 1 minute.

3 Drain the cooked swede and carrots thoroughly, then mash together or purée in a food processor. Season liberally with black pepper and stir in half of the mustard and ginger mixture.

4 Transfer the mashed swede and carrots to a warmed serving dish and drizzle the remaining mustard and ginger mixture over the top. Garnish with parsley or chervil and serve at once.

COOK'S TIP
As a variation, make a mustard and ginger cauliflower cheese by tossing cooked cauliflower florets in half of the mustard mixture. Transfer to a gratin dish and spoon on the cheese sauce. Top with the remaining mustard mixture and grated cheese, then brown high in the ROASTING OVEN.

Roast New Potatoes with Garlic and Parmesan

PREPARATION TIME:
5 MINUTES

COOKING TIME:
40 MINUTES

FREEZING:
UNSUITABLE

180 CALS PER
SERVING

SERVES 6

As you open the Aga door, the fragrance of these potatoes will really hit you.

900 g (2 lb) small new potatoes
12 garlic cloves, peeled
30 ml (2 tbsp) olive oil

50 g (2 oz) Parmesan cheese, finely grated
coarse sea salt
rosemary sprigs, to garnish

1 Place the potatoes in a large roasting tin with the garlic cloves, then toss in the olive oil and Parmesan cheese.

2 Cook on the bottom runners of the ROASTING OVEN for 30-40 minutes. Season with coarse sea salt and garnish with rosemary sprigs just before serving.

Crunchy Topped Mash

PREPARATION TIME:
10 MINUTES

COOKING TIMES:
45 MINUTES

FREEZING:
UNSUITABLE

260 CALS PER
SERVING

SERVES 6

Everyday mashed potato is lifted to a new level with this bacon and chestnut topping. This wonderfully fragrant dish is ideal for cooking on the Aga.

1.25 kg (12½ lb) potatoes
100 g (3½ oz) bacon, diced
15 ml (1 tbsp) oil
200 g (7 oz) peeled chestnuts, broken into pieces (see Cook's Tips)

40 g (1½ oz) butter
75 ml (5 tbsp) milk
30 ml (2 tbsp) rosemary
salt and freshly ground black pepper

1 Scrub the potatoes and peel thickly using a knife. Reserve the peel. Cut the potatoes into large pieces, place in a pan, cover with water and bring to the boil on the BOILING PLATE. Tip off all but 1 cm (½ in) of the water, sprinkle with a little salt, cover and place in the SIMMERING OVEN for 20-30 minutes until tender.

2 Roughly chop the potato peel, place in a roasting tin and toss with the bacon, oil and black pepper. Roast on the top runners of the ROASTING OVEN for 15-20 minutes until the potato skins are almost cooked, then scatter over the chestnuts and toss together.

3 Drain the potatoes, add the butter and milk and place on the SIMMERING PLATE until the milk boils. Remove from the heat and mash to a creamy texture. Season to taste and tip into a shallow dish. Top with the bacon and chestnut topping.

4 Bake on the grid shelf on the floor of the ROASTING OVEN for 7-10 minutes until the potatoes are piping hot and the topping is golden.

COOK'S TIPS

To prepare ahead, complete to the end of step 3 up to 24 hours ahead. To use, complete the recipe, allowing an extra 20 minutes.

Buy ready peeled vacuum-packed chestnuts to save time. Alternatively, cook 300 g (11 oz), making a slit in each chestnut, in the ROASTING OVEN for about 20 minutes. Allow to cool, then peel when hand hot.

Pumpkin and Cheese Bake

PREPARATION TIME:
15 MINUTES

COOKING TIME:
45 MINUTES

FREEZING:
UNSUITABLE

656 CALS PER
SERVING

SERVES 4

Few will be able to resist this dish of potatoes, pumpkin and cheese baked in deliciously rich crème fraîche. With its crisp golden edges and melting sauce, it's perfect for Hallowe'en.

450 g (1 lb) new potatoes, halved
450 g (1 lb) pumpkin, peeled and thinly sliced
1 large onion, about 175 g (6 oz), finely sliced
salt and freshly ground black pepper

125 g (4 oz) thinly sliced smoked ham
225 g (8 oz) buttery cheese, eg Taleggio, Gruyère or Fontina, thinly sliced
300 ml (½ pint) crème fraîche
baguette and green salad, to serve (optional)

1 Boil the potatoes, pumpkin and onion together in a little salted water in a shallow flameproof casserole on the BOILING PLATE for 3-4 minutes. Drain off all the liquid and roughly mix in the ham and cheese.

2 Beat a little cold water into the crème fraîche to give a thick pouring consistency. Season with pepper, then pour over vegetables. Place the casserole on the SIMMERING PLATE and bring to the boil.

3 Transfer to the ROASTING OVEN and cook uncovered on the grid shelf on the second runners for 40 minutes or until bubbling and golden. Two or three times during the cooking time, stir the crust that forms on top into the dish to add to the flavour. To check the dish is cooked, press the tip of a knife into the centre of a potato, which should be tender. Serve with a baguette and green salad if wished.

COOK'S TIPS

To prepare ahead, complete the recipe, reserving a little of the crème fraîche mixture. Cool, cover and chill overnight in the fridge. To use, brush on the reserved crème fraîche, then reheat on the grid shelf on the floor of the ROASTING OVEN for 15-20 minutes.

This recipe can be adapted to make a great vegetarian dish. Omit the ham and use an extra 125 g (4 oz) of potatoes or pumpkin. Sweet potatoes and celeriac are delicious, too – simply peel and slice the sweet potato thinly and the celeriac a little thicker, and boil with the potatoes and pumpkin.

Vegetables à la Grecque

PREPARATION TIME:
40-50 MINUTES,
PLUS 15 MINUTES
COOLING

COOKING TIME:
40 MINUTES

FREEZING:
UNSUITABLE

330 CALS PER
SERVING

SERVES 4

To save time, you could use fresh vegetable stock (available from supermarkets), instead of making the bouillon. If you do this, omit step 1.

FOR THE BOUILLON
30 ml (2 tbsp) virgin olive oil
2 shallots, peeled and finely chopped
1 garlic cloves, peeled and crushed
150 ml (¼ pint) dry white wine
15 ml (1 tbsp) white wine vinegar
2 fresh thyme sprigs, bruised
2 bay leaves
6 coriander seeds, bruised
large pinch of saffron threads
2 strips of orange rind
1.25 ml (¼ level tsp) sea salt
6 white peppercorns, lightly crushed

FOR THE VEGETABLES
900 g (2 lb) mixed baby vegetables, such as carrots, turnips, fennel, broccoli, asparagus, courgettes and broad beans, trimmed, peeled, halved and quartered
75 ml (5 tbsp) virgin olive oil
salt and freshly ground black pepper
juice of ½ lemon
diced yellow pepper, to garnish

1 For the bouillon, heat the oil in a pan on the SIMMERING PLATE; add shallots and garlic and cook gently for 2-3 minutes until soft and translucent. Add remaining ingredients and 300 ml (½ pint) water. Bring to the boil, then transfer to the SIMMERING OVEN for 30-45 minutes.

2 Meanwhile, prepare the vegetables. Peel and cut the carrot into thumb-sized pieces. Peel and quarter the turnip. Quarter the fennel. Break the broccoli into florets. Snap off the coarse end of the asparagus. Thickly slice the courgette.

3 Cook the vegetables: heat the oil in a large sauté pan on the SIMMERING PLATE, then add the slower-cooking root vegetables (carrots and turnips) and cook for 4-5 minutes. Add the broccoli, fennel and carrot and cook for 2-3 minutes. Finally, add the asparagus, courgettes and beans and cook for a final 2-3 minutes.

4 Pour the bouillon into the pan, bring to the boil and poach the vegetables in the SIMMERING OVEN for 5 minutes, then cool slightly. To serve, season and add lemon juice to taste. Garnish with yellow pepper.

COOK'S TIP
To prepare ahead, complete to the end of step 1, cool, cover and chill. To use, complete the recipe.

Roasted Vegetable Ratatouille

PREPARATION TIME:
30 MINUTES

COOKING TIME:
1 HOUR 30 MINUTES

FREEZING:
UNSUITABLE

335 CALS PER
SERVING

SERVES 6

The addition of goat's cheese makes this almost a meat in itself – especially good for any vegetarian guests.

225 g (8 oz) each plum tomatoes, aubergines, courgettes, red peppers and onions
350 g (12 oz) sweet potatoes, peeled and roughly chopped
salt and freshly ground black pepper
2 garlic cloves, peeled
5 ml (1 level tsp) chopped fresh thyme
50 ml (2 fl oz) olive oil

50 ml (2 fl oz) white wine
225 g (8 oz) passata or 400 g can chopped plum tomatoes
5 ml (1 level tsp) caster sugar
175 g (6 oz) firm goat's cheese, thickly sliced
thyme sprigs and roasted garlic slivers, to garnish

1 Halve the tomatoes, thickly slice the courgettes, quarter and seed the peppers, cut the aubergine and onions into large chunks.

2 Cook the sweet potatoes in a pan of boiling salted water, bringing it to the boil then tipping off all but 1 cm (½ in) of water and transferring it to the SIMMERING OVEN for 10-15 minutes. Transfer the sweet potatoes to a large roasting tin with the remaining vegetables, garlic, thyme and oil; season and toss together. Cook on the top runners of the ROASTING OVEN for 45 minutes-1 hour, until golden brown, turning the tin round and stirring the vegetables after 30 minutes to ensure even colouring.

3 Meanwhile, place the wine, passata or tomatoes and sugar in a pan. Bring to the boil on the BOILING PLATE and bubble for a few minutes until thick, stirring constantly, then season well.

4 Place the roasted vegetables in an ovenproof dish. Peel and mash the roasted garlic and mix into the tomato sauce. Spoon over the vegetables and arrange cheese on top.

5 Return to the top of the ROASTING OVEN for 20 minutes or until golden. Leave for 5 minutes, then garnish and serve.

COOK'S TIP
To prepare ahead, complete to the end of step 3, then cover and chill for up to one day. To use, complete the recipe, allowing an extra 5-10 minutes cooking time.

Roast Sweet Pepper with Sage

PREPARATION TIME:
20 MINUTES

COOKING TIME:
30-35 MINUTES

FREEZING:
UNSUITABLE

170 CALS PER
SERVING

SERVES 4

Roast peppers flavoured with fresh herbs make a tasty vegetable accompaniment which will enhance a wide variety of main course dishes. You could even serve them cold as a side salad or starter, if preferred.

2 large red peppers
2 large orange or yellow peppers
1 small onion
1 garlic clove
30 ml (2 tbsp) olive oil

about 8 fresh sage leaves
25 g (1 oz) pine nuts
coarse sea salt and freshly ground black pepper

1 Roast the whole peppers in a roasting tin on the top runners of the ROASTING OVEN for 20 minutes until the skin is blistered and blackened. Cover with a damp cloth and leave to cool slightly.

2 While the peppers are cooking, peel and chop the onion. Peel and finely slice the garlic. Heat the oil in a small saucepan, add the onion and garlic, cover and cook on the SIMMERING PLATE until softened. Add the sage leaves and cook for 2-3 minutes until frazzled. Remove the sage with a slotted spoon and set aside. Add the vegetable stock to the pan and boil rapidly on the BOILING PLATE or on the floor of the ROASTING OVEN until reduced to a quarter of the original volume.

3 Spread the pine nuts on a baking sheet.
■■ Toast on the grid shelf on the floor of the ROASTING OVEN.
■■■■ Toast on the grid shelf on the floor of the BAKING OVEN.

4 When the peppers are ready, peel away the skins. Cut off the stalk, then halve the peppers and scrape out the core and seeds but reserve the juices. Cut the peppers into broad strips, and add to the garlic and onion mixture with their juices. Toss lightly to mix.

5 Arrange the peppers on a warmed serving dish and sprinkle with the pine nuts and sage leaves. Serve immediately, or leave to cool and serve cold.

COOK'S TIP
To make vegetable stock, use 1 onion, peeled and sliced; 1 leek, cleaned and sliced; 6 spring onion tops, chopped; 1 celery stick, chopped; and 1 carrot, peeled and chopped. Heat 15 ml (1 tbsp) vegetable oil in a saucepan. Add the vegetables and fry gently for 4-5 minutes. Season with salt and pepper, add 1 bay leaf and 1 litre (1¾ pints) water. Bring to the boil, then cook in the SIMMERING OVEN for 2-3 hours. Strain, then cool and use as required.

Gingerbread Tree Decorations

PREPARATION TIME:
30 MINUTES, PLUS
COOLING

COOKING TIME:
10 MINUTES

FREEZING: SUITABLE
AT THE END OF
STEP 6. THAW AT
ROOM
TEMPERATURE FOR
ABOUT 2 HOURS.

125 CALS PER
BISCUIT

MAKES ABOUT 25

Fun to make and to give to friends, these little biscuits look lovely hanging on a Christmas tree. You can also decorate them with glacé or royal icing.

350 g (12 oz) plain white flour
5 ml (1 level tsp) bicarbonate of soda
30 ml (2 level tbsp) ground ginger
15 ml (1 level tbsp) ground cinnamon
2.5 ml (½ level tsp) ground cloves
125 g (4 oz) butter
175 g (6 oz) soft light brown (muscovado) sugar

60 ml (4 tbsp) golden syrup
1 egg, size 4

FOR THE ICING
1 egg white
sifted icing sugar
food colouring

1 Line two baking sheets with non-stick baking parchment.

2 Sift the flour with the bicarbonate of soda and spices into a large bowl. Rub in the butter until the mixture resembles fine breadcrumbs. Stir in the sugar.

3 Place the syrup tin in the SIMMERING OVEN to warm the syrup very slightly, then measure into a bowl and beat in the egg. Cool slightly, then pour onto the flour mixture. Beat with a wooden spoon to a soft dough or mix in a food processor. Bring together with your hands and knead until smooth.

4 Roll out the mixture on a lightly floured surface to a 5 mm (¼ in) thickness and cut out shapes with cutters. Make a small hole in the top of each one to enable ribbon to be threaded through after baking. Carefully transfer the shapes to the baking sheets.

5 ■■ Bake on the grid shelf on the floor of the ROASTING OVEN and on the bottom runners with a cold roasting tin placed on the top runners for 5 minutes, then turn the sheets round, remove the roasting tin and cook for a further 2-5 minutes until golden brown.

■■■■ Bake in the middle of the BAKING OVEN for 10-12 minutes until golden brown, turning the trays round after 5 minutes to ensure even colouring.

Leave to cool and harden for 10 minutes on the baking sheet, then transfer to a wire rack to cool completely.

6 To make the icing, beat the egg white until frothy and gradually add enough sifted icing sugar to make a stiff coating or piping consistency. Colour the icing as required.

Marinated Olives and Spiced Nuts

PREPARATION TIME:
20 MINUTES, PLUS
MARINATING
OLIVES

COOKING TIME:
NUTS: 30 MINUTES

FREEZING:
UNSUITABLE

50 CALS PER 25 G
(1 OZ) OF OLIVES;
195 CALS PER 25 G
(1 OZ) OF NUTS

MAKES 450 G (1 LB)
EACH

Make these perfumed olives at least a month before Christmas to allow the olives to fully absorb the flavours. Serve with drinks or layer in small pots to use as gifts. The deliciously spicy nuts are wonderful served almost straight from the oven while still warm. Alternatively, cool them and store in an airtight tin for up to 2 weeks – any longer and they go stale.

OLIVES
200g (7 oz) each black, green and stuffed olives
30 ml (2 tbsp) coriander seeds
finely pared rind of 1 orange, shredded
few fresh coriander sprigs
450-750 ml (¾-1¼ pints) extra-virgin olive oil (depending on the size of jar)

NUTS
350 g (12 oz) mixed skinned nuts, such as almonds, pecans, hazelnuts
125 g (4 oz) shelled mixed pumpkin and sunflower seeds
45 ml (3 tbsp) sunflower oil
15 ml (1 level tbsp) curry powder or garam marsala
5 ml (1 level tsp) coarse sea salt

1 Using a rolling pin, lightly hit each black and green olive to split without crushing completely. Alternatively, slit with a small sharp knife. (Stoned olives do not need cracking.)

2 Arrange the black, green and stuffed olives in layers in an attractive 1.2 litre (2 pint) glass jar. Sprinkle each layer with coriander seeds and orange rind shreds. Tuck a few sprigs of coriander down the side of the jar.

3 Warm the olive oil in a saucepan on the SIMMERING PLATE to release the aroma, then pour sufficient into the jar to cover the olives completely. Tapping the jar to release any air bubbles, seal tightly and allow to cool. Leave in a cool dark place for 1 month to mature.

4 To prepare the nuts, toss them in the oil with the curry powder in a small roasting tin. Place on the grid shelf on the floor of the ROASTING OVEN with the cold plain shelf on the second runners. Cook for 8 minutes, then turn the tray round. Add the seeds, toss well and return to the ROASTING OVEN. Check them after 8 minutes. If they are not light brown, stir well and cook for a further 3-10 minutes (see Aga Tip).

COOK'S TIPS
The nicest stuffed olives are those filled with anchovies or almonds.

For a variation with an oriental accent, flavour the nuts with 10 ml (2 tsp) Chinese five-spice powder instead of the curry powder.

AGA TIP
Leave the oven door slightly open during cooking so you can smell when the nuts are cooked.

Christmas Morning Muffins

PREPARATION TIME:
15 MINUTES

COOKING TIME:
15-20 MINUTES

FREEZING:
UNSUITABLE

175 CALS PER
MUFFIN

MAKES 12

Moist muffins bursting with cranberries make a wonderful start to the celebrations! Have all the dry ingredients mixed together, and prepare the muffin tin the night before. On Christmas morning, just stir in the liquids and cranberries, fill the tin and bake. Serve from the oven – these muffins do not reheat well.

175 g (6 oz) fresh cranberries
50 g (2 oz) icing sugar, sifted
150 g (5 oz) plain wholemeal flour
150 g (5 oz) plain white flour
15 ml (1 level tbsp) baking powder
5 ml (1 level tsp) ground mixed spice

2.5 ml (½ tsp) salt
50 g (2 oz) soft light brown sugar
1 egg
250 ml (8 fl oz) milk
60 ml (2 fl oz) vegetable oil

1 Halve the cranberries and place in a bowl with the icing sugar. Toss gently to mix.

2 Line up a twelve-cup muffin tin with paper cases or simply grease with butter. Sift together the flours, baking powder, mixed spice, salt and soft brown sugar into a large bowl. Make a well in the centre.

3 Beat the egg with the milk and oil. Add to the dry ingredients and stir just until blended, then lightly and quickly stir in the cranberries. The mixture should look roughly mixed, with lumps and floury pockets. Two-thirds fill the muffin cups with the mixture.

4 ■■ Bake at the front of the grid shelf on the floor of the ROASTING OVEN for 15-18 minutes until well risen and golden brown.

■■■■ Bake in the middle of the BAKING OVEN for 20 minutes until well risen and golden brown.

Transfer the muffins to a wire rack to cool slightly. Serve whilst still warm.

COOK'S TIPS

If using a greased (rather than lined) muffin tin, on removing from the oven turn it upside down onto a wire rack and leave for 2 minutes to allow the steam to loosen the muffins. Lift off the tray and turn the muffins up the right way.

For a variation, substitute 225 g (8 oz) mincemeat for the cranberries. Add to the well in the middle of the dry ingredients with the liquid. Stir until just moistened but still lumpy. Fill the muffin tins and bake as above.

Savoury Stars

PREPARATION TIME: 40 MINUTES, PLUS CHILLING

COOKING TIME: 12-20 MINUTES PLUS 10 MINUTES

FREEZING: SUITABLE. THAW IN THE SIMMERING OVEN FOR 15-20 MINUTES. THEN COOL ON A WIRE RACK FOR A FRESH FLAVOUR.

35 CALS PER STAR

MAKES ABOUT 40

These stars work well when served with crunchy vegetables and filled with cream cheese to provide a delicious contrast in taste and texture.

75 g (3 oz) plain white flour
75 g (3 oz) freshly grated Parmesan cheese
75 g (3 oz) butter
2.5 ml (½ tsp) salt
2.5 ml (½ tsp) cayenne pepper

25 g (1 oz) sun-dried tomatoes
25 g (1 oz) pistachio nuts
25 g (1 oz) pitted black olives
1 beaten egg, to glaze
15 ml (1 level tbsp) poppy seeds, caraway seeds or sesame seeds

1 In a food processor, blend the flour, cheese, butter, salt and cayenne pepper until the pastry forms a ball shape. Knead lightly, wrap in cling film and chill for about 10 minutes if it is too soft to roll out easily.

2 Meanwhile, finely chop the tomatoes, nuts and olives.

3 Roll out the pastry on a floured worksurface until it is about 5 mm (¼ in) thick. Brush with beaten egg, then sprinkle on an even layer of tomato, nuts and olives. Fold the pastry into a neat parcel shape to enclose the filling completely.

4 Roll out the parcel of pastry to a 1 cm (½ in) thickness. Use a star cutter to stamp out shapes, than place on baking sheets. Brush lightly with beaten egg and sprinkle on poppy, caraway or sesame seeds. Chill the pastry shapes for about 20 minutes.

5 ■■ Place the baking sheets on the grid shelf on the floor of the ROASTING OVEN with a cold roasting tin on the second runners. Cook for about 10 minutes until beginning to brown, then turn the tray round for even colouring and cook for a further 2-5 minutes. Transfer to the SIMMERING OVEN for 10 minutes to ensure the biscuits will be really crisp when cooked.

■■■■ Bake in the middle of the BAKING OVEN for 15-20 minutes. If you wish, transfer to the SIMMERING OVEN for an extra 10 minutes to ensure the biscuits will be really crisp when cooked.

Leave on the baking sheets for about 5 minutes before removing to a cooling rack.

COOK'S TIP

Omit the tomatoes, pistachio nuts and olives and replace with half a can of anchovy fillets soaked in milk for 30 minutes, then drained and finely chopped, or with freshly chopped herbs.

Roasted Turkey

These are general instructions for roasting a turkey in the Aga.

1 To make carving easier, first remove the wishbone from the turkey. Loosen the skin at the neck end, ease your fingers up between the skin and the breast and, using a sharp knife, remove the wishbone. Remove the giblets and reserve. Season the inside of the turkey, then stuff with thyme and rosemary sprigs and a few pieces of lemon and onion. Spoon a cold stuffing into the neck end only (see Cook's Tip), neaten the shape, tuck the skin under and secure with metal skewers or cocktail sticks. Weigh the turkey to calculate the cooking time (see the chart below). Decide which method suits you. Slower roasting results in a more succulent bird and frees the roasting oven for roast potatoes, sausages, bacon rolls, etc. However, you do not necessarily want to get up in the middle of the night to put a small bird in the oven for lunch or a large bird in for dinner.

2 Place the turkey in a large roasting tin, spread with a little butter and arrange slices of bacon on the breast. Pour in 150-450 ml (¼-¾ pint) of stock and arrange all the giblets except the liver around the bird. Cover with a loose tent of foil. If the butcher has tied the legs together tightly, loosen after the first hour so they cook through more evenly. Roast according to the chart, basting from time to time. Remove the foil and bacon for the last 30 minutes in the ROASTING OVEN or the last 45 minutes in the BAKING OVEN.* For the SIMMERING OVEN, transfer the turkey to the BAKING OVEN for 45 minutes or the ROASTING OVEN for 30 minutes when almost cooked to brown the bird. Slow cooking in the SIMMERING OVEN is not recommended for roasting small turkeys (or chickens).

3 When the turkey is cooked (the juices should run clear when a skewer is insert deep into the thigh), tip the turkey so the juices run into the tin, then place the turkey on a dish. Replace the bacon on the breast. Cover the turkey with foil and a thick towel. Set aside to rest for 30 minutes (small birds, 15 minutes).

COOK'S TIP
To prepare ahead, complete to the end of step 1, then cover and chill for up to 24 hours. To use, take the turkey out of the fridge 1 hour before cooking. Complete the recipe. Stuffing the cavity of the bird is not recommended.

TURKEY ROASTING TIMES					
Oven-ready weight	Approx no of servings	Approx thawing time	Cooking times		
			BAKING OVEN	2 or 4 Aga SIMMERING OVEN	2 or 4 Aga ROASTING OVEN
550 g-1.4 kg (1¼-3 lb)	2-4	4-10 hours	1-1½ hours		¾-1 hour
1.4-2.3 kg (3-5 lb)	4-6	10-15 hours	1½-2 hours		1-1½ hours
2.3-3.6 kg (5-8 lb)	6-10	15-18 hours	2-3 hours		1½-1¾ hours
3.6-5 kg (8-11 lb)	10-15	18-20 hours	3-3¼ hours	10 hours*	1¾-2 hours
5-6.8 kg (11-15 lb)	15-20	20-24 hours	3¼-4 hours	12 hours*	2½ hours
6.8-9 kg (15-20 lb)	20-30	24-30 hours	4-5½ hours	14 hours*	3 hours

* Transfer to hotter oven to brown, as in step 2 above.
NB With the individuality of Agas and possible loss of heat if hobs are used a lot, these times can be considered only a guide.

Lemon and Herb Roasted Turkey

PREPARATION TIME:
20 MINUTES

COOKING TIME:
ABOUT 3 HOURS,
PLUS AT LEAST
30 MINUTES
RESTING

FREEZING:
UNSUITABLE

644-515 CALS PER
SERVING

SERVES 8-10

Cooking the turkey with a little white wine in the roasting tin ensures it stays succulent and moist.

4.5 kg (10 lb) oven-ready turkey with giblets
450 g (1 lb) Mushroom and Olive Stuffing (see page 92)
125 g (4 oz) butter, softened
375 g (13 oz) pancetta or thinly sliced streaky bacon
salt and freshly ground black pepper
1 large bunch fresh thyme

1 large bunch fresh rosemary
3 lemons, preferably unwaxed, cut into chunks
1 large Spanish onion, about 450 g (1 lb), cut into chunks
150 ml (¼ pint) white wine
fresh thyme and rosemary sprigs, to garnish

1 Follow the instructions in step 1 of the general turkey roasting instructions on the left and stuff the neck end only with the Mushroom and Olive Stuffing.

2 Place the turkey in a large roasting tin, spread with a little butter and arrange slices of pancetta over the breast. Place the herbs, lemon and onion chunks around the bird, season and pour over the wine. Cover with a loose tent of foil and roast according to the chart. Baste from time to time. Loosen the leg joints if they are tied together tightly after 1 hour. Remove the foil and the pancetta to allow the bird to brown 30 minutes before the end of the cooking time in the ROASTING OVEN; 45 minutes if using the BAKING OVEN.

3 Check the turkey is cooked (see step 3, left). Place the pancetta back on the breast, cover with foil and a thick towel and set aside to rest for 20-30 minutes before carving. Serve with Turkey Gravy, below.

Turkey Gravy

PREPARATION TIME:
5 MINUTES

COOKING TIME:
15 MINUTES

FREEZING:
UNSUITABLE

40 CALS PER
SERVING FOR 8;
32 CALS PER
SERVING FOR 10

MAKES ABOUT
900 ML (1½ PINTS)

juices from the roast turkey
60 ml (4 level tbsp) plain flour

1.1 litres (2 pints) turkey or chicken stock (see Cook's Tips)
salt and freshly ground black pepper

1 Strain the juices from the turkey and skim off the fat, reserving 60 ml (4 tbsp). Place the reserved fat in the roasting tin and stir in flour to make a smooth paste. Place on the BOILING PLATE and cook, stirring, until the flour turns russet brown.

2 Off the heat, add the turkey juices, stir until smooth, then stir in the stock. Return to the BOILING PLATE, bring to the boil and bubble for 5-10 minutes or until reduced and thickened (skim off fat). Season, strain and serve.

COOK'S TIPS
To make stock, cook the turkey giblets (minus the liver) or five chicken wings in a pan with 1.5 litres (2 ½ pints) water, a few slices of onion, celery and leek, and seasoning, in a covered pan overnight in the SIMMERING OVEN. Strain, cool quickly and chill.

You can pour the gravy into a thermos flask to keep it piping hot and skin-free. Pour it into heated sauce boats moments before serving.

Sausage and Bacon Rolls

PREPARATION TIME:
15 MINUTES

COOKING TIME:
45-50 MINUTES

FREEZING:
UNSUITABLE

320 CALS PER
SERVING

SERVES 6

A traditional accompaniment to roast turkey and stuffing, these are easy to prepare ahead.

700 g (1½ lb) sausagemeat

450 g (1 lb) thinly sliced, rindless streaky bacon

1   Divide sausagemeat into 20 rounds; wrap each one in a rasher of bacon (see Cook's Tips).
2   Place in a shallow roasting tin with the ends of the bacon tucked under.
3   Roast on the top runners or on the floor of the ROASTING OVEN for about 15 minutes or until golden on one side, then turn over to brown the other side and cook for a further 15-30 minutes. (The cooking time will depend how much heat the Aga has lost in cooking the turkey.)

COOK'S TIPS
To prepare ahead, prepare to the end of step 2, place in a roasting tin and chill overnight. To use, follow step 3, allowing an extra 10-15 minutes.

Lay the rashers on a chopping board, then flatten and stretch them with the back of a knife. This makes the bacon thinner so it crisps well and doesn't shrink.

AGA TIP
Oven space is always at a premium at Christmas. You can cook these rolls 1-2 hours ahead, then reheat in any of the ovens until piping hot.

Couscous and Herb Stuffing

PREPARATION TIME:
20 MINUTES, PLUS
20 MINUTES
STANDING

COOKING TIME:
6 MINUTES

FREEZING:
COMPLETE THE
RECIPE, THEN PACK
AND FREEZE. THAW
AT COOL ROOM
TEMPERATURE
OVERNIGHT AND
USE AS PREFERRED.

115 CALS PER
SERVING FOR 8;
94 CALS PER
SERVING FOR 10

MAKES ABOUT
450 G (1 LB),
SERVES 8-10

LEMON AND HERB
ROASTED TURKEY
(PAGE 89)

An unusual but tasty stuffing recipe which makes a change from the more traditional versions.

30 ml (2 tbsp) oil
225 g (8 oz) onions, roughly chopped
1 garlic clove, crushed
100 g (3½ oz) couscous
salt and freshly ground black pepper

5 ml (1 level tsp) paprika
zested rind of 1 lemon
15 ml (1 level tbsp) chopped fresh herbs
1 medium egg

1   Heat the oil in a saucepan and gently fry the chopped onion with the lid on for 3-5 minutes on the SIMMERING PLATE until soft but not coloured. Add garlic and cook for 30 seconds.
2   Place the couscous in a heatproof bowl with the pepper and 5 ml (1 level tsp) salt. Pour boiling water over to cover the couscous by 5 mm (¼ in). Cover the leave in the SIMMERING OVEN for 20 minutes, then fluff up with a fork.
3   Stir onions and remaining ingredients into couscous and season. Cool, then spoon into a buttered 450 g (1 lb) loaf tin. Cover with buttered foil and bake in the ROASTING OVEN for 45 minutes or in the BAKING OVEN for 1 hour if space is limited. Turn out to serve.

COOK'S TIPS
To prepare ahead, complete the recipe, then cover and chill for up to two days. To use, cook as in step 3.

Stuffing the central cavity of a turkey is not recommended as it is hard to be sure that sufficient heat has penetrated the thickest part of the bird to avoid food poisoning.

Mushroom and Olive Stuffing

PREPARATION TIME:
20-30 MINUTES

COOKING TIME:
1¼ HOURS

FREEZING: SUITABLE

410 CALS PER
SERVING

SERVES 8

Bacon, mushrooms and juicy olives make perfect partners in this Christmas stuffing mixture.

450 g (1 lb) streaky bacon
3 small onions or shallots
60 ml (4 tbsp) oil
350 g (12 oz) small brown-cap mushrooms
125 g (4 oz) risotto (arborio) rice
pinch powdered saffron

600 ml (1 pint) hot chicken stock
125 g (4 oz) pitted green olives
30 ml (2 level tbsp) chopped flat-leaf parsley
2 eggs
salt and freshly ground black pepper

1 Coarsely chop the bacon; peel and chop the onions or shallots.

2 Place 15 ml (1 tbsp) oil in a deep ovenproof frying pan or shallow flameproof casserole dish and cook the bacon on the floor of the ROASTING OVEN for 7-10 minutes until crisp. Remove with a slotted spoon. Add 15 ml (1 tbsp) oil to the pan and cook the mushrooms on the BOILING PLATE for 4-5 minutes. Add the mushrooms to the bacon.

3 Heat a further 30 ml (2 tbsp) oil and add the onions. Cook, stirring, on the SIMMERING PLATE for 3-5 minutes, add the rice and saffron and stir over the heat for a further minute. Add a quarter of the boiling stock, cover the pan and transfer to the SIMMERING OVEN to allow the rice to absorb the stock. Repeat with the remaining stock, allowing the rice to swell after each addition.

4 Mix together all the ingredients and season well with salt and pepper; cool.

5 Cook the stuffing in a small dish covered with foil in the SIMMERING OVEN for about 1 hour, then transfer to the ROASTING OVEN for 10-15 minutes.

Crumb Roasted Rosemary and Garlic Potatoes

PREPARATION TIME:
5 MINUTES

COOKING TIME:
1¼-2 HOURS

FREEZING:
UNSUITABLE

275 CALS PER
SERVING

SERVES 8

These fragrant potatoes are delicious with turkey, chicken or lamb.

1.8 kg (4 lb) old medium sized potatoes
150 g (5 oz) fresh white breadcrumbs
salt and freshly ground black pepper

45 ml (3 tbsp) fresh rosemary, chopped
4 cloves garlic, crushed
about 150 ml (5 fl oz) olive oil

1 Peel the potatoes and quarter lengthwise. Cover with cold water and bring to the boil on the BOILING PLATE; cook for 2-3 minutes. Drain well, then return the potatoes to the pan. Cover the pan; shake to roughen up the surface of the potatoes.

2 Stir the breadcrumbs, rosemary, salt, pepper, garlic and oil into the potatoes until well mixed.

3 Place in a large a roasting tin just large enough to hold the potatoes, sprinkling over stray crumbs.

4 ■■ Cook on the top runners of the ROASTING OVEN for 30 minutes, then transfer to the floor of the ROASTING OVEN for 40-55 minutes.

■■■■ Cook in the BAKING OVEN for about 2 hours, turning occasionally.

Glazed Carrots and Turnips

PREPARATION TIME:
10 MINUTES

COOKING TIME:
15 MINUTES

FREEZING:
UNSUITABLE

75 CALS PER
SERVING

SERVES 8

Deliciously glazed and sweet, root vegetables retain maximum flavour and nutrients when cooked by this method.

900 g (2 lb) carrots	**15 ml (1 tbsp) lemon juice**
450 g (1 lb) turnips	**30 ml (2 level tbsp) granulated sugar**
25 g (1 oz) butter or margarine	**salt and freshly ground black pepper**

1 Peel the carrots with a potato peeler. Peel the turnips more thickly with a knife. Cut the vegetables into thick, fat sticks (about the size of your little finger).

2 Place in a large saucepan and add 1 cm (½ in) cold water. Add 25 g (1 oz) butter, lemon juice and sugar. Season with salt and pepper to taste.

3 Bring to a fast boil on the BOILING PLATE, then cover and place in the SIMMERING OVEN for 10 minutes. Transfer to the BOILING PLATE, uncover and bubble for about 5 minutes or until all the liquid has evaporated and the vegetables are tender and glazed. Shake the pan to prevent sticking.

4 Cover and keep warm in the SIMMERING OVEN until required. Grind over black pepper to serve.

COOK'S TIP
Whole shallots, quartered onions, parsnips, sweet potatoes, fennel, Jerusalem artichokes and swede can all be cooked by this method.

Parsnips in a Lime Glaze

PREPARATION TIME:
5 MINUTES

COOKING TIME:
17 MINUTES

FREEZING:
UNSUITABLE

225 CALS PER
SERVING

SERVES 4

The sweet nature of parsnips will complement almost any meal. Here the tang of lime is used to enhance their flavour. If possible, use young tender parsnips and choose the whitest. The sharp glaze can be used with any sweet root vegetables to excellent effect – try it with sweet potatoes or carrots, for example.

675 g (1½ lb) parsnips	**coarse sea salt and freshly ground black pepper**
1 lime	**thyme sprigs, to garnish**
50 g (2 oz) butter	
25 g (1 oz) light muscovado sugar	

1 Peel the parsnips and trim off the tops and roots. Cut in half lengthways. (If using older, tougher parsnips cut into quarters and remove the woody core.) Add to a pan of boiling salted water and cook on the BOILING PLATE for 2 minutes.

2 Meanwhile, using a canelle knife or a vegetable peeler, carefully pare thin slivers of rind from the lime; set aside for the garnish. Halve the lime and squeeze out the juice.

3 Melt the butter in a large saucepan together with the sugar. Add the lime juice and heat gently, stirring, to dissolve the sugar.

4 Drain the parsnips thoroughly in a colander, then add to the lime mixture in the saucepan. Toss in the buttery lime mixture and cook on the BOILING PLATE until hot, then place in the SIMMERING OVEN for 10 minutes. Transfer to the SIMMERING PLATE and cook for about 5 minutes, shaking the pan frequently, until golden brown.

5 Transfer to a warmed serving dish and garnish with the slivers of lime zest and thyme sprigs.

COOK'S TIP
You can use carrots or turnips instead of parsnips. A handful of walnuts tossed in towards the end of the cooking time adds a delicious crunch.

Creamy Brussels Sprouts

PREPARATION TIME:
15 MINUTES

COOKING TIME:
25 MINUTES, PLUS
30 MINUTES
INFUSING

FREEZING:
COMPLETE TO THE
END OF STEP 4 BUT
DON'T REHEAT.
PACK AND FREEZE.
THAW OVERNIGHT
AT COOL ROOM
TEMPERATURE,
THEN REHEAT AS IN
COOK'S TIP.

170 CALS PER
SERVING FOR 8;
135 CALS FOR 10

SERVES 8-10

A delicious updated version of a traditional Christmas vegetable.

600 ml (1 pint) milk
1 thick slice each onion and celery
6 peppercorns
1 small bay leaf
1.1 kg (2½ lb) Brussels sprouts, lightly trimmed
salt and freshly ground black pepper

40 g (1½ oz) butter
40 g (1½ oz) plain flour
½ whole nutmeg, grated – about 5 ml (1 level tsp)
60 ml (4 tbsp) single cream
oregano sprigs, flat-leafed parsley and grated nutmeg, to garnish

1 Place the milk in a saucepan with the onions, celery, peppercorns and bay leaf. Bring to the boil, transfer to the SIMMERING OVEN and leave to infuse for 20-30 minutes.

2 Meanwhile, cook the sprouts in a pan of boiling salted water until just tender. Drain and plunge into a bowl of icy cold water. Drain again and dry well.

3 Strain and reserve the milk. Melt the butter in a heavy-based saucepan on the SIMMERING PLATE. Off the heat, add the flour and stir until smooth. Stir in the milk and mix until smooth. Return to the SIMMERING PLATE and bring to the boil, stirring. Simmer for 1-2 minutes, add the nutmeg and season. Float the cream on top.

4 In a food processor, pulse the sprouts briefly until roughly chopped. Combine with the sauce. Place in a pan on the SIMMERING PLATE and stir until hot. Garnish to serve.

COOK'S TIP
To prepare ahead, complete to the end of step 4 but don't reheat. Cover and chill overnight. To use, reheat the sprout mixture in a heavy-based saucepan, stirring, for 7-10 minutes or until hot.

CREAMY BRUSSELS SPROUTS

Turkey Pot Pie

PREPARATION TIME:
40 MINUTES

COOKING TIME:
40 MINUTES

FREEZING: SUITABLE
AT STEP 7

735-550 CALS PER
SERVING

SERVES 6-8

This tempting supper dish is loosely based on an American recipe in which the 'pie' is topped with 'biscuits' or cobblers to make a homely crust. It is an excellent way of using up turkey and ham leftovers, combining them in a delicious creamy sauce. You will need a chunky piece of ham.

700 g (1½ lb) cooked boneless turkey
225 g (8 oz) cooked ham
2 carrots
1 large leek
125 g (4 oz) baby corn cobs
225 g (8 oz) chestnut or button mushrooms
900 ml (1½ pints) chicken stock
150 ml (¼ pint) dry white wine
1 bay leaf
2 fresh rosemary sprigs
75 g (3 oz) butter

60 ml (4 level tbsp) plain flour
300 ml (½ pint) single cream
salt and freshly ground black pepper

FOR THE HERB COBBLERS
350 g (12 oz) self-raising flour
30 ml (2 level tbsp) chopped parsley
30 ml (2 level tbsp) chopped chives
75 g (3 oz) butter
about 200 ml (7 fl oz) milk
coarse sea salt and rosemary leaves, to garnish

1 Cut the turkey into bite-sized pieces. Cut the ham into large cubes. Place the meat in a 1.7 litre (3 pint) ovenproof dish.

2 Peel and cut the carrots into thick sticks. Thickly slice the leek. Halve the baby corn. Quarter the mushrooms.

3 Pour the stock into a saucepan and add the wine, bay leaf and rosemary. Bring to the boil on the BOILING PLATE, add the carrots and cook for 20 minutes in the SIMMERING OVEN. Add the leeks and baby corn and cook on the SIMMERING PLATE for 5 minutes until all the vegetables are tender. Strain the stock into a jug; set the vegetables aside.

4 Melt the butter in a saucepan, add the mushrooms and cook on the BOILING PLATE until beginning to colour. Sprinkle in the flour. Take off the heat and mix well. Stir in the stock and cream. Return to the heat and slowly bring to the boil, stirring all the time. Simmer for 3 minutes, taste and season. Cover the surface closely with dampened greaseproof paper or a pan lid to prevent a skin forming, and allow to cool.

5 To make the herb cobblers, sift the flour with 2.5 ml (½ tsp) salt into a bowl and stir in the chopped herbs. Rub in the butter until the mixture resembles fine breadcrumbs. Stir in enough milk to make a soft scone dough. (Alternatively, you can prepare the dough in a food processor.) Turn out onto a floured surface and knead lightly.

6 Roll out the dough to a 22 cm (9 in) square and cut out into nine squares with a sharp knife. Halve these diagonally to make triangles.

7 Add the vegetables and sauce to the meat and mix well. Arrange the herb cobblers, overlapping, around the edge of the dish and sprinkle with coarse sea salt.

8 Bake on the third runners of the ROASTING OVEN for 10 minutes until the cobblers are risen and browning, then transfer to the floor of the ROASTING OVEN for 10 minutes. Brush with milk again and sprinkle with about 15 ml (1 level tbsp) rosemary leaves. Bake for a further 10-15 minutes. Serve piping hot with green vegetables.

COOK'S TIP
If fresh chives or parsley are unavailable, use freeze-dried herbs but halve the quantities.

Traditional Christmas Pudding

PREPARATION TIME:
40 MINUTES PLUS
MATURING FOR AT
LEAST 6 WEEKS FOR
THE BEST FLAVOUR

COOKING TIME:
8-10 HOURS PLUS
2 HOURS

FREEZING:
SUITABLE BUT
DOES KEEP ALMOST
INDEFINITELY IN A
COOL, DARK
PLACE.

790 CALS PER
SERVING

SERVES 10

One of the advantages of cooking this Christmas pudding in the simmering oven is the lack of anxiety that the steamer may boil dry and ruin the pudding.

butter, for greasing
finely grated rind of 1 lemon
75 g (3 oz) chopped mixed peel
225 g (8 oz) each seedless raisins, currants and sultanas
225 g (8 oz) suet (see Cook's Tips)
225 g (8 oz) fresh breadcrumbs
225 g (8 oz) soft light brown (muscovado) sugar

75 g (3 oz) plain flour
2.5 ml (½ level tsp) mixed spice
1.25 ml (¼ level tsp) salt
4 large eggs
150 ml (¼ pint) brandy, dark rum or medium sherry
100 ml (4 fl oz) milk
Brandy Butter or cream, to serve (see Cook's Tips)

1 Grease and base-line a 1.6-litre (2¾-pint) pudding basin (see Cook's Tips).

2 Place the finely grated lemon rind in a bowl with the mixed peel, raisins, currants and sultanas, suet, breadcrumbs, brown sugar, plain flour, mixed spice and salt. Whisk together the eggs, 100 ml (4 fl oz) brandy, rum or sherry and the milk. Stir the egg mixture into the fruit mixture until well blended, then spoon into the greased and lined pudding basin. Press the mixture down, cover with greaseproof paper and foil and secure with string. Cook within 24 hours of completing this step.

3 Lower the basin into a large pan. Pour in boiling water to come halfway up the side of the basin. Cover tightly, bring to the boil and simmer gently for 15 minutes on the SIMMERING PLATE, then transfer to the SIMMERING OVEN for 8-10 hours (overnight is ideal, except some electric Agas with hotter than average simmering ovens where 5-6 hours will be sufficient).

4 Lift out the basin; allow to cool. Re-cover with fresh greaseproof paper and foil and secure with string. Store for at least six weeks in a cool, dark place.

5 To reheat, follow step 3, but allow the pudding to cook in the SIMMERING OVEN for only 2-3 hours, or simply place the bowl in the SIMMERING OVEN for 1-2 hours without steaming. Remove the covering, run a palette knife around the inside of the bowl and turn the pudding out on to a warmed serving plate. Warm the remaining brandy, rum or sherry in a pan or ladle and ignite it. While still flaming, pour it over the pudding and serve with Brandy Butter or cream.

COOK'S TIPS
When making this pudding, you can use beef or vegetarian suet or melted butter. If you are concerned about the calorie count or want to make a lighter pudding, use half the quantity of fat.

As well as Brandy Butter or cream, you could also serve this pudding with bottled fruit, such as mandarins in brandy syrup.

To make an old-fashioned round Christmas pudding, use a spherical 2.3-litre (4-pint) mould.

AGA TIPS
If short of cooking space in your Aga, place the pudding directly in the SIMMERING OVEN for 1-2 hours, then on the back of the Aga to keep warm while the turkey is resting in the simmering oven. Return the pudding to the simmering oven whileeating the turkey, then turn out just before serving.

Slices of leftover pudding may be reheated wrapped in foil and placed in the SIMMERING OVEN for 30-40 minutes.

If using the SIMMERING OVEN it is not usually necessary to top up the pan with boiling water during the cooking time to prevent it from boiling dry.

Light Christmas Pudding

PREPARATION TIME:
30 MINUTES

COOKING TIME:
2-2½ HOURS

FREEZING:
COMPLETE TO END
OF STEP 3, THEN
COOL, WRAP AND
FREEZE. THAW
OVERNIGHT AT
COOL ROOM
TEMPERATURE.
PLACE PUDDING IN
THE SIMMERING
OVEN FOR ¾-1
HOUR UNTIL HOT
TO THE CENTRE.

470-375 CALS PER
SERVING

SERVES 8-10

If you find the dark treacly flavours of a traditional pudding too much, then this one is for you. It has a buttery, orange and spice sponge base and is packed with fruit.

175 g (6 oz) unsalted butter at room temperature, plus extra for greasing
grated rind of 2 oranges
175 g (6 oz) caster sugar
3 large eggs
175 g (6 oz) self-raising flour
pinch of salt

5 ml (1 level tsp) ground cinnamon
75 g (3 oz) each ready-to-eat dried figs, dates and apricots, roughly chopped
75 g (3 oz) unsalted, shelled pistachio nuts, roughly chopped
Sticky Kumquat Compote, to serve (see below)

1 Grease and base-line a 1.4 litre (2½ pint) pudding basin. Place the butter and grated orange rind in a large bowl and, using an electric hand mixer, whisk the butter until smooth. Gradually add the caster sugar and whisk until the mixture is pale and fluffy. Lightly whisk the eggs, then gradually whisk into the butter mixture until smooth and fluffy.

2 Sift together the self-raising flour, salt and cinnamon, then carefully fold into the butter mixture with the dried fruit and nuts. Spoon the mixture into the prepared pudding basin and smooth the top.

3 Cover the top of the basin with a circle of buttered greaseproof paper and foil. Tie string securely around the top of the basin, just under the lip. Place in a large saucepan and pour in sufficient boiling water to come two-thirds of the way up the sides of the basin. Cover the saucepan with a tight-fitting lid, then bring back to the boil on the BOILING PLATE.

■■ Cook on the grid shelf on the floor of the ROASTING OVEN for 2 hours.

■■■ Cook on the grid shelf on the floor of the BAKING OVEN for 2½ hours.

Test the centre of the pudding with a skewer to check it is cooked right through.

ILLUSTRATED OVERLEAF

4 Turn out the pudding and serve with the compote.

COOK'S TIP
To prepare ahead, complete to the end of step 3, then cool and store in a cool place for up to four days. To use, place the pudding in the SIMMERING OVEN for ¾-1 hour until hot to the centre.

Sticky Kumquat Compote

PREPARATION TIME:
5 MINUTES

COOKING TIME:
30-40 MINUTES

FREEZING:
UNSUITABLE

160-190 CALS PER
SERVING

SERVES 8-10

The perfect accompaniment to Christmas pudding.

450 g (1 lb) kumquats
200 g (7 oz) caster sugar
1 cinnamon stick, crumbled
2 whole cloves

nutmeg, grated
50 g (2 oz) unsalted pistachio nuts, chopped

1 Cut the kumquats in half lengthways, place in a saucepan of cold water, bring to the boil and cook on the SIMMERING PLATE for 10-15 minutes or until soft.

2 Drain the saucepan, then return the kumquats to the pan with the caster sugar, 450 ml (¾ pint) water, crumbled cinnamon stick, cloves and a generous grating of nutmeg. Gently bring to the boil and bubble on the SIMMERING PLATE for 20 minutes or until the liquid is reduced by half and syrupy. Add the chopped pistachio nuts and serve warm.

LEFT: LIGHT CHRISTMAS PUDDING

ABOVE: OLD-TIME MINCE PIES

Old-Time Mince Pies

PREPARATION TIME:
30 MINUTES

COOKING TIME:
25 MINUTES

FREEZING:
SUITABLE. THAW
OVERNIGHT AT
COOL ROOM
TEMPERATURE.
REFRESH IN THE
SIMMERING OVEN
FOR 5 MINUTES
BEFORE SERVING.

105 CALS PER MINCE
PIE

MAKES 24

It just wouldn't be Christmas without these all-time favourites.

125 g (4 oz) butter
225 g (8 oz) plain white flour
about 225 g (8 oz) Spicy Apple Mincemeat
(see page 100)

1 egg white, lightly beaten
caster sugar, for dusting
cream, to accompany

1 Rub the butter into the flour and bind to form a firm dough with about 60 ml (4 tbsp) water. Knead lightly until just smooth. Roll out the pastry thinly and, using a 5.5 cm (2¼ in) round cutter, cut out about 48 rounds, re-rolling as necessary.

2 Place half the rounds on baking sheets and spoon mincemeat onto the centre of each. Moisten the pastry edges. Cover with the remaining pastry rounds, sealing the edges well, flute, if wished. Make a tiny hole in the top to allow the air to escape.

3 Bake on the grid shelf on the floor of the ROASTING OVEN for 10-15 minutes until just set but not browned.

4 Take the pies out of the oven and brush with lightly beaten egg white and dust with caster sugar. Return to the oven for a further 5-7 minutes or until well browned. Serve the mince pies warm with cream.

Spicy Apple Mincemeat

PREPARATION TIME:
20 MINUTES, PLUS
STANDING

COOKING TIME:
ABOUT 15 MINUTES

FREEZING:
UNSUITABLE

50 CALS PER 15 ML
(1 LEVEL TBSP)

MAKES ABOUT
1.8 KG (4 LB)

A jar of home-made mincemeat makes a delightful traditional Christmas gift. Attach a circle of gingham fabric to the top of the jar with an elastic band and decorate with ribbon to give a festive finishing touch.

550 g (1¼ lb) cooking apples
butter
50 g (2 oz) walnut pieces
125 g (4 oz) blanched almonds
225 g (8 oz) seedless raisins
225 g (8 oz) sultanas
225 g (8 oz) currants
125 g (4 oz) mixed peel
225 g (8 oz) soft dark brown sugar

grated rind and juice of 1 lemon
grated rind and juice of 1 orange
5 ml (1 level tsp) ground cinnamon
2.5 ml (½ level tsp) ground nutmeg
2.5 ml (½ level tsp) ginger
pinch ground cloves
125 g (4 oz) vegetable suet
150 ml (5 fl oz) brandy

1 Peel, core and roughly chop the apples. Place in a saucepan with 60 ml (4 tbsp) water and a knob of butter. Cook, uncovered, on the SIMMERING PLATE for 5 minutes, then transfer to the SIMMERING OVEN until very soft and mushy. Uncover and cook, stirring, on the BOILING PLATE for 2-3 minutes, or until there is very little excess liquid. Transfer to a bowl and allow to cool.

2 Roughly chop the walnuts and almonds. Stir into the cold apple purée with all the remaining ingredients. Cover and leave the mixture to stand overnight.

3 Stir the mincemeat mixture well before spooning into sterilised jars. Press down well to exclude any air, then seal. Store in a cool dark place for up to 6 months.

COOK'S TIP
This particular blend of mincemeat keeps well and provides an excellent filling for mince pies – see the recipe on page 99.

AGA TIP
Before potting the mincemeat, wash the jars in hot water, drain, and then leave to dry in the SIMMERING OVEN.

Bûche de Noël

PREPARATION TIME:
45 MINUTES, PLUS
COOLING

COOKING TIME:
10 MINUTES

FREEZING:
UNSUITABLE

720 CALS PER
SERVING

MAKES ABOUT
8 SLICES

Bûche de Noël is traditionally eaten in France at Christmas time. This and the English Yule Log date back to the days when a huge log used to be burnt on Christmas Eve.

oil, for greasing
125 g (4 oz) caster sugar, plus extra for dredging
75 g (3 oz) plain flour, plus extra for dredging
3 eggs
30 ml (2 tbsp) cocoa powder
440 g (15½ oz) can sweetened chestnut purée

icing sugar, for dusting
holly sprigs, to decorate

FOR THE BUTTER CREAM
225 g (8 oz) unsalted butter, softened
50 g (2 oz) plain chocolate
450 g (1 lb) icing sugar

1 To make the cake, grease a 33 x 23 cm (13 x 9 in) Swiss-roll tin. Line with greaseproof paper and grease the paper. Dredge with a little caster sugar, then with a little flour, knocking out any excess.

2 Put the eggs and sugar in a deep heatproof bowl and place in the SIMMERING OVEN until fairly hot to the touch. Using a mixer or a hand-held electric whisk, whisk until thick enough to leave a trail on the surface when the whisk is lifted.

3 Sift in the flour and cocoa and gently fold into the mixture with 15 ml (1 tbsp) hot water.

4 Pour the mixture gently into the prepared tin and lightly level the surface. Bake on the grid shelf on the floor of the ROASTING OVEN for 7-10 minutes or until slightly shrunk away from the sides of the tin. Turn the tin around and bake for a further 2-3 minutes to ensure even cooking.

5 Meanwhile, place a sheet of greaseproof paper on top of a tea-towel. Dredge the paper with caster sugar and turn the cake out onto it. Trim off the crusty edges on the short ends with a sharp knife. Roll up the cake with the paper inside. Transfer to a wire rack, seam-side down, and leave to cool for 20 minutes.

6 To make the butter cream, melt the chocolate with 15 ml (1 tbsp) water in a bowl in the SIMMERING OVEN for 5-10 minutes, then leave to cool slightly. Beat the butter until soft. Gradually sift and beat the icing sugar into the softened butter, then add the melted chocolate.

7 Unroll the cold Swiss roll and spread the chestnut purée over the surface. Roll up again without the paper inside. Place on a cake board or plate.

8 Cut a thick diagonal slice off one end of the Swiss roll and attach with butter cream to the side of the roll to give the classic forked log shape.

9 Using a piping bag and a large star nozzle, pipe thin lines of butter cream over the log. Pipe one or two swirls of butter cream to represent knots in the wood. Decorate with sprigs of holly and dust lightly with icing sugar.

Luxury Christmas Cake

PREPARATION TIME:
1 HOUR, PLUS
MACERATING

COOKING TIME:
12 HOURS

FREEZING: SUITABLE
AT STAGE 5

315-235 CALS PER
SLICE

MAKES 30-40 SLICES

Make this Christmas cake any time from mid-November to mid-December. Don't be tempted to use margarine – the butter gives a wonderful flavour and improves the cake's keeping qualities. Store tightly wrapped to prevent the cake from drying out; spear occasionally with a skewer and 'feed' with a drop of brandy.

1 lemon
1 orange
225 g (8 oz) dried apricots
175 g (6 oz) stoned prunes
175 g (6 oz) unblanched almonds
175 g (6 oz) glacé cherries
225 g (8 oz) currants
125 g (4 oz) sultanas
225 g (8 oz) raisins
150 ml (¼ pint) brandy, rum, port or sweet stout
125 g (4 oz) chopped candied peel

350 g (12 oz) self-raising white flour
10 ml (2 level tsp) mixed spice
salt
300 g (10 oz) unsalted butter, softened
300 g (10 oz) soft dark muscovado sugar
6 eggs, size 3, beaten
60 ml (4 tbsp) treacle

TO DECORATE
apricot glaze (see Cook's Tips)
450 g (1 lb) almond paste
450 g (1 lb) ready-to-roll fondant icing

1 Grate the rind from the lemon and orange and squeeze the juice. Roughly chop the apricots, prunes and almonds. Wash, dry and halve the cherries. Mix the apricots, prunes and citrus rinds and juices together in a large bowl, with the currants, sultanas and raisins. Add the brandy (or other liquor), cover and leave to macerate overnight, stirring occasionally.

2 The next day, line a 25 cm (10 in) round or 23 cm (9 in) square cake tin with a double or triple layer of greaseproof paper. Grease with butter.

3 Add the cherries, nuts and peel to the macerated fruit mixture and stir well. Sift the flour, spice and 2.5 ml (½ level tsp) salt together. In a large bowl, cream together the butter and sugar until fluffy. Gradually beat in the eggs, beating well between each addition to prevent curdling. Stir in the treacle, then fold in the flour and fruit. Spoon the mixture into the cake tin, level the surface, then make a slight hollow in the middle.

4 Bake on the grid shelf on the floor of the SIMMERING OVEN for approximately 12 hours. Test by inserting a skewer into the centre of the cake – if it comes out clean, the cake is cooked. The top of the cake does not brown, but this will be covered by icing. If you wish, you can cover the tin and bake the cake the following day.

5 Leave in the tin until cool enough to handle, then turn out onto a wire rack to cool completely in the paper. When cold, keep one layer of greaseproof paper on the cake, then wrap in foil. Store in a cool dry place.

6 Set the cake on a board. Up to 1 week before Christmas, brush the cake with apricot glaze and cover with almond paste (see below). Leave to dry for 24 hours, then cover with fondant icing and apply the decorations (see right). Secure a ribbon around the cake if desired.

COOK'S TIPS
Use seedless muscatel raisins if obtainable. Avoid using 'no-need-to-soak' dried apricots and prunes as you want them to soak up the brandy.

To make the apricot glaze, gently heat 125 g (4 oz) apricot jam in a small pan with 30 ml (2 tbsp) water until melted. Boil for 1 minute, then sieve. Use warm.

APPLYING THE ALMOND PASTE AND FONDANT ICING
1 Dust the worksurface with icing sugar. Roll out the almond paste into a round or square 7.5 cm (3 in) larger all round than the cake. With the help of a rolling pin, lift the almond paste on top of the cake and allow it to drape over the edge(s). Press the almond paste onto the side(s) of the cake, working it down to the board. Trim off the excess.

2 Repeat step 1 to apply the fondant icing. Dust your fingers with a little sifted icing sugar and gently rub the surface of the cake in a circular movement to buff the icing and make it smooth.

DECORATING THE CAKE

1 To make star decorations, knead 450 g (1 lb) fondant icing on a surface dusted with icing sugar until pliable. Knead in 5 ml (1 tsp) gum tragacanth or dental fixative (which helps the fondant to dry and harden). Roll the fondant icing out to a thickness of 3 mm (⅛ in).

2 Using a star-shaped cutter, stamp out about 40 stars and transfer to a baking sheet lined with non-stick baking parchment.

3 Sprinkle a little edible gold lustre powder on a plate and press some of the stars gently onto it. A little power will stick to the surface. Place on the baking sheet and leave in a warm place for at least 24 hours to dry out and harden.

4 When dry, paint some of the plain stars with gold or silver edible food colouring.

5 If using gold leaf (see Cook's Tip), lightly brush a few stars with a little beaten egg white. Press the gold leaf sparingly onto the stars.

6 Arrange all of the stars around the edge of the cake as soon as it is iced if possible, pushing them lightly into the icing. Or if the icing is dry, use a little royal icing to secure them.

COOK'S TIP
If using gold leaf, it must be pure 24 carat gold, otherwise it should not be eaten. Edible gold leaf, gum tragacanth, food colourings and lustre powders are available from specialist mail order suppliers.

Pannetone

PREPARATION TIME:
25 MINUTES, PLUS
RISING

COOKING TIME:
35 MINUTES

FREEZING:
SUITABLE. THAW
OVERNIGHT AT
COOL ROOM
TEMPERATURE.

415-320 CALS PER
SERVING

MAKES 10-12 SLICES

This classic Italian favourite is really a cross between a bread and a cake, and, because of the high butter content, it keeps well. Pannetone is normally eaten with coffee, or a glass of dessert or fortified wine. It is delicious served slightly warm.

15 ml (1 level tbsp) active dried yeast
150 ml (5 fl oz) warm milk
450 g (1 lb) strong plain white flour
1 egg
4 egg yolks
10 ml (2 level tsp) salt
75 g (3 oz) caster sugar

finely grated rind of 1 lemon
finely grated rind of 1 orange
175 g (6 oz) unsalted butter, softened
75 g (3 oz) chopped mixed candied orange and citron peel
125 g (4 oz) raisins

1 Line a 15 cm (6 in) deep cake tin with a double layer of non-stick baking parchment which projects 10 cm (4 in) above the rim.

2 Dissolve the yeast in 60 ml (4 tbsp) warm milk. Cover and leave in a warm place near the Aga for 10 minutes until frothy. Stir in 125 g (4 oz) flour and the remaining warm milk. Cover and leave to rise for 30 minutes.

3 Beat the egg and egg yolks together. Sift the remaining flour and salt onto the yeast mixture. Make a well in the centre and add the sugar, beaten eggs and grated citrus rinds. Mix to an elastic dough, adding a little more flour if necessary, but keeping the dough quite soft. Work in the softened butter.

4 Cover and leave to rise at room temperature for 2-4 hours until doubled in volume. Meanwhile, chop the candied peel.

5 Knock the dough down and knead in the chopped peel and raisins. Place in the prepared tin and cut an X on the top with an oiled scalpel or very sharp knife. Cover and leave to rise until the dough is about 2.5 cm (1 in) above the top of the cake tin.

6 ■■■ Bake on the grid shelf on the floor of the ROASTING OVEN for 15 minutes. Then place the cold baking sheet above and secure a collar of a single folded sheet of newspaper around the tin and bake for a further 35-40 minutes until well risen and golden.

■■■■ Bake on the grid shelf on the floor of the ROASTING OVEN for 15 minutes, then transfer to the grid shelf in the BAKING OVEN for 40 minutes until well risen and golden.

Leave in the tin for 10 minutes, then transfer to a wire rack to cool.

7 Serve cut into horizontal slices. To store, wrap the whole pannetone in cling film or foil. Keep in the refrigerator. Bring to room temperature to serve.

Mulled Wine

PREPARATION TIME:
5 MINUTES

COOKING TIME:
1½-2 HOURS

MAKES 16 GLASSES

The tantalising fragrances of spices and citrus fruit make warm mulled wine a great favourite. For the best results, avoid using very cheap wines.

2 oranges, thinly sliced
1 lemon, thinly sliced
12 cloves, bruised
15 ml (1 tbsp) allspice, bruised
1-2 sticks cinnamon

1 cm (½ in) fresh ginger, thinly sliced
2 bottles red wine (see Cook's Tips)
100-150 g (3½-5 oz) golden granulated syrup

1 Place the sliced oranges, lemon and spices in a large pan (preferably stainless steel) with 500 ml (¾ pint) water. Bring to the boil on the SIMMERING PLATE, then cover and transfer to the SIMMERING OVEN for 1-1½ hours for the flavours to infuse.

2 Add the wine and sweeten to taste. This will depend on the sharpness that the citrus fruit imparts as well as your preference and the wine used. Return the covered pan to the SIMMERING OVEN for 30 minutes. Check that the wine does not overheat (hot bath temperature is about right). If preferred, you can heat on the SIMMERING PLATE.

3 Pour into a warm jug to serve (you may wish to strain the mulled wine first).

COOK'S TIPS
A wide variety of wines can be used. Merlot, Shiraz and Cabernet Sauvignon wines are particularly suitable, but don't choose the cheapest, poorest quality wines that can lead to a hangover.

If you wish, up to 3 measures of brandy can be added at the same time as the wine.

Bruise the spices by placing them in a strong polythene bag and crushing with a rolling pin.

Spiced Rum

PREPARATION TIME:
5 MINUTES, PLUS
STANDING

COOKING TIME:
20 MINUTES

SERVES 6

This drink comes from Mauritius where it is served at the end of a meal or poured over ice cream.

1 large orange
5 ml (1 level tsp) whole cloves
5 ml (1 level tsp) cardamom pods
1 stick cinnamon
1 vanilla pod, split lengthways

40 g (1½ oz) raisins
40 g (1½ oz) sultanas
125 g (4 oz) muscovado sugar
1 bottle white rum

1 Cut the orange into small chunks. Place in a small pan with the spices, dried fruits and sugar. Add 200 ml (7 fl oz) water, bring slowly to the boil and then transfer to the SIMMERING OVEN for 30 minutes.

2 Add the rum, cool and bottle. Store in a dark, cool, dry place for at least 1 week before using. Serve warmed.

AGA TIP
Store the spiced rum in a bottling jar. To serve it warm after a meal, place the jar with the lid slightly loosened on the back of the Aga at the beginning of the meal so it can gently heat.

DESSERTS

Chocolate and Orange Truffle Torte

PREPARATION TIME:
30 MINUTES, PLUS
2-4 HOURS OR
OVERNIGHT
CHILLING

COOKING TIME:
20-30 MINUTES

FREEZING:
COMPLETE RECIPE
TO END OF THE
STEP 5, WRAP AND
FREEZE. THAW AT
COOL ROOM
TEMPERATURE
OVERNIGHT.
COMPLETE RECIPE.

560 CALS PER
SERVING

SERVES 12

Inspired by a favourite chocolate that breaks into perfect orange segments, this pudding will finish the meal with a flourish. This recipe is large enough for second servings.

FOR THE BASE
4 large eggs
125 g (4 oz) caster sugar
40 g (1½ oz) plain flour; sifted with 30 ml (2 level tbsp) cocoa powder
20 g (¾ oz) butter, melted and cooled
60 ml (4 tbsp) Grand Marnier or brandy

FOR THE CHOCOLATE AND ORANGE TRUFFLE MIXTURE
450 g (1 lb) plain chocolate, preferably 70% cocoa content, roughly chopped
568 ml carton double cream
4 large egg yolks
50 g (2 oz) caster sugar
rind of 3 large oranges
cocoa to dust

1 First make the base. Using a food mixer, whisk the eggs and the caster sugar together on high until the mixture has doubled in volume and is very thick. (If you don't have a food mixer, place the eggs and sugar in a large heatproof bowl and whisk the mixture using an electric whisk or large balloon whisk over a saucepan of simmering water until thick, then remove from the heat and whisk until cool.)

2 Lightly fold in the sifted flour and cocoa, then the melted butter, folding until just combined. Take care not to overfold as the air will be knocked out of the mixture and the resulting cake will be flat.

3 Grease a 25.5 cm (10 in) loose-bottomed cake tin and base-line with non-stick baking parchment. Pour mixture into the tin and bake.

■■ Cook at the front of the grid shelf on the floor of the ROASTING OVEN with the cold plain shelf set on the third runners for about 20 minutes.

■■■■ Cook in the middle of the BAKING OVEN for 25-30 minutes.

Cool for 10 minutes before turning out on to a rack. Drizzle with Grand Marnier or brandy, allow to cool, then return, upside down, to the clean tin. Press firmly into base.

4 For the chocolate and orange truffle mixture, place the chocolate in a heatproof bowl with half the cream, and place on the floor of the SIMMERING OVEN for 20-30 minutes. Once the chocolate has melted, stir until smooth, remove from the heat and leave to cool.

5 Whisk the remaining cream to soft peaks. Using an electric whisk, beat the egg yolks and sugar together until pale and fluffy. Beat the egg mixture into the cooled chocolate, then fold the chocolate mixture into the whipped cream with the orange rind. Immediately pour over the cake in the cake tin and chill for at least 2-4 hours or until the truffle mixture is set firm. The torte is best left overnight before serving.

6 To serve, remove the torte from the tin and dust with cocoa powder.

COOK'S TIPS
To prepare ahead, complete recipe to the end of step 5. Cover with foil and chill for up to four days. To use, complete the recipe.

The young, the elderly, pregnant women and those with immune-deficiency diseases should avoid raw or lightly cooked eggs, which may contain salmonella.

Apple and Blackberry Oat Crunch

PREPARATION TIME:
25 MINUTES

COOKING TIME:
35 MINUTES, PLUS
1 HOUR COOLING

FREEZING:
COMPLETE TO THE
END OF STEP 3,
WRAP AND FREEZE.
THAW OVERNIGHT
AT COOL ROOM
TEMPERATURE.
COMPLETE THE
RECIPE.

400 CALS PER
SERVING

SERVES 8

This delicious, hearty pudding is a wonderful combination of hedgerow fruits and toasted oats.

1.4 kg (3 lb) eating apples, such as Braeburns, peeled, cored and roughly chopped (see Cook's Tips)
225 g (8 oz) fresh or frozen blackberries
25 g (1 oz) caster sugar
200 g (7 oz) mixed nuts, such as hazelnuts, pecan nuts or almonds, roughly chopped

100 g (3½ oz) porridge oats
125 g (4 oz) butter
25 g (1 oz) plain flour
100 g (3½ oz) soft brown sugar

1 Base-line a 20 cm (8 in) spring-release tin (see Cook's Tips). Place the apples in a large saucepan with the blackberries, caster sugar and 100 ml (3½ fl oz) water. Cover and cook on the BOILING PLATE for 1-2 minutes, then uncover and cook briskly, stirring occasionally, for about 10 minutes until the apples are tender and most of the liquid has evaporated. Set aside.
2 Place nuts, oats and butter in a roasting tin. Bake on the grid shelf on the floor of the ROASTING OVEN for 10-15 minutes, stirring occasionally, until golden. Stir in sugar and flour.
3 Press half of the nut mixture into the base of the prepared tin. Spoon the fruit over then cover with the remaining nut mixture.
4 Cook on the floor at the front of the ROASTING OVEN for 15 minutes or until golden and crisp. Check after 7-10 minutes and if already brown, place the cold baking sheet above on the bottom runners. Leave in the tin to cool completely before turning out.

COOK'S TIPS
If you prefer, replace the apples with pears, and the blackberries with blackcurrants or raspberries.
You can use any combination of nuts – try a mixture of walnuts, pistachios and hazelnuts.

Wrap foil around the loose-bottomed base of the tin before clipping it into position – this will make unmoulding easier once the pudding is cooked and ready to serve.

Chocolate Puddings with White Chocolate Custard

PREPARATION TIME:
20 MINUTES

COOKING TIME:
20-25 MINUTES

FREEZING: SUITABLE

280 CALS PER
SERVING

SERVES 6

These wonderful dark chocolate individual puddings are a decadent treat.

125 g (4 oz) half-fat butter, plus a little extra for greasing

25 g (1 oz) hazelnuts

75 g (3 oz) each soft brown (muscovado) sugar and self-raising flour

2.5 ml (½ level tsp) baking powder

30 ml (2 level tbsp) cocoa powder, plus extra for dusting

25 g (1 oz) plain chocolate, roughly chopped

2 large eggs, beaten

20 ml (4 level tsp) each custard powder and sugar

450 ml (¾ pint) skimmed milk

40 g (1½ oz) white chocolate drops

1 Grease and base-line six 120-150 ml (4-5 fl oz) ramekins with non-stick baking parchment. Lightly brown the hazelnuts in a roasting tin on the bottom runners of the BAKING OVEN for 4-10 minutes (watch them carefully so they do not burn), cool and roughly chop.

2 Place the butter and sugar in a pan and heat gently until combined. Cool.

3 Sift the flour, baking powder and cocoa into a bowl. Stir in the nuts and chocolate. Make a well in the centre; pour in the butter mixture and eggs and beat well.

4 Pour into the ramekins and place in a small roasting tin.

■■ Bake at the front of the ROASTING OVEN on the bottom runners with a cold plain shelf above on the second runners for 20 minutes or until just firm to the touch.

■■■ Bake on the middle runners of the BAKING OVEN for 25 minutes or until just firm to the touch.

Cool slightly and turn out; keep warm for 15-20 minutes in the SIMMERING OVEN.

5 Meanwhile, place the custard powder and sugar in a bowl; add enough milk to make a smooth paste. Heat the remaining milk until almost boiling, pour into the custard powder, then return to the pan. Add the white chocolate and stir until the chocolate has melted and the custard thickened. Just before serving, whisk the custard until foaming.

6 Trim the top from each pudding; place upside down in a serving dish. Dust with cocoa powder, pour custard around and serve immediately.

COOK'S TIP

To prepare ahead, complete recipe to end of step 4 up to one day ahead; store in an airtight container. To use, place puddings on a baking sheet; cover with foil. Reheat in the SIMMERING OVEN for 30-40 minutes. Complete step 6.

Plums with Caramelised Fruit Bread

PREPARATION TIME:
10 MINUTES

COOKING TIME:
16 MINUTES

FREEZING:
UNSUITABLE

250 CALS PER
SERVING

SERVES 4

This simple-to-make dish is also perfect for a special breakfast.

700 g (1½ lb) dessert plums, stoned and cut into quarters

60 ml (4 level tbsp) caster sugar

8 slices fruit or cinnamon bread, about 5 mm (¼ in) thick (see Cook's Tips)

1 large egg

45 ml (3 tbsp) milk

25 g (1 oz) unsalted butter

Greek yogurt, to accompany

1 Place the plums in a shallow pan, sprinkle over 30 ml (2 level tbsp) caster sugar and cook on the SIMMERING PLATE, stirring occasionally, for 3-4 minutes, then transfer to the SIMMERING OVEN until the plums begin to soften.

2 Meanwhile, using a large plain cutter or upturned tumbler as a guide, cut the fruit or cinnamon bread into circles. Beat together the egg and the milk.

3 Heat the butter in a non-stick frying pan on the BOILING PLATE. Dip the bread into the egg mixture, making sure it is well coated. Once the butter is hot, add the bread and sprinkle with 15 ml (1 level tbsp) of the caster sugar. Fry until golden underneath, turn over and sprinkle with remaining 15 ml (1 level tbsp) sugar; fry until golden on the other side. Repeat with the remaining slices of bread.

4 Place the cooked fruit bread on a plate, then top with the warm plums and a spoonful of Greek yogurt.

COOK'S TIPS

Make sure you choose ripe fruit as it will be sweeter and have a better flavour, which means you can cut down on sugar. Alternatively, buy the fruit a few days in advance and keep in a dark, warm place to ripen further. A ripe banana gives off ethylene gas which helps other fruit ripen, so try adding one to the fruit bowl.

You can also use four tea cakes for this recipe. Just split them in half and add a little mixed spice to the egg mixture.

Apricot and Cardamom Crumble

PREPARATION TIME:
15 MINUTES

COOKING TIME:
1 HOUR

FREEZING: SUITABLE

230 CALS PER
SERVING

SERVES 6

A really good fruit crumble is delicious but can often be high in calories and fat. This version is lighter than most but it won't disappoint.

700 g (1½ lb) fresh apricots, stoned and cut into quarters
30-45 ml (2-3 level tbsp) caster sugar
3-4 green cardamom pods, split, seeds reserved and crushed (see Cook's Tips)
50 g (2 oz) plain flour
50 g (2 oz) jumbo rolled oats

50 g (2 oz) light brown sugar
50 g (2 oz) butter, cut into cubes
25 g (1 oz) hazelnuts, browned and roughly chopped
thick Greek yogurt, to accompany (optional)

1 Mix the apricots with the caster sugar and place in a 1.3 litre (2¼ pint) capacity ovenproof dish or divide between six individual dishes.

2 Place the crushed cardamom seeds, flour, oats and light brown sugar in a large bowl, then rub in the butter. Mix in the chopped hazelnuts.

3 Spoon the crumble mixture over the fruit. Bake on the floor of the ROASTING OVEN for 15-20 minutes, then transfer to the SIMMERING OVEN for 40-50 minutes until the fruit is tender. Serve warm with a little thick Greek yogurt, if wished.

COOK'S TIPS

To prepare ahead, complete to the end of step 2 up to 6 hours in advance. Cover and store in a cool place. To use, complete the recipe.

If you don't have a pestle and mortar to crush the cardamom seeds, wrap them in a small piece of cling film, place on a chopping board and crush with the base of a heavy pan.

Choose apricots with the warmest colour – a slight pink blush means they're ripe.

RHUBARB AND
RASPBERRY MERINGUES

Rhubarb and Raspberry Meringues

PREPARATION TIME:
15 MINUTES

COOKING TIME:
10-15 MINUTES

FREEZING:
UNSUITABLE

90 CALS PER
SERVING

SERVES 4

Rhubarb has a delicate flavour which marries well with ginger, but you could use a pinch of cinnamon as an alternative. These puddings are low in calories, but if you use low-calorie sweetener to replace the sugar when cooking the rhubarb it will reduce the calories to just 65 cals per serving.

450 g (1 lb) rhubarb
2.5 cm (1 in) piece stem ginger or
chopped glacé ginger (optional)
75 g (3 oz) caster sugar

finely grated rind and juice of 1 orange
75 g (3 oz) frozen raspberries
1 large egg white

1 Clean and cut the rhubarb into 2.5 cm (1 in) pieces. Finely chop the ginger, if using.

2 Place the rhubarb in a large saucepan with 25 g (1 oz) caster sugar, the chopped stem ginger, if using, and the orange rind. Cover and cook gently on the SIMMERING PLATE for 2-3 minutes, adding a little orange juice if necessary. Add the raspberries. Spoon the mixture into four 150 ml (5 fl oz) ramekin or ovenproof tea cups.

3 Whisk the egg white and remaining sugar together until foamy. Place the bowl over a saucepan of simmering water and continue to whisk for 5 minutes or until stiff and shiny.

4 Place a spoonful of meringue mixture on top of each ramekin.

■■ Bake in the SIMMERING OVEN for 15-20 minutes until firm when touched with a wet finger. Then place briefly on the grid shelf on the floor of the ROASTING OVEN until pale gold.

■■■■ Bake on the grid shelf on the floor of the BAKING OVEN for 5-10 minutes until golden.

COOK'S TIP
To prepare ahead, complete the recipe to the end of step 2 up to 3 hours ahead. To use, complete the recipe.

BUTTER AND RUM-
BAKED APPLES

Butter and Rum-Baked Apples

PREPARATION TIME:
30 MINUTES, PLUS
MARINATING AND
CHILLING

COOKING TIME:
1 HOUR 15 MINUTES

FREEZING:
UNSUITABLE

400 CALS PER
SERVING

SERVES 6

Baked apples are always a winter favourite. The quick topping and delicious spicy rum butter sauce turn them into festive fare.

50 g (2 oz) dried mango or pineapple
75 ml (5 tbsp) dark rum or brandy
grated rind of 1 lemon
50 g (2 oz) butter
75 g (3 oz) soft brown sugar
2.5 ml (½ level tsp) ground cinnamon

6 small eating apples
250 g (9 oz) puff pastry
1 egg
30 ml (2 level tbsp) caster sugar
double cream, to serve

1 Roughly chop the dried mango or pineapple, add the rum or brandy, cover and marinate for at least 4 hours or place in a covered jam jar for 1 hour in the SIMMERING OVEN. Beat the grated lemon rind, butter, sugar and cinnamon together until pale and light. Drain fruit, reserving marinade, then beat the marinade into the flavoured butter.

2 Slice tops off the apples and remove core and seeds. Prick apples. Fill each with drained fruit and top with 5 ml (1 tbsp) rum butter. Place in a small roasting tin with 150 ml (¼ pint) water. Cover with foil. Bake on the grid shelf on the floor of the ROASTING OVEN for 35 minutes or until tender. Set aside to cool.

3 Roll out puff pastry thinly on a lightly floured worksurface. Cut out six 10 cm (4 in) rounds. Brush with some beaten egg and place, egg-side down, on the cooled apples; press to seal. Brush pastry with remaining egg, decorate with pastry trimmings and sprinkle with sugar. Refrigerate for 30 minutes.

4 Cook on the grid shelf on the floor of the ROASTING OVEN for 20-25 minutes or until pastry is golden brown. Lift on to a serving dish. Add remaining rum butter to roasting tin and bring to the boil on the SIMMERING PLATE, stirring continuously (add water if sauce is too thick). Serve apples with the sauce and cream.

Cinnamon and Orange Stack

PREPARATION TIME:
30 MINUTES, PLUS
MACERATING AND
CHILLING

COOKING TIME:
30 MINUTES

FREEZING:
UNSUITABLE

654 CALS PER
SERVING

SERVES 6

This is an excellent winter recipe as it makes good use of dried fruits.

FOR THE DRIED FRUIT SALAD
15 ml (1 level tbsp) Earl Grey tea leaves
200 g (7 oz) ready-to-eat dried apricots, cut into chunks
150 g (5 oz) ready-to-eat dried prunes, cut into chunks
50 g (2 oz) each ready-to-eat dried figs and dates, cut into chunks
45 ml (3 tbsp) Grand Marnier
rind and juice of 1 lemon
juice of 1 orange
1 vanilla pod, split
1 star anise

FOR THE CINNAMON CREAM
142 ml carton double cream
250 g (9 oz) mascarpone
2.5 ml (½ level tsp) ground cinnamon
grated rind of 1 lemon and 1 orange
5 ml (1 level tsp) caster sugar

FOR THE FILO STACK
9 sheets of filo pastry, about 125 g (4 oz) total weight
25 g (1 oz) butter, melted
2 small bananas, peeled and sliced
25 g (1 oz) icing sugar, sieved, to dust
5 ml (1 level tsp) ground cinnamon, to dust
Honey and Orange Syrup (see below)

1 Pour 450 ml (¾ pint) boiling water over the tea leaves and leave to stand for 5 minutes. Place the dried fruits in a bowl, pour the strained tea over and add the Grand Marnier. Leave to macerate overnight.

2 Place dried fruits and liquid in a pan with the lemon juice and rind, orange juice, vanilla and star anise. Bring slowly to the boil and cook, uncovered, on the SIMMERING PLATE for 10 minutes, then transfer to the SIMMERING OVEN for a further 10 minutes. Remove and discard the lemon rind and star anise and set fruits aside to cool. Scrape the seeds out of the vanilla pod, cover and reserve separately for the cinnamon cream.

3 To make the cinnamon cream, whip the cream until it just holds its shape, then whisk in the mascarpone. Mix in the ground cinnamon, lemon and orange rind, caster sugar and reserved vanilla seeds. Cover and chill.

4 Cut the filo into nine 10 x 25 cm (4 x 10 in) rectangles, then brush each sheet with the melted butter. On the plain shelf, create three stacks, each made of three sheets placed one on top of the other. On one of the stacks score the filo lightly into six equal portions. Cook on the bottom runners of the ROASTING OVEN for 4-5 minutes. Turn the shelf around and cook for a further 1-2 minutes. When pale gold in colour, place in the SIMMERING OVEN to ensure the slices are crisp and dry. Cool.

5 To assemble, drain the fruit and mix with the banana slices. Place an unmarked filo stack on a large serving dish, cover with half the dried fruit mixture and top with half the cinnamon cream. Place a second unmarked filo stack on top and repeat the layering, finishing with the marked filo stack. Dust with sieved icing sugar and ground cinnamon and serve with the warm Honey and Orange Syrup (see Cook's Tips).

COOK'S TIPS
To prepare ahead, complete steps 1, 2 and 4; cover and chill the fruit and store the filo pastry in an airtight container for up to two days. Complete step 3, cover and chill for up to one day. To use, complete the recipe.

To make the honey and orange syrup, place 50 ml (2 fl oz) runny honey, the finely shredded rind and juice of two oranges, one cinnamon stick and a sprig of fresh rosemary in a saucepan, then bring to the boil and bubble on the BOILING PLATE for 4-6 minutes until the mixture is syrupy. Remove the cinnamon stick and rosemary.

Apple and Mincemeat Tart

PREPARATION TIME:
45 MINUTES, PLUS
MINIMUM 3 HOURS
MARINATING,
1 HOUR COOLING
AND 30 MINUTES
CHILLING

COOKING TIME:
55 MINUTES

FREEZING:
COMPLETE THE
RECIPE, THEN WRAP
AND FREEZE. THAW
AT COOL ROOM
TEMPERATURE FOR
5-6 HOURS. WARM
AS IN COOK'S TIP.

695 CALS PER
SERVING

SERVES 6

If you don't have enough time to make your own mincemeat, use 450 g (1 lb) good-quality ready-made mincemeat and add a little brandy or port to the mixture.

FOR THE MINCEMEAT
125 g (4 oz) each raisins and sultanas
125 g (4 oz) ready-to-eat dried apricots, chopped
125 g (4 oz) dark, soft brown sugar
2.5 ml (½ level tsp) ground cinnamon
1.25 ml (¼ level tsp) grated nutmeg
5 ml (1 level tsp) ground mixed spice
juice and finely grated rind of 1 lemon
finely grated rind of 1 orange
30 ml (2 tbsp) brandy
30 ml (2 tbsp) port
25 g (1 oz) butter

FOR THE PASTRY
175 g (6 oz) plain white flour, plus extra for dusting

25 g (1 oz) icing sugar
125 g (4 oz) unsalted butter, chilled and cut into cubes
pinch of salt

FOR THE APPLE PURÉE
450 g (1 lb) cooking apples, peeled, quartered, cored and diced
15 g (½ oz) unsalted butter
juice of 1 small orange
15 ml (1 level tbsp) caster sugar

FOR THE CRUMBLE TOPPING
50 g (2 oz) unsalted butter
75 g (3 oz) self-raising flour
25 g (1 oz) ground almonds
25 g (1 oz) granulated sugar

1 To make the mincemeat, place all the ingredients in a bowl, except for the brandy, port and butter. Add 15 ml (1 tbsp) each of the brandy and port. Mix well, cover and leave for at least 3 hours or overnight. Put the mincemeat in a saucepan, bring to the boil and simmer gently for 5-10 minutes or until it is thick and rich-looking. Stir in remaining brandy, port and the butter. Cool for 1 hour.

2 To make the pastry, place all the ingredients in a food processor and process until mixture resembles crumbs. Add 10 ml (2 tsp) cold water to bind. Turn pastry out on to a floured worksurface; knead lightly. Roll out the pastry thinly and line a 11.5 × 34 cm (4½ × 13½ in) oblong, fluted flan tin. The pastry sides need to be 4 cm (1½ in) deep, so pinch up the pastry above the level of the tin if necessary. (A 20 cm (8 in) round loose-bottomed flan tin can also be used.)

3 To make the purée, place the apples, butter and orange juice in a saucepan. Cover and cook gently on the SIMMERING PLATE for 5 minutes or until beginning to soften. Uncover and transfer to the BOILING PLATE and cook briskly, stirring, for 1-2 minutes or until most of the liquid has evaporated. Stir in caster sugar; cool.

4 To make the crumble topping, place all the ingredients, except the sugar, in a food processor and process to a crumble mixture. Add the granulated sugar.

5 To assemble the tart, spread the mincemeat over the pastry, then the apple purée and finally sprinkle with the crumble topping.

6 Place the tart tin on the floor of the ROASTING OVEN on the cooler right-hand side. Bake for 20-25 minutes or until golden brown. Slip the plain shelf underneath when lifting out loose-bottomed tins. Cool in the tin for 10-15 minutes, then unmould, leaving on the base of the tin to serve.

COOK'S TIP
To prepare ahead, complete the recipe, then pack and chill for up to two days. To use, warm through on the grid shelf on the floor of the ROASTING OVEN for 7-10 minutes.

Chocolate Pancakes

PREPARATION TIME:
15 MINUTES, PLUS
30 MINUTES
CHILLING

COOKING TIME:
30-40 MINUTES

FREEZING: MAKE
AND WRAP THE
PANCAKES AS IN
THE COOK'S TIP.
FREEZE FOR UP TO
ONE MONTH. THAW
AT COOL ROOM
TEMPERATURE FOR
3 HOURS.
COMPLETE AS IN
COOK'S TIP.

115-75 CALS PER
PANCAKE

MAKES 8-12
PANCAKES;
SERVES 4-6

This low-calorie dessert is ideal for those watching their waistlines. You can use any fruit instead of the banana filling, or serve the pancakes with chocolate sauce and vanilla ice cream or frozen yogurt.

150 g (5 oz) plain chocolate
100 g (3½ oz) plain flour
I large egg
pinch of salt
300 ml (½ pint) skimmed milk
25 g (I oz) butter
15 ml (I level tbsp) light brown sugar

4 medium bananas, thickly sliced
120 ml (8 tbsp) brandy
vegetable oil, for brushing
icing sugar, to dust
Greek yogurt, to serve
chocolate shavings, to decorate

1 Place 50 g (2 oz) chocolate in a food processor and chop. Add the flour, egg, salt and milk and process until smooth. Pour into a measuring jug. Cover and chill for 30 minutes.

2 Melt the butter and sugar in a frying pan. Add the bananas and stir-fry on the BOILING PLATE for 2 minutes. Add the brandy (take care when doing this as it may ignite in the warm pan) and continue to simmer until bananas soften and the liquid is syrupy (about 1-2 minutes). Set aside.

3 Lightly wipe an 18 cm (7 in) non-stick crêpe or small frying pan with oil on kitchen paper and heat on the BOILING PLATE. Wipe the SIMMERING PLATE with oil. Stir the batter and coat the base of the pan thinly with about 60 ml (4 tbsp). Cook for 1 minute or until golden brown, then turn onto the SIMMERING PLATE. Put the lid down for 30 seconds-1 minute to cook on the other side. Cook for a further minute. Transfer to a plate, cover and keep warm. Cook remaining batter in the same way, stirring the batter each time before cooking.

4 Chop the remaining chocolate. Place two spoonfuls of banana filling over one half of each pancake; sprinkle with some of the chocolate. Fold in half, then in half again. Arrange in a dish, cover with buttered foil and place in the SIMMERING OVEN for 15-20 minutes to keep warm. Dust, decorate and serve warm with yogurt.

COOK'S TIP
To prepare ahead, make the pancakes (steps 1 and 3). When cold, interleave with greaseproof paper, then wrap in cling film and a polythene bag. Chill for up to 48 hours. To use, fill the pancakes, cover with buttered foil and warm in the SIMMERING OVEN for 20-30 minutes.

AGA TIP
By using both plates when frying pancakes, they can be cooked in half the time with less heat loss.

Apple Strudel with Maple Fudge Sauce

PREPARATION TIME:
30 MINUTES

COOKING TIME:
40 MINUTES

FREEZING: SUITABLE

230-170 CALS PER
SERVING

SERVES 6-8

A delicious pudding with a wicked sauce, but surprisingly low in calories.

I lemon
25 g (I oz) fresh white breadcrumbs
30 ml (2 level tbsp) caster sugar
700 g (1½ lb) cooking apples
6 sheets filo pastry, about 50 g (2 oz)
25 g (I oz) low-fat spread

FOR THE MAPLE FUDGE SAUCE
75 g (3 oz) butter
150 g (5 oz) light brown (muscovado) sugar
30 ml (2 tbsp) maple syrup
75 ml (3 fl oz) half-fat double cream
icing sugar, to dust

APPLE STRUDEL WITH MAPLE FUDGE SAUCE

1 Grate the rind and squeeze the juice of the lemon. Mix the rind with the breadcrumbs and 15 ml (1 level tbsp) of the caster sugar. Peel, quarter and thickly slice the apples. Drizzle with a little lemon juice to prevent them from browning. Mix the apple with the breadcrumb mixture.

2 Lay three pieces of filo pastry side by side on a clean tea towel, overlapping the longest edges by 5 cm (2 in). Brush with a little melted low-fat spread. Place three remaining sheets of filo on top and brush again.

3 Place the apple mixture on the filo pastry. Using the tea towel to help, roll the filo from the longest edge to form a thick roll. Roll it on to a non-stick baking sheet, seam-side down, curling it slightly, if necessary, to fit the sheet. Brush with the remaining low-fat spread and sprinkle with the remaining sugar.

4 ■■ Bake on the grid shelf on the floor of the ROASTING OVEN for 10-12 minutes, then transfer to the SIMMERING OVEN for 30 minutes until the pastry is golden brown and apples are soft. If necessary, cover the pastry loosely with foil to prevent it becoming too brown.

■■■■ Bake in the middle of the BAKING OVEN for 40 minutes until the pastry is golden brown and the apples are soft.

5 Meanwhile, make the Maple Fudge Sauce: melt the butter in a small, heavy-based pan, then add the sugar and maple syrup and cook on the SIMMERING PLATE until the sugar dissolves completely. Stir in the cream and bring to the boil. Allow the sauce to cool slightly before serving with slices of strudel, dusted with icing sugar.

COOK'S TIP
To prepare one day ahead, prepare the strudel to the end of step 3 and prepare the sauce as in step 5. Cover both and chill. To use, bake the strudel as in step 4 and warm the Maple Fudge Sauce in the SIMMERING OVEN. Serve as in step 5.

Chocolate Meringue Roulade

PREPARATION TIME:
30 MINUTES, PLUS
COOLING

COOKING TIME:
1 HOUR

FREEZING: MAKE
THE ROULADE TO
THE END OF STEP 5,
THEN WRAP AND
FREEZE. THAW AT
COOL ROOM
TEMPERATURE FOR
2 HOURS, THEN
DECORATE AND
SERVE.

260-195 CALS PER
SERVING

SERVES 6-8

It's hard to believe this delicious pudding has so few calories.

5 egg whites
175 g (6 oz) caster sugar
5 ml (1 level tsp) cornflour
60 ml (4 level tbsp) half-fat crème fraîche
125 g (4 oz) chocolate spread

50 g (2 oz) cooked, vacuum-packed chestnuts (optional)
icing sugar and cocoa powder, to dust
chocolate shavings, to decorate
half-fat crème fraîche, to serve

1 Use non-stick baking parchment to line a 31.5 x 21.5 cm (12½ x 8½ in) Swiss-roll tin.

2 With an electric whisk, whip the egg whites in a large bowl until frothy, then whisk in the sugar. Stand the bowl over a pan of gently simmering water and whisk at high speed until very thick and shiny – about 4-5 minutes. Take off the heat and whisk in the cornflour.

3 Spoon the mixture into the prepared tin and level the surface. Bake on the grid shelf on the floor of the SIMMERING OVEN for ¾-1 hour or until just firm on the surface. Cool, uncovered, for 1 hour (see Cook's Tips).

4 Beat the crème fraîche into the chocolate spread. Roughly chop the chestnuts, if using, and fold in.

5 Lightly dust a sheet of baking parchment with icing sugar. Turn the meringue out on to the paper, upside down. Carefully peel off the parchment. Make a shallow cut in the meringue about 2.5 cm (1 in) in from the edge of the nearest short end. Spread the chocolate mixture over the meringue and roll it up as you would a Swiss roll, starting from the end with the cut.

6 Dust with a little more icing sugar and cocoa powder and sprinkle over the chocolate shavings. Serve with half-fat crème fraîche.

COOK'S TIPS
To prepare ahead, make the roulade to the end of step 5. Cover lightly with cling film and chill for up to two days. To use, decorate and serve.

The cooked meringue mixture will weep a little as it's cooling – don't worry.

Figs in Cinnamon Syrup

PREPARATION TIME:
15 MINUTES

COOKING TIME:
35 MINUTES, PLUS
COOLING AND
CHILLING

FREEZING:
UNSUITABLE

370 CALS PER
SERVING

SERVES 6

These figs are delicious served either warm or cold with mascarpone cheese or a good-quality vanilla ice cream.

1 orange
1 lemon
300 ml (½ pint) red wine
50 g (2 oz) caster sugar

1 cinnamon stick
450 g (1 lb) ready-to-eat dried figs
200 g tub mascarpone cheese or vanilla ice cream, to serve

1 Pare the rind from the orange and lemon and place in a medium saucepan. Squeeze and add the orange and lemon juice with the wine, sugar and cinnamon stick. Bring slowly to the boil on the SIMMERING PLATE, stirring occasionally.

2 Add the figs to the pan, return to the boil, cover and cook in the SIMMERING OVEN for 20 minutes until plump and soft. Remove figs, rind and cinnamon with a slotted spoon; transfer to a serving bowl.

3 Return the liquid to the BOILING PLATE and bubble until syrupy (about 5 minutes). Pour over the figs, then cool, cover and refrigerate (see Cook's Tip).

4 If wished, warm figs in the syrup for 3-4 minutes, then serve with mascarpone or ice cream.

COOK'S TIP
The figs can be kept, covered, in the fridge for up to one week. Just stir occasionally. Or place in jar and shake from time to time to keep the top of the fruit moist.

Pears in Malmsey Madeira

PREPARATION TIME:
15 MINUTES

COOKING TIME:
30 MINUTES-1
HOUR, PLUS 2
HOURS COOLING

FREEZING:
COMPLETE THE
RECIPE, THEN PACK
AND FREEZE. THAW
AT COOL ROOM
TEMPERATURE
OVERNIGHT.

290 CALS PER
SERVING

SERVES 6

If you have a bottle of sweet sherry lurking in the cupboard, turn it into an elegant dessert with this trouble-free Aga recipe.

300 ml (½ pint) Malmsey Madeira or dark cream sherry
225 g (8 oz) caster sugar

pared rind of 2 lemons
1 vanilla pod, split
6 firm underripe pears (see Cook's Tips)

1 Pour the Malmsey and 150 ml (¼ pint) water into a pan and add the caster sugar, lemon rind and vanilla pod. Heat gently on the SIMMERING PLATE until the sugar is dissolved and boil for 3 minutes. Set aside.

2 Decorate the pears by using a canelle knife to etch spirals or stripes into the skin of the fruit, retaining the stalks (see Cook's Tips).

3 Stand the pears in the smallest saucepan that will take them. Pour the syrup over the top and tuck the lemon rind and vanilla pod among them. Cover tightly, bring to the boil and cook on the floor of the SIMMERING OVEN until tender – anything from 30 minutes-1 hour, depending on the ripeness of the pears.

4 Lift the pears out of the syrup and set aside. Boil syrup hard on the BOILING PLATE for 5-8 minutes until reduced by half. Strain over the pears. Serve at room temperature with ice cream.

COOK'S TIPS
Slightly underripe pears will keep their shape better when poaching.

If you don't have a canelle knife, you can use a vegetable peeler to peel away thin strips of skin from the pears.

If wished, carefully remove the core of the pears by using the tip of a vegetable peeler, working from the base of the fruit.

Chocolate, Prune and Orange Soufflés

PREPARATION TIME:
20 MINUTES

COOKING TIME:
20 MINUTES

FREEZING:
UNSUITABLE

140 CALS PER
SOUFFLÉ

MAKES 8

These wonderful individual soufflés are great for entertaining, yet the low calorie count makes them ideal for those watching their waistlines. The perfect accompaniment is prunes in brandy (see below).

a little butter, for greasing	**grated rind of 1 orange**
75 ml (5 level tbsp) caster sugar	**5 egg whites**
175 g (6 oz) pitted, ready-to-eat prunes	**1.25 ml (¼ level tsp) cream of tartar**
30 ml (2 tbsp) vegetable oil	**pinch of salt**
75 ml (3 fl oz) unsweetened orange juice	**icing sugar, to dust**
50 g (2 oz) plain chocolate	**Prunes in Brandy to serve (see below)**

1 Lightly grease eight 130-150 ml (4-5 fl oz) ramekins and sprinkle with 15 ml (1 level tbsp) of the caster sugar (see Cook's Tips).

2 Place the prunes, vegetable oil and the orange juice in a blender and liquidise for 2-3 minutes (see Cook's Tips) to form a purée.

3 Using a sharp knife, chop the plain chocolate into small pieces and mix with the prune purée, 30 ml (2 level tbsp) of the remaining caster sugar and the orange rind.

4 Place the egg whites, cream of tartar and salt in a clean bowl and whisk until stiff but not dry. Add the remaining 30 ml (2 level tbsp) sugar and continue to whisk until the mixture becomes very stiff and shiny.

5 Using a large metal spoon, beat one-quarter of the egg whites into the prune mixture, then gently fold in the remainder. Spoon into the prepared ramekins.

6 Stand the ramekins in a roasting tin and add enough hot water to come halfway up the sides.

■■ Cook on the grid shelf on the floor of the ROASTING OVEN with the cold plain shelf on the top runners for 7-10 minutes or until soufflés are just set.

■■■■ Cook on the grid shelf on the floor of the BAKING OVEN for 15-20 minutes or until soufflés are just set.

Serve immediately, dusted with icing sugar and accompanied by Prunes in Brandy (see below).

COOK'S TIPS
If you'd prefer to make one large soufflé instead of eight small ones, place the mixture in a 1.7-litre (3-pint) soufflé dish and cook for 40-45 minutes in the ROASTING OVEN or 50-55 minutes in the BAKING OVEN, covering loosely after 30 minutes, if necessary, to prevent soufflé becoming too brown.

Prune purée can be made up to three days ahead and chilled, covered, until needed.

Prunes in Brandy

PREPARATION TIME:
10 MINUTES, PLUS
SOAKING

45 CALS PER
SERVING

This makes the perfect accompaniment to the soufflé recipe above. Place 225 g (8 oz) pitted, ready-to-eat prunes in a jar or bowl. Cover the prunes with 200 ml (7 fl oz) brandy, then cover with a lid or cling film and leave for two or three days.

Treacle Tart

PREPARATION TIME:
25 MINUTES, PLUS
CHILLING

COOKING TIME:
25-50 MINUTES

FREEZING:
SUITABLE. THAW
AT ROOM
TEMPERATURE FOR
4 HOURS.

620-495 CALS PER
SERVING

SERVES 8-10

This robust pudding illustrates how the simplest ingredients can be transformed into the most heavenly dessert. Here, breadcrumbs are mixed with plenty of golden syrup and lemon to cut the sweetness, then baked in a semi-sweet pastry case. Spoonfuls of slightly melting clotted cream ice cream are the perfect indulgence accompaniment. Alternatively, serve with crème fraîche.

FOR THE PASTRY
225 g (8 oz) plain white flour
150 g (5 oz) unsalted butter
1 egg yolk
15 g (½ oz) caster sugar

FOR THE FILLING
700 g (1½ lb) golden syrup
175 g (6 oz) white breadcrumbs
grated rind of 3 lemons
2 eggs

1 To make the pastry, sift the flour and put in a food processor. Add the butter, cut into small pieces, and work until the mixture resembles breadcrumbs. Add the egg yolk, sugar and about 30 ml (2 tbsp) cold water; process briefly to a firm dough. Turn onto a lightly floured surface and knead lightly, then wrap in cling film and chill in the refrigerator for 30 minutes.

2 Roll out the pastry on a lightly floured surface and use to line a 25 cm (10 in) shallow fluted flan tin, about 4 cm (1½ in) deep (it is easiest to slip the base of the tin under the pastry and lift it into the tin). Trim off the excess pastry and flute the edges. Prick the base with a fork.

3 For the filling, warm the golden syrup in a saucepan on the floor of the SIMMERING OVEN or on the SIMMERING PLATE until thinned in consistency. Remove from the heat and mix with the breadcrumbs and lemon rind. Lightly beat the eggs and stir into the syrup mixture. Pour the filling into the pastry case.

4 ■■ Bake on the floor of the ROASTING OVEN, in the front right-hand corner, with the cold plain shelf on the bottom runners for 30-35 minutes until the filling is lightly set and turning golden.

■■■■ Bake on the floor of the BAKING OVEN for 45-50 minutes until the filling is lightly set and turning golden.

Allow to cool slightly. Serve warm, with ice cream or crème fraîche.

Spiced Raisin Puddings with Demerara Lemon Butter Sauce

PREPARATION TIME:
25 MINUTES

COOKING TIME:
40-45 MINUTES

FREEZING: FREEZE
PUDDINGS
UNCOOKED. BAKE
AS IN STEP 4,
ALLOWING AN
EXTRA 5 MINUTES
COOKING TIME.

560 CALS PER
SERVING

SERVES 8

Few of us with a passion for food can resist the temptation of a hot, steaming pudding. There are many wonderful versions, but this light-as-air spicy sponge specked with raisins and stem ginger is one of the best. A sweet, syrupy lemon-flavoured butter is the perfect complement.

1 piece preserved stem ginger in syrup, about 15 g (½ oz)
175 g (6 oz) unsalted butter, softened
175 g (6 oz) caster sugar
3 eggs, lightly beaten
225 g (8 oz) self-raising flour
7.5 ml (1½ level tsp) baking powder
5 ml (1 level tsp) ground mixed spice

2.5 ml (½ level tsp) ground cinnamon
75 g (3 oz) raisins
a little milk

FOR THE SAUCE
75 g (3 oz) unsalted butter
175 g (6 oz) demerara sugar
grated rind and juice of 2 small lemons

1 Grease the base and sides of eight individual 185 ml (6 fl oz) metal pudding basins. Chop the ginger into tiny pieces.

2 In a bowl, cream together the butter and sugar until pale and fluffy. Add the egg, a little at a time, beating well after each addition, and adding a little of the flour to prevent curdling.

3 Sift the remaining flour, baking powder and spices over the bowl. Add the raisins and chopped ginger and gradually fold in, using a large metal spoon. Stir in sufficient milk to give a soft, dropping consistency. Divide the mixture among the prepared tins and level the surfaces.

4 Stand the tins in a roasting tin and pour boiling water around the tins to a depth of 1 cm (¾ in). Cover the roasting tin with foil.

■■■ Bake on the grid shelf on the floor of the ROASTING OVEN with the cold plain shelf on the second runners for 25-30 minutes or until the sponges have risen and feel firm to the touch.

■■■■ Bake on the grid shelf on the floor of the BAKING OVEN for 40-45 minutes or until the sponges have risen and feel firm to the touch.

5 Meanwhile, make the sauce. Melt the butter in a small saucepan on the SIMMERING PLATE. Add the sugar and heat gently for 2-3 minutes until bubbling. Add the lemon rind and juice and cook gently to make a buttery syrup.

6 Loosen the edges of the puddings with a knife, then invert onto warmed serving plates. Pour a little sauce over each one and serve with cream or crème fraîche.

COOK'S TIP
As a variation, use chopped dates, dried figs or prunes instead of raisins. Replace the lemon in the sauce with orange rind and juice.

Chocolate Bread and Butter Pudding

PREPARATION TIME:
15 MINUTES, PLUS
STANDING

COOKING TIME:
45-55 MINUTES

FREEZING:
UNSUITABLE

500 CALS PER
SERVING

SERVES 6

This irresistible recipe has all the comforting qualities of a traditional bread and butter pudding – it's sweet, eggy, soft-textured and so difficult to resist. The bonus here is the generous pockets of dark, gooey chocolate sauce, melting into the spiced vanilla custard to create a perfect balance of flavours.

200 g (7 oz) plain chocolate
75 g (3 oz) unsalted butter
225 g (8 oz) fruited bun loaf or light teabread
5 ml (1 tsp) vanilla essence
2.5 ml (½ level tsp) ground cinnamon
3 eggs
25 g (1 oz) caster sugar
600 ml (1 pint) milk
cocoa powder and icing sugar, for dusting

1 Lightly grease the sides of a 1.7 litre (3 pint) ovenproof dish. Break up the chocolate and put into a heatproof bowl. Add 25 g (1 oz) of the butter and place in the SIMMERING OVEN for 15-20 minutes until melted. Stir lightly.

2 Cut the fruited bread into thin slices and arrange a third of the slices, overlapping, in the prepared dish. Spread with half the chocolate sauce. Arrange half the remaining bread in the dish and spread with the remaining sauce. Finally arrange the last of the bread slices in the dish.

3 Melt remaining butter. Remove from heat and stir in vanilla essence, cinnamon, eggs, sugar and milk. Beat thoroughly, then pour over the bread. Leave to stand for 1 hour.

4 ■■ Set the pudding in a roasting tin containing 2.5 cm (1 in) of hot water and place on the grid shelf on the floor of the ROASTING OVEN for 40-45 minutes until the custard has set and the bread is deep golden brown.

■■■■ Cook in the middle of the BAKING OVEN for 40-45 minutes until the custard has set and the bread is deep golden brown.

Leave to stand for 5 minutes. Dust with cocoa powder and icing sugar before serving.

COOK'S TIP
Use a teabread that is lightly dotted with fruits or the pudding will be too heavy. Allow to stand for a full hour before baking to ensure a really good texture. You can substitute the fruited bread with brioche or ordinary unsliced bread. Lightly scatter with raisins when layering the bread in the dish.

AGA TIP
The pudding can be reheated in the SIMMERING OVEN for 20-30 minutes.

BAKING

Almond Bakewell Tarts with Plum Sauce

PREPARATION TIME:
25 MINUTES, PLUS
30 MINUTES
CHILLING

COOKING TIME:
50 MINUTES

FREEZING:
COMPLETE THE
RECIPE BUT DON'T
DECORATE. COOL,
WRAP AND FREEZE
TARTS, TOPPING
AND SAUCE
SEPARATELY. THAW
AT COOL ROOM
TEMPERATURE FOR
4-5 HOURS;
DECORATE.

935 CALS PER
SERVING

SERVES 6

This is a variation on that all-time favourite, Bakewell tart.

FOR THE PASTRY
200 g (7 oz) plain white flour, plus extra for dusting
100 g (3½ oz) butter, cut into cubes
75 g (3 oz) caster sugar
3 large egg yolks
2.5 ml (½ tsp) vanilla essence

FOR THE FILLING
125 g (4 oz) butter
125 g (4 oz) caster sugar
3 large eggs
125 g (4 oz) ground almonds

2-3 drops almond essence
90 ml (6 level tbsp) redcurrant jelly

FOR THE PLUM SAUCE
450 g (1 lb) ripe plums, halved and stoned
50-75 g (2-3 oz) soft brown sugar, plus extra to taste
150 ml (¼ pint) sweet white wine

FOR THE CRUMBLE TOPPING
25 g (1 oz) butter
75 g (3 oz) plain flour
25 g (1 oz) caster sugar

1 To make the pastry, place the flour and butter in a processor and process until it resembles fine breadcrumbs. Add the remaining pastry ingredients and process until the dough resembles very coarse breadcrumbs. Lift out the blade and gather the dough together. Turn out on to a floured worksurface and knead lightly until smooth. Divide into six balls, flatten slightly, wrap and chill for 30 minutes if too soft to roll out immediately.

2 On a floured worksurface roll out the pastry thinly and line six 10 cm (4 in) diameter, 3 cm (1¼ in) deep tart tins. Prick the pastry bases and line with well crumpled and softened greaseproof paper and baking beans. Bake blind on the floor of the ROASTING OVEN for 5 minutes or until lightly coloured. Remove the paper and beans and return to the oven for 2 minutes. Cool.

3 To prepare the filling, beat the butter until soft, then gradually beat in the caster sugar until mixture is light and fluffy. Slowly beat in two eggs, then the remaining egg with one-third of the ground almonds. Fold in the remaining ground almonds and the almond essence.

4 Warm the redcurrant jelly in a heatproof bowl in the SIMMERING OVEN and brush generously over the insides of the pastry cases. Spoon in the almond filling. Place the tarts on a baking sheet.

■■ Bake on the grid shelf on the floor of the ROASTING OVEN for 12-16 minutes until golden and just firm.

■■■■ Bake on the grid shelf on the second runners of the BAKING OVEN for 20-25 minutes until golden and just firm. Leave in tins for 10 minutes, unmould and cool.

5 To make the plum sauce, place all the ingredients in a saucepan with 150 ml (¼ pint) water and bring to the boil. Remove three plum halves when soft to reserve for decoration. Cook the remaining plums until very soft – about 15 minutes. Place in a food processor or blender and process until smooth. Sieve, if wished, adding more sugar to taste. Cool.

6 For the crumble topping, rub the butter into the flour and add the sugar to make a crumble mix. Spread evenly on a small roasting tin. Place on the bottom runners at the front of the ROASTING OVEN for 4-8 minutes until golden. Cool.

7 Sprinkle the crumble on the top of each tart. Decorate with reserved plums, cut into strips, and serve with the plum sauce.

ALMOND BAKEWELL
TARTS WITH PLUM
SAUCE

Coconut Squares

PREPARATION TIME:
10 MINUTES, PLUS
COOLING

COOKING TIME:
35 MINUTES

FREEZING:
UNSUITABLE

500 CALS PER
SQUARE

MAKES 10 SQUARES

These lovely, textured nutty squares are bound to become family favourites. They are gluten-wheat free so this is a useful recipe for those on special diets.

75 g (3 oz) butter, plus extra for greasing
200 g (7 oz) demerara sugar
175 g (6 oz) ground rice
2 large eggs
pinch of salt

1-2 drops vanilla essence
75 g (3 oz) desiccated coconut
75 g (3 oz) chopped hazelnuts
45 ml (3 level tbsp) apricot or raspberry jam, plus extra for brushing

1 Base-line a small roasting tin with non-stick baking parchment.

2 Cream together the butter and 75 g (3 oz) of the sugar until light and fluffy. Stir in 150 g (5 oz) of the ground rice. Pat the mixture into the prepared tin.

■■ Bake for 7-10 minutes on the floor of the ROASTING OVEN until beginning to colour.

■■■■ Bake for 15 minutes in the middle of the BAKING OVEN until beginning to colour. Leave in the tin to cool for a few minutes.

3 Lightly beat the eggs. Add the remaining sugar, rice, salt, vanilla essence, desiccated coconut and chopped hazelnuts. Mix well. Spread the jam over the base, followed by the egg mixture.

■■ Place on the grid shelf on the floor of the ROASTING OVEN with the cold plain shelf on the second runners. Bake for 17-20 minutes until pale golden.

■■■■ Bake in the middle of the BAKING OVEN for 20 minutes until pale golden.

4 Allow to cool, then brush with a little warmed jam. Cut the cake into squares. Leave in the tin to cool completely before serving (see Cook's Tip).

COOK'S TIP
The coconut squares can be wrapped in greaseproof paper and stored in an airtight container for three to five days.

Sticky Ginger Flapjacks

PREPARATION TIME:
10 MINUTES

COOKING TIME:
40 MINUTES

FREEZING:
UNSUITABLE

512-255 CALS PER
SERVING

MAKES 12 LARGE
SQUARES OR 24
SMALL TRIANGLES

Because these flapjacks are cooked in a deep tin, they have a delicious crumbly, moist texture. The addition of the ground ginger adds a subtle spice flavour which cuts through the richness of the buttery oat mixture.

350 g (12 oz) unsalted butter, plus extra for greasing
275 g (10 oz) caster sugar

225 g (8 oz) golden syrup
450 g (1 lb) rolled oats
15 ml (1 level tsp) ground ginger

1 Grease and base-line a small roasting tin with non-stick baking parchment. Put the butter, caster sugar and golden syrup in a large pan and heat them together gently on the SIMMERING PLATE until melted. Mix in the rolled oats and ground ginger until they are thoroughly combined.

2 Pour the mixture into the tin and level the surface.

■■ Bake on the grid shelf on the floor of the ROASTING OVEN with the cold plain shelf on the second runners for 30-35 minutes or until golden brown round the edges (see Cook's Tip). If browning too quickly, lower the plain shelf.

■■■■ Bake in the middle of the BAKING OVEN for 30-35 minutes.

3 Leave to cool in the tin for 15 minutes. While still warm, score into squares or triangles with a sharp knife. Leave in the tin to cool completely, then turn out and cut into the required shape.

COOK'S TIP
Don't overcook the flapjacks or they will be hard and dry. Once cooked, they should still be sticky and slightly soft when pressed in the middle.

Sesame Prune Slices

PREPARATION TIME: 20 MINUTES, PLUS COOLING

COOKING TIME: 35 MINUTES

FREEZING: SUITABLE

295 CALS PER SLICE

MAKES 16 SLICES

Here deliciously sweet, sticky prunes are sandwiched between a buttery shortbread base and a moist, syrupy oatmeal layer. At least you can take comfort from the proportion of healthy ingredients in this tempting traybake!

FOR THE BASE
175 g (6 oz) plain white flour
125 g (4 oz) unsalted butter or margarine
50 g (2 oz) caster sugar

FOR THE FILLING
225 g (8 oz) no-need-to-soak dried prunes
15 g (½ oz) dark muscovado sugar
2.5 ml (½ tsp) cornflour

FOR THE TOPPING
125 g (4 oz) unsalted butter or margarine
75 g (3 oz) caster sugar
15 ml (1 tbsp) honey
125 g (4 oz) no-need-to-soak dried prunes
125 g (4 oz) self-raising white flour
2.5 ml (½ tsp) bicarbonate of soda
125 g (4 oz) medium oatmeal
50 g (2 oz) sesame seeds

1 Grease a small roasting tin.

2 To make the base, sift the flour into a bowl. Add butter or margarine, cut into small pieces, and rub in the sugar using fingertips or a food processor until mixture begins to cling together.

3 Turn into the tin and pack the mixture down well with the back of a tablespoon.

■■ Bake on the front of the grid shelf on the floor of the ROASTING OVEN with the plain shelf on the second runners for 15 minutes until turning golden around the edges. Turn the tin around after the first 5 minutes to ensure even cooking.

■■■ Bake in the middle of the BAKING OVEN for 10 minutes, then turn the tin around and bake for a further 6 minutes until turning golden around the edges.

4 For the filling, roughly chop the prunes and place in a small saucepan with the sugar and 150 ml (¼ pint) water. Bring to the boil, cover and place in the SIMMERING OVEN for 20 minutes. Blend the cornflour with 15 ml (1 tbsp) water and add to the pan. Cook for 1 minute on the SIMMERING PLATE, stirring until the juices have thickened. Leave to cool slightly, then spread over the shortbread base.

5 For the topping, place the butter or margarine, sugar and honey in a small pan and heat in the SIMMERING OVEN until dissolved. Finely chop the prunes and stir into the mixture.

6 Sift the flour and bicarbonate of soda into a bowl. Add the oatmeal and all but 30 ml (2 tbsp) of the sesame seeds. Add the melted mixture and beat until evenly combined.

7 Spoon the topping over the prunes in the tin and level the surface. Sprinkle over the remaining seeds. Bake as in step 3 for 20 minutes, turning halfway through the cooking time, until the topping is golden and slightly risen. Leave to cool in the tin, then cut into bars. Store in an airtight tin for up to 5 days.

COOK'S TIP
Use other plump dried fruit such as apricots, figs or dates instead of prunes. Add a pinch of mixed spice or grated lemon rind to the topping.

Manhole Cover Biscuits

PREPARATION TIME:
5-10 MINUTES

COOKING TIME:
30-35 MINUTES

FREEZING:
UNSUITABLE

425 CALS PER
BISCUIT

MAKES 10

Children love these giant-sized biscuits and they are fun for them to make. You can wrap them individually and pop them in your pocket for nibbling on long winter walks.

175 g (6 oz) soft margarine
225 g (8 oz) soft light brown sugar
I medium egg
225 g (8 oz) self-raising flour

100 g (3½ oz) plain chocolate chips
100 g (3½ oz) roasted hazelnuts, chopped
25 g (I oz) desiccated coconut

I Place the margarine in a bowl, stir in the sugar and egg until smooth – there is no need to beat hard. Fold or stir in the flour, half the chocolate chips, and half the chopped nuts and the coconut. Mix to an even texture, then divide the mixture into 10 even balls.

2 Place the remaining nuts on a saucer. Lightly roll the dough balls in the nuts, then place the balls well spaced out on two large baking trays. Dip a fork in water, then pat out the dough into circles 10 cm (4 in) across. Sprinkle the biscuits with the remaining chocolate chips.

3 ■■ Place one tray on the grid shelf on the top runners of the ROASTING OVEN and the second tray on the bottom runners. Set a cold roasting tin on the second runners above. Bake for 15-20 minutes until pale golden, turning the tray round after 10 minutes for even colouring. ■■■■ Set one tray on the bottom runners and one tray on the second runners of the BAKING OVEN. Bake for 15-20 minutes. Then transfer the trays to the SIMMERING OVEN for 15 minutes to complete cooking.

MANHOLE COVER
BISCUITS

Orange Biscuits with Seville Curd

PREPARATION TIME:
35 MINUTES, PLUS
CHILLING

COOKING TIME:
12-15 MINUTES

FREEZING: MAKE
THE DOUGH ROLLS
TO THE END OF
STEP 2 AND FREEZE.
THAW, SLICE AND
BAKE. IF FREEZING
THE DOUGH
SLICED, COOK
FROM FROZEN,
ALLOWING AN
EXTRA 1-2
MINUTES.

185 CALS PER
BISCUIT

MAKES 30

Storing ready-to-bake biscuits in the freezer is a great asset. If you store dough ready sliced, you can produce home-baked biscuits in the time that it takes to prepare tea or coffee for unexpected visitors.

450 g (I lb) plain flour
125 g (5 oz) caster sugar
350 g (12 oz) butter
grated rind of 2 Seville oranges
I egg
few drops vanilla essence

FOR THE SEVILLE CURD
grated rind of I Seville orange
60 ml (4 tbsp) Seville orange juice
50 g (2 oz) butter
90 g (3 oz) caster sugar
I large egg

I To make the biscuits, combine the flour, sugar and butter in a food processor or rub together. Add the orange rind, egg and vanilla essence and work to a smooth dough.

2 Divide the dough into four and roll each piece to a sausage shape 10 cm (4 in) long. Wrap individually and chill in the freezer for 10 minutes.

3 Slice one dough roll into 20 slices and space out on a baking tray or the plain shelf covered with silicon baking parchment.

4 ■■ Bake on the grid shelf on the floor of the ROASTING OVEN with the cold plain shelf on the bottom runners or a cold roasting tin on the third runners for 12-15 minutes until pale golden. Turn halfway through the cooking time for even colouring. ■■■■ Bake on the bottom runners of the BAKING OVEN for 12-15 minutes until pale golden. Turn halfway through the cooking time for even colouring.

5 Leave the biscuits to cool on the baking tray for 15 minutes, then cool on a wire rack. Cook the remaining biscuits as required. Sandwich the biscuits together with a teaspoon of Seville curd.

6 To make the Seville curd, place the orange rind, juice and butter in a small pan and heat to boiling on the SIMMERING PLATE. Stir to ensure the sugar has dissolved. Whisk the egg thoroughly, then gradually whisk in the hot orange mixture.

7 Return the orange curd to the pan, place in the SIMMERING OVEN for 12-15 minutes until well thickened, giving it a stir every 5 minutes. Pour into a clean screw-top jam jar and chill.

Moist Fruit Cake with Glacé Fruits

PREPARATION TIME:
20 MINUTES, PLUS
COOLING

COOKING TIME:
1¾ HOURS

FREEZING: SUITABLE
BEFORE
DECORATING

515 CALS PER SLICE

MAKES 12 SLICES

An impressive arrangement of colourful glacé fruits perfectly offsets this crumbly and exceptionally moist fruit cake. To enhance the moist texture, dried fruits are first simmered in a buttery syrup to plump and sweeten them. Look for quality glacé fruits in good confectioners and specialist food stores – they are well worth the expense! For a less costly alternative, try one of the variations.

200 g (7 oz) dried apple rings
300 g (10 oz) mixed dried fruit
200 g (7 oz) molasses sugar
175 g (6 oz) unsalted butter or margarine
275 ml (9 fl oz) cold black tea
350 g (12 oz) self-raising white flour
5 ml (1 level tsp) baking powder
15 ml (1 level tbsp) ground mixed spice

1 egg
30 ml (2 tbsp) black treacle
100 g (3½ oz) glacé ginger pieces

TO DECORATE
60 ml (4 level tbsp) apricot jam
450 g (1 lb) mixed glacé fruits (pears, plums, cherries, pineapple, etc)

1 Grease and line a deep 23 cm (9 in) round cake tin. Roughly chop the apples and place in a saucepan with the other dried fruit, sugar, butter or margarine and tea. Bring to the boil on the SIMMERING PLATE and simmer gently for 3-5 minutes. Remove from the heat and leave to cool completely.

2 Sift the flour, baking powder and mixed spice into a bowl. Add the cooled fruit mixture, egg, treacle, ginger and liquid; stir well until the ingredients are evenly combined.

3 Turn the cake mixture into the prepared tin and level the surface.

■■ Bake on the grid shelf on the floor of the ROASTING OVEN with the cold plain shelf on the second runners for 35-45 minutes until deep golden. Turn once during the cooking time for even colouring. Transfer the hot shelf to the second runners in the SIMMERING OVEN and place the cake tin on this at the back of the oven. Bake for 45 minutes-1 hour or until a skewer inserted in the centre comes out clean.

■■■■ Bake on the grid shelf on the floor of the BAKING OVEN with the cold plain shelf on the top runners for 1-1¼ hours or until a skewer inserted into the centre comes out clean. Leave in the tin for 15 minutes, then transfer to a wire rack to cool.

4 To finish the cake, heat the apricot jam in a small bowl in the SIMMERING OVEN until softened, then press through a sieve into another bowl. Brush a little of the apricot glaze over the cake.

5 Cut any larger pieces of glacé fruit into small wedges or slices. Arrange the fruits over the cake, then brush with the remaining glaze.

COOK'S TIPS
If more convenient, the dried fruit mixture can be cooked and cooled a day in advance.

For a more everyday fruit cake omit the glacé fruit topping. Instead, generously sprinkle the top of the cake with demerara sugar or decorate with whole blanched almonds before baking.

Turkish Yogurt Cake with Poached Pumpkin

PREPARATION TIME:
10 MINUTES, PLUS
1 HOUR COOLING
AND 15 MINUTES
SOAKING

COOKING TIME:
55 MINUTES

FREEZING:
UNSUITABLE

340 CALS PER SLICE

SERVES 6;
MAKES 12 SLICES

This moist, light-textured cake improves with keeping and may be served with any fresh fruit. Don't be put off by the combination of cake and pumpkin – it's quite delicious.

175 g (6 oz) butter, plus extra for greasing
200 g (7 oz) thick Greek yogurt
2 large eggs, beaten
300 g (11 oz) caster sugar
few drops vanilla essence
30 ml (2 level tbsp) desiccated coconut
225 g (8 oz) self-raising flour, sieved
2.5 ml (½ level tsp) baking powder

75 g (3 oz) sultanas
juice of 2 lemons and 1 orange
1 cinnamon stick
225 g (8 oz) pumpkin flesh, cut into thin slices (see Cook's Tips)
rosewater (optional)
pumpkin seeds, to decorate

1 Grease and base-line a 900 g (2 lb) loaf tin with non-stick baking parchment. Melt the butter and leave to cool a little before beating into the yogurt. In a bowl, whisk together the eggs and 175 g (6 oz) sugar with an electric whisk until very light and fluffy. Fold in the yogurt mixture, vanilla essence and coconut. Sieve in the self-raising flour and baking powder and fold in the sultanas. Spoon the mixture into the prepared tin.

2 ■■ Bake at the front of the grid shelf on the floor of the ROASTING OVEN for 45-50 minutes, turning the tin round after about 30 minutes to ensure even colouring.

■■■ Bake on the grid shelf on the floor of the BAKING OVEN for 50-55 minutes or until a skewer inserted into the centre comes out clean.

Leave to cool in the tin for 10 minutes before turning out onto a cooling rack.

3 Meanwhile, in a saucepan dissolve 75 g (3 oz) caster sugar in 60 ml (4 tbsp) water. Add the juice of 1 lemon, the orange juice and crumbled cinnamon stick and bring to the boil. Add the pumpkin, then place in the SIMMERING OVEN for 20-30 minutes or until soft. Leave the pumpkin to cool in the syrup.

4 Slowly dissolve the remaining 50 g (2 oz) caster sugar in 30 ml (2 tbsp) water. Add the juice of the remaining lemon or a few drops of rosewater, if using, and warm in the SIMMERING OVEN to a light syrup. Allow to cool a little.

5 Return the cake to the clean tin. Make fine holes all over the cake with a skewer and pour the warm syrup over. Remove the cake from the tin and cut into thick slices. Decorate with pumpkin seeds and serve with slices of the poached pumpkin.

COOK'S TIPS
To prepare up to one week ahead, make cake to end of step 2; wrap in foil; freeze or store in an airtight container. The day before, cook pumpkin as in step 3; thaw cake, if frozen. To use, complete the recipe.

If pumpkin is unavailable, use turban, kabocha or butternut squash instead.

Spiced Apricot Cake

PREPARATION TIME:
45 MINUTES, PLUS
20 MINUTES
CHILLING AND
1 HOUR COOLING

COOKING TIME:
1 HOUR 45 MINUTES

FREEZING:
COMPLETE TO THE
END OF STEP 5 BUT
DON'T DECORATE;
FREEZE. THAW AT
ROOM
TEMPERATURE
OVERNIGHT.

450 CALS PER
SERVING

SERVES 10

Inspired by the classic Simnel cake, this has a layer of sticky almond paste running through the middle and a delicious fresh spiced taste that improves with keeping. Home-made almond paste tastes wonderful and can be made in minutes, but if you're pressed for time, use shop-bought white marzipan.

FOR THE ALMOND PASTE FILLING
50 g (2 oz) ground almonds
40 g (1½ oz) icing sugar, plus extra for sprinkling
25 g (1 oz) caster sugar
grated rind of 1 lemon
15 ml (1 tbsp) egg, beaten

FOR THE CAKE
4 eggs
300 g (11 oz) plain white flour
10 ml (2 level tsp) baking powder
pinch of salt
2.5 ml (½ level tsp) ground coriander

2.5 ml (½ level tsp) ground cloves
5 ml (1 level tsp) ground ginger
5 ml (1 level tsp) ground cinnamon
175 g (6 oz) softened butter, preferably unsalted
grated rind of 1 lemon
225 g (8 oz) soft brown sugar, such as muscovado
apricot glaze or jam
15 ml (1 tbsp) Kirsch or Grand Marnier
kumquats, ready-to-eat dried apricots or mangoes cut into pieces, physalis (Cape gooseberries) dipped in edible gold dust and ribbon, to decorate

1 Line a deep 23 cm (9 in) round tin with greaseproof paper. To make the filling, place the ground almonds, icing sugar, caster sugar and lemon rind in a small bowl. Mix thoroughly; stir in 15 ml (1 tbsp) beaten egg (from the cake ingredients). Mix to a smooth paste, cover and chill.

2 To make the cake, sift together flour, baking powder, salt and the spices. Place butter in a bowl with the lemon rind; beat until creamy. Add sugar a spoonful at a time, beating well (or use the beater attachment in a food mixer).

3 Beat the remaining eggs, spoonful by spoonful, into the sugar and butter mixture until light and fluffy (see Cook's Tips). Using a large metal spoon, fold in the flour and spices.

4 Put half the cake mixture in the tin; smooth the surface. Roll almond paste out between two pieces of cling film or on a worksurface sprinkled with icing sugar to a 20.5 cm (8 in) round. Peel off one piece of cling film; use the other to help lay the almond paste on the cake mixture. Spoon remaining cake mixture on top of the almond paste and smooth.

■■ Cook on the front of the grid shelf on the floor of the ROASTING OVEN with the cold plain shelf on the third runners. Bake for 30-45 minutes until golden, turning once for even colouring. Then put the hot plain shelf on the second runners of the SIMMERING OVEN and put the cake at the back of the oven for 15-30 minutes.

■■■ Cook on the grid shelf on the floor of the BAKING OVEN with the cold plain shelf on the top runners. Bake for 1 hour, turning once for even colouring. Then put the hot plain shelf on the second runners of the SIMMERING OVEN and cook the cake for a further 15-30 minutes.

Cool for 30 minutes in the tin, then turn out on to a wire rack to cool completely.

5 To decorate the cake, warm the apricot glaze in the SIMMERING OVEN, add the Kirsch, kumquats and apricots and spoon over the top of the cake in a thin layer. Cool for about 30 minutes until set. Top with physalis dipped in gold dust and tie with ribbon to serve.

COOK'S TIPS
Take care when you add the last 15-30 ml (1-2 tbsp) egg – the mixture may be runny enough and not need it.

If the cake begins to overbrown as it cooks, cover it with greaseproof paper.

CHOCOLATE
MOUSSE CAKE

Chocolate Mousse Cake

PREPARATION TIME:
20 MINUTES

COOKING TIME:
1 HOUR

FREEZING:
UNSUITABLE

570 CALS PER
SERVING

SERVES 6

A real 'death by chocolate' recipe that chocoholics will adore. Serve with a dish of sliced clementines for those that need a little light relief!

375 g (13 oz) plain chocolate	**3 eggs**
5 ml (1 level tsp) instant coffee granules	**50 g (2 oz) caster sugar**
175 ml (6 fl oz) double cream	**25 g (1 oz) butter**
15 ml (1 tbsp) brandy	**single cream, to serve**

1 Break 200 g (7 oz) chocolate into small pieces. Place in a small bowl with the instant coffee. Melt in the SIMMERING OVEN for 15 minutes, then stir until it is dissolved.

2 Grease and base-line a 16 cm (6½ in) square base measurement and 4 cm (1½ in) deep tin with non-stick baking parchment.

3 Whisk eggs and sugar together until pale and thick (see Cook's Tip). In a separate bowl, whip 100 ml (4 fl oz) double cream until it just holds its shape, then whisk in the brandy.

4 Fold a little egg mixture into the warm melted chocolate to give a soft mixture, then fold the chocolate into the egg mixture, followed by the whipped cream, ensuring the ingredients are thoroughly mixed. Pour into prepared tin and place in a small roasting tin. Pour in enough hot water to come at least halfway up the sides of the tin.

5 ■■ Place at the font of the grid shelf on the floor of the ROASTING OVEN with the cold plain shelf on the second runners. Bake for 45 minutes-1 hour or until just firm to the centre.
■■■■ Place on the bottom runners of the BAKING OVEN and bake for 45 minutes-1 hour or until just firm to the centre.
Allow to cool in tin.

6 When the cake is cool, make the topping. Place the remaining chocolate and cream in a small bowl, add the butter. Melt in the SIMMERING OVEN for 15 minutes. Cool, stirring occasionally, until spreadable.

7 Turn cake out onto cutting board when cool; spread with topping. Chill until just firm. Serve at room temperature or topping may be too solid. Serve with cream.

COOK'S TIP
If you whisk the eggs with a clean whisk first, there is no need to stop and wash the whisk before whipping the cream. The cream and egg mixtures should be whipped to the same texture so that they are easy to fold together.

Citrus Eccles Cakes

PREPARATION TIME:
35 MINUTES, PLUS
CHILLING

COOKING TIME:
12-15 MINUTES

FREEZING: SUITABLE

160 CALS PER CAKE

MAKES 20

Flaky, light and oozing butter, these delicate lattice-topped pastries are a far cry from some dry and heavy shop-bought versions. In this recipe they are filled with currants, citrus peel and muscovado sugar, and drizzled with melted butter after cooking. For maximum enjoyment serve with that freshly baked lingering warmth.

175 g (6 oz) firm unsalted butter
225 g (8 oz) plain white flour
pinch of salt
5 ml (1 tsp) lemon juice

FOR THE FILLING
175 g (6 oz) currants
50 g (2 oz) chopped mixed peel

50 g (2 oz) muscovado sugar
finely grated rind of 2 lemons
beaten egg, to glaze
caster sugar, for dusting
50 g (2 oz) unsalted butter, for melting

1 To make the pastry, cut the butter into small dice. Sift the flour and salt into a bowl. Add the butter, lemon juice and 100 ml (3½ fl oz) iced water. Using a round-bladed knife mix to a soft dough, adding a little extra water if it is too dry.

2 Knead lightly, then roll out on a lightly floured surface to an oblong, about 30 cm (12 in) long and 10 cm (4 in) wide. Fold the bottom third up and the lower third down, keeping the edges straight, then give the pastry a quarter turn. Repeat the rolling, folding and turning four more times. Wrap in greaseproof paper and leave to rest in the refrigerator for 30 minutes.

3 For the filling, mix the currants, mixed peel, sugar and lemon rind together in a small bowl.

4 Lightly grease two baking sheets. Roll out half of the pastry on a lightly floured surface to a 50 × 20 cm (20 × 8 in) rectangle. Cut in half lengthways, then cut each strip into five equal pieces, making squares 10 × 10 cm (4 × 4 in).

5 Using a knife, make three 2 cm (¾ in) cuts, 5 mm (¼ in) apart down the centre of one piece of pastry. Make three more rows of cuts either side of the first row so when the pastry is pulled apart it creates a lattice. Repeat with remaining pieces of pastry. Brush edges with beaten egg.

6 Set aside half of the filling. Divide the remainder between the latticed pastries, placing it in the centres. Bring the edges of the pastry up over the filling, pinching them together to seal. Invert onto one baking sheet, so the latticed sides face upwards.

7 Repeat with remaining pastry and filling to make ten more pastries. Brush the pastries with beaten egg and sprinkle with sugar. Bake on top and third runners of the ROASTING OVEN for 12-15 minutes, until golden, turning the trays around halfway through the cooking time to ensure even cooking. Melt the butter and pour a little into each cake, through the lattice. Serve warm.

COOK'S TIP
To make cherry and almond cakes, replace currants, peel and lemon rind with 125 g (4 oz) chopped glacé cherries, 50 g (2 oz) chopped blanched almonds and 125 g (4 oz) grated almond paste.

Saffron Scones

PREPARATION TIME:
15 MINUTES, PLUS
INFUSING

COOKING TIME:
10-12 MINUTES

FREEZING: SUITABLE

110 CALS PER
SCONE

MAKES ABOUT 12

With its golden colour, wonderful aroma and intriguing taste, real saffron gives an exciting lift to the humble scone. Serve warm with melting butter or generous scoops of thick clotted cream. Slices of juicy melon and mango would make the perfect accompaniment.

½-1 sachet or 2.5-5 ml (½-1 level tsp)
saffron strands (see Cook's Tips)
150 ml (¼ pint) milk (approximately)
225 g (8 oz) self-raising white flour
pinch of salt

5 ml (1 level tsp) baking powder
40 g (1½ oz) firm unsalted butter or
margarine
30 ml (2 tbsp) caster sugar
beaten egg, to glaze

1 Lightly grease a baking sheet. Roughly break up the saffron strands and place in a saucepan with half of the milk. Bring just to the boil, then remove from the heat and leave to infuse for 20 minutes and cool.

2 Sift the flour, salt and baking powder into a bowl. Add the butter, cut into small pieces, and rub in using the fingertips until the mixture resembles fine breadcrumbs. Stir in the sugar.

3 Using a round-bladed knife, stir in the saffron milk and half of the remaining milk. Mix to a soft dough, adding the rest of the milk if the mixture is too dry; it should be soft and slightly sticky.

4 Knead lightly and roll out to a 2 cm (¾ in) thickness. Cut out rounds, using a 5 cm (2 in) cutter. Place on the baking sheet and brush the tops with the beaten egg. Bake on the top runners of the ROASTING OVEN for 10-12 minutes until well risen and golden brown. Transfer to a wire rack to cool. Serve split, with butter, or clotted cream and fruits.

COOK'S TIPS
Use either ½ or 1 sachet saffron strands, depending on the strength of flavour required. As with any recipe using baking powder, scones should be baked immediately as the baking powder is activated as soon as it comes into contact with liquids.

If you wish, replace the saffron with the finely grated rind of 1 orange and 15 ml (1 level tbsp) finely snipped rosemary leaves. Do not heat the milk before mixing.

Herb and Soured Milk Scones

PREPARATION TIME:
10 MINUTES

COOKING TIME:
15 MINUTES

FREEZING: SUITABLE

115 CALS PER
SCONE

MAKES ABOUT
18 SCONES

You can also make this recipe using butter milk, milk and yogurt mixed together or real sour milk instead of the milk and lemon juice mixture.

450 g (1 lb) self-raising flour
5 ml (1 level tsp) baking powder
2.5 ml (½ level tsp) salt
freshly ground black pepper
15 ml (1 level tbsp) chopped fresh flat-leafed parsley
15 ml (1 level tbsp) chopped fresh thyme

50 g (2 oz) butter, cut into cubes
300 ml (½ pint) milk
45 ml (3 tbsp) lemon juice
flour, for dusting
toasted crushed Parmesan cheese, to serve (see Cook's Tips)

1 Place the first six ingredients in a bowl, add the cubed butter and, using two knives, 'cut' it into the flour until the mixture resembles breadcrumbs. Mix the milk with the lemon juice, then add to the bowl. Mix together quickly with your hands until the dough comes into a ball (see Cook's Tips).

2 Place the dough on a well-floured surface and lightly roll out to a thickness of 2.5 cm (1 in). Stamp out into rounds with a 5 cm (2 in) pastry cutter and place on a lightly floured baking sheet.

3 Bake on the top runners of the ROASTING OVEN for 12-15 minutes until risen and light brown. Cool on a wire rack and sprinkle with toasted crushed Parmesan cheese.

COOK'S TIPS
Grate 50 g (2 oz) Parmesan cheese on to a non-stick baking sheet and bake in the ROASTING OVEN for just a few minutes until pale golden. Leave it to harden, then crush with the end of a rolling pin.

When making dough, work quickly and lightly – if it's overworked, the scones will be tough.

Rustic Walnut Bread

PREPARATION TIME:
25 MINUTES, PLUS
RISING

COOKING TIME:
35 MINUTES

FREEZING: SUITABLE

1080 CALS PER
LOAF

MAKES 2

Freshly baked home-made bread is always delicious – these walnut loaves particularly so. A variety of nuts, seeds or herbs may be added to or substituted for the walnuts to make your own speciality.

15 g (½ oz) fresh yeast or 7 g sachet fast-action dried yeast
600 g (1 lb 5 oz) strong plain white flour

5 ml (1 level tsp) salt
25 g (1 oz) butter or margarine
125 g (4 oz) walnuts, roughly chopped

1 If using fresh yeast, blend it with 350 ml (12 fl oz) tepid water.

2 Mix the flour and salt together in a large bowl. Rub in the butter, then stir in the fast-action dried yeast if using, and the chopped walnuts.

3 Make a well in the centre of the flour mixture and pour in the yeast liquid, or 350 ml (12 fl oz) tepid water if using fast-action dried yeast. Mix to a smooth dough, then turn out onto a lightly floured surface and knead for 10 minutes until smooth and elastic, adding a little more flour if the dough becomes too sticky. If kneading in a large food processor or other machine, work for 2 minutes.

4 If using fresh yeast, put the dough in a large oiled bowl and cover with oiled cling film. Leave to rise in a warm place for about 1 hour until doubled in size. Turn out and knead the dough again for 2-3 minutes. (If fast-action dried yeast has been used, this stage is not necessary.)

5 Divide the dough in half and shape each piece into a roll about 33 cm (13 in) long. Place on oiled baking sheets, cover with a damp tea towel, and leave to rise in a warm place for about 1 hour, or until doubled in size.

6 Uncover the loaves and slash the tops with a sharp knife. Bake on the second runners of the ROASTING OVEN for 10 minutes.

■■ Turn the tray round and transfer to the grid shelf on the floor of the ROASTING OVEN. Place the cold plain shelf or a roasting tin above and bake for a further 25 minutes or until the loaves are crusty and feel hollow when tapped on the bottom.

■■■■ Turn the tray round and bake on the second runners of the BAKING OVEN for 25-30 minutes or until the loaves are crusty and feel hollow when tapped on the bottom.
Cool on a wire rack.

AGA TIP
To serve warm, heat in the SIMMERING OVEN for 10 minutes, or for 30 minutes if frozen.

Granary and Rosemary Batch Loaves

PREPARATION TIME:
15 MINUTES, PLUS
RISING

COOKING TIME:
20-25 MINUTES

FREEZING: WRAP
AND FREEZE AND
AS SOON AS THE
BREAD HAS
COOLED. THAW IN
THE SIMMERING
OVEN FOR
20 MINUTES.

1200 CALS PER LOAF

MAKES 3

Herb loaves such as this one are excellent to serve with soups, starters and salads.

1 kg (2 lb 3 oz) fresh granary flour
1 medium potato
10 ml (2 tsp) salt
25 g (1 oz) fresh yeast or 1 sachet fast-action dried yeast

50 g (2 oz) butter, at room temperature
15 ml (1 tbsp) fresh rosemary, chopped
oil, for greasing

1 Warm the bag of flour of the back of the Aga. Peel and chop the potato; place in a measuring jug and make up to 700 ml (1¼ pints) with water. Pour into a pan, add the salt and bring to the boil on the BOILING PLATE. Transfer to the SIMMERING OVEN for about 20 minutes or until tender. Mash well in the liquid and cool until hand-hot.

2 Tip the flour into a large bowl, reserving one handful for kneading. Combine the fresh yeast with the warm potato mixture, or combine the dry yeast with the bowl of flour. Mix well.

3 Pour the potato mixture into the flour, beat with a wooden spoon to make an even dough –

you may need to add a little extra water. Work well in the bowl, then sprinkle the reserved flour on the worksurface and knead the dough on top for about 10 minutes.

4 Wipe a bowl around with oil. Place the dough in the bowl and cover with clingfilm or a damp tea towel. Leave to rise beside the Aga until doubled in size. (This stage is not essential if using fast-action yeast.)

5 Scatter the rosemary on the worksurface. Tip the dough on top and flatten to a disk. Dot with soft butter. Roll up, then knead to an even texture without using any extra flour. Divide the dough into three and shape into oblong loaves. Oil the small roasting tin and set the loaves in it side by side. Leave in a warm place beside the Aga for about 30 minutes to double in size.

6 Bake on the second runners of the ROASTING OVEN for 15 minutes until golden, then transfer to the floor of the ROASTING OVEN for 5 minutes for a crisp base.

COOK'S TIP
Adding potatoes and potato water to bread dough gives a very good flavour and texture.

AGA TIP
When leaving the dough to rise, the ideal place is to set it on top of an oven glove on top of the SIMMERING PLATE lid.

135

Lemon Seed Loaf

PREPARATION TIME:
20 MINUTES

COOKING TIME:
1 HOUR

FREEZING:
COMPLETE TO THE
END OF STEP 3,
WRAP AND FREEZE.
THAW FOR 4
HOURS AT COOL
ROOM
TEMPERATURE.
COMPLETE AS IN
STEP 5.

200 CALS PER
SERVING

MAKES 12 SLICES

This lemon cake is deliciously light and lemony and very low in fat, making it ideal for anyone watching their weight.

3 lemons
50 g (2 oz) butter, plus a little extra for greasing
250 g (9 oz) caster sugar
250 g (9 oz) self-raising white flour
5 ml (1 level tsp) baking powder

1 egg
100 ml (4 fl oz) semi-skimmed milk
30 ml (2 level tbsp) plain yogurt
30 ml (2 level tbsp) poppy seeds

1 Remove the zest from 1 lemon. Lightly grease, and base-line a 900 g (2 lb) loaf tin.

2 Process the butter in a food processor until soft. Add the lemon zest, 200 g (7 oz) sugar, the flour, baking powder, egg, milk, yogurt and poppy seeds. Process until smooth.

3 Turn the mixture into the tin; level the top.

■■ Bake on the grid shelf on the floor of the ROASTING OVEN for 7-10 minutes until golden, then place the cold plain shelf on the second runners and cook for a further 35-40 minutes.

■■■ Bake on the grid shelf on the floor of the BAKING OVEN for 55 minutes-1 hour until golden. Place the cold plain shelf above if it is sufficiently brown after 40 minutes.

Cool in the tin for 10 minutes.

4 For the syrup, squeeze the juice from the lemon with zest removed, plus 1 more lemon. Thinly slice the third lemon. Place together in a pan with remaining sugar and 150 ml (¼ pint) water. Bring to the boil; bubble for 4-5 minutes on the SIMMERING PLATE or until syrupy. Remove from the heat. Cover and place on the floor of the SIMMERING OVEN until the cake is cooked.

5 Loosen the sides of the cake with a knife and turn out onto a plate. Using a cocktail stick, pierce cake in several places. Spoon the syrup and lemon slices over.

Quick Cheese and Apple Bread

PREPARATION TIME:
20 MINUTES

COOKING TIME:
45 MINUTES

FREEZING:
UNSUITABLE

225 CALS PER SLICE

MAKES 8 SLICES

This bread makes a perfect accompaniment for soups and salads. A wide variety of fruits, vegetables, cheeses, nuts and seeds can be used, so you can make this bread with whatever you have available.

225 g (8 oz) self-raising flour
1.25 ml (¼ level tsp) freshly ground black pepper
25 g (1 oz) butter
1 small crisp eating apple, about 125 g (4 oz)

125 g (4 oz) mature Cheddar cheese, coarsely grated
50 g (2 oz) roasted salted peanuts, chopped
1 egg
60-75 ml (4-5 tbsp) milk

1 Mix the flour and pepper together in a large bowl and rub in the butter.

2 Peel, quarter, core and chop the apple, then stir into the dry ingredients with the cheese and chopped nuts. Make a well in the centre

3 Whisk together the egg and milk, then pour into the well and mix to a soft dough.

4 Turn out onto a lightly floured surface and knead quickly into a small neat round, about 15-18 cm (6-7 in) in diameter. Mark a lattice on top of the round.

5 Place on a lightly greased baking sheet and bake on the grid shelf on the floor of the ROASTING OVEN with the cold plain shelf on the top runners for about 40 minutes or until well risen and golden brown. Cool on a wire rack.

COOK'S TIP
This bread is best eaten on the day of making.

Honey and Yogurt Muffins

PREPARATION TIME:
15 MINUTES

COOKING TIME:
15-20 MINUTES

FREEZING:
SUITABLE

180 CALS PER
MUFFIN

MAKES 12

American-style muffins rise considerably during baking to produce a wonderful craggy texture and typically 'top heavy' appearance. This honey and yogurt version is light, airy and perfect served with just a dot of butter while still warm. For a sweeter variation, try the rippled chocolate and banana version.

225 g (8 oz) plain white flour
7.5 ml (1½ level tsp) baking powder
5 ml (1 level tsp) bicarbonate of soda
pinch of salt
2.5 ml (½ level tsp) ground mixed spice
1.25 ml (¼ level tsp) ground nutmeg
50 g (2 oz) medium oatmeal

50 g (2 oz) light muscovado sugar
50 g (2 oz) butter
225 g (8 oz) Greek-style yogurt
125 ml (4 fl oz) milk
1 egg
60 ml (4 tbsp) clear honey
medium oatmeal, for dusting

1 Line 12 deep bun tins or muffin tins with paper muffin cases. Sift the flour, baking powder, bicarbonate of soda, salt, mixed spice and nutmeg into a bowl. Stir in the oatmeal and sugar.
2 Melt the butter in a bowl in the SIMMERING OVEN, then beat in the yogurt, milk, egg and honey.
3 Pour over the dry ingredients and stir in quickly until only just blended; do not over-mix.
4 Divide the mixture equally between the paper cases. Sprinkle with oatmeal and bake for 15-20 minutes on the bottom runners of the ROASTING OVEN until well risen and just firm to the touch. Remove from the oven and leave in the tins for 5 minutes, then transfer to a wire rack. Serve warm or cold, with a little butter if desired.

Wholemeal Banana Muffins

PREPARATION TIME:
15 MINUTES, PLUS
1 HOUR SOAKING

COOKING TIME:
15-20 MINUTES

FREEZING: SUITABLE

370 CALS PER
MUFFIN

MAKES 8

These muffins are good for those on cholesterol-lowering diets.

butter, for greasing (optional)
50 g (2 oz) raisins
grated rind and juice of 1 orange
125 g (4 oz) wholemeal flour
25 g (1 oz) wheatgerm
45 ml (3 level tbsp) caster sugar
10 ml (2 level tsp) baking powder
pinch of salt
1 large egg, beaten

50 ml (2 fl oz) milk
50 ml (2 fl oz) sunflower oil
2 medium-sized ripe bananas (about 225 g
(8 oz) when peeled), roughly mashed

FOR THE TOPPING
75 ml (5 level tbsp) orange marmalade
50 g (2 oz) banana chips
50 g (2 oz) roughly chopped walnuts

1 Line 8 muffin tins with paper muffin cases or grease the tins well. Place the raisins in a bowl, pour the orange juice over and leave to soak for 1 hour or overnight.
2 Place the orange rind in a bowl with the next five ingredients and mix together. Make a well in the centre.
3 In a separate bowl, mix the egg, milk and oil, then pour into the flour mixture. Drain the raisins, reserving 15 ml (1 tbsp) juice, and stir into the mixture with the bananas. Don't over-mix.
4 Fill each muffin case two-thirds full. Bake on the bottom runners of the ROASTING OVEN for 15-20 minutes or until a skewer inserted into the centre comes out clean. Transfer the muffins to a wire rack to cool slightly.
5 While the muffins are baking, prepare the topping. Gently heat the orange marmalade with the reserved orange juice in a saucepan on the SIMMERING PLATE until melted. Simmer for 1 minute, then add the banana chips and chopped walnuts. Spoon on top of the muffins. Serve while still warm.

PRESERVING

COOK'S TIPS FOR JAM MAKING

SETTING AGENTS
■ Preserving sugar produces less scum, dissolves easily and produces sparkling clear jellies and jams. (Jam sugar is used for fruits with low pectin and acid level.)
■ Pectin makes jam set when fruit is heated with sugar. However, many summer fruits are low in natural pectin, so if your jam is not setting, add extra lemon juice. Alternatively, use an artificial pectin which helps extract the maximum pectin.

SETTING POINT
When jam reaches setting point, it's ready to pot. There are two good ways of testing this stage:
1. Spoon a little jam on to a chilled plate, then chill for 1-2 minutes. If it crinkles when you run your finger through it, setting point has been reached
2. Use a jam thermometer – when it reaches at least 104°C /230°F the jam is at setting point.

POTTING TIPS
■ Before use, wash jars in hot water, drain, then leave to dry in the SIMMERING OVEN. Boil the lids. Alternatively,

a fast wash in the dishwasher is ideal.
■ Always pour hot jam into warm jars.
■ Always fill to the rim to allow for shrinkage on cooling.
■ Cover with waxed discs, waxed side down, and dampened Cellophane covers, dampened side up.
■ For longer-term storage, cover with screw-on lids too.
■ For best results, store jams in a cool dark place.

AGA TIPS
■ Where possible, cook in the ovens rather than on top to save heat. This is possible in the early stages of cooking fruits or vegetables. Chutneys can be reduced in the ROASTING OVEN.

■ Heat sugar in the SIMMERING OVEN to reduce the time required for dissolving.

■ When using other recipes which specify 'boil the fruit pulp down until reduced by half', try halving the quantity of water and then cooking the fruit with the lid on in the Aga ovens.

Blackberry, Apple and Cardamom Jam

PREPARATION TIME:
10 MINUTES

COOKING TIME:
35 MINUTES

35 CALS PER 15 ML
(1 LEVEL TBSP)

MAKES ABOUT
1.4 KG (3 LB) JAM

Blackberries and apples are a winning combination and the cardamom adds an unusual twist. This is great for old-fashioned jam tarts.

700 g (1½ lb) granulated or preserving sugar
350 g (12 oz) green cooking apples, peeled and cut in chunks

900 g (2 lb) blackberries
3 cardamom pods, seeds removed and lightly crushed, tied in muslin
juice of ½ lemon

1 Place the sugar in a roasting tin and warm in the SIMMERING OVEN for 10 minutes. Meanwhile, place the apples and 150 ml (¼ pint) water in a large pan, bring to the boil and simmer very gently until the apples are soft. Transfer to the SIMMERING OVEN to complete the cooking if the juices evaporate before the apples are soft.
2 Add the blackberries and cook for about 5 minutes or until soft and the juices run. Add the sugar, crushed cardamom seeds and lemon juice. Bring to the boil and bubble on the BOILING PLATE for 20 minutes or until the jam is set. Remove the cardamom seeds and pot hot or cool (not warm), then cover and label the jars.

BLACKBERRY, APPLE
AND CARDAMOM JAM

Plum and Armagnac Jam with Pecans

PREPARATION TIME:
10 MINUTES

COOKING TIME:
35 MINUTES PLUS 20
MINUTES

25 CALS PER 15 ML
(1 LEVEL TBSP)

MAKES ABOUT
2.25 KG (5 LB)

Everyday plum jam is made extra-special with the addition of a dash of Armagnac and pecan nuts.

700 g (1½ lb) plums
700 g (1½ lb) sugar

100 g (3½ oz) pecans, roughly chopped
75 ml (5 tbsp) Armagnac

1 Quarter the plums, twisting the sections off the stones. Tie the stones loosely in a cotton muslin cloth. Place the fruit and stones in a very large pan with 150 ml (¼ pint) water. Cover the pan and bring slowly to the boil on the SIMMERING PLATE, stirring occasionally (see Cook's Tip). When boiling, transfer to the SIMMERING OVEN for 30 minutes or until the fruit is very soft.

2 Place the sugar in a heatproof bowl in the SIMMERING OVEN to warm while the fruit is cooking.

3 Meanwhile, wash the jam jars and scald the lids. When the fruit and sugar are taken out of the SIMMERING OVEN, put the jars in to warm.

4 Return the pan of fruit to the SIMMERING PLATE, stir in the warm sugar and allow to dissolve. Transfer to the BOILING PLATE and boil very briskly for about 20 minutes, adding the pecans after 10 minutes. Cook until setting point is reached (see page 138). Lift the bags of stones into a sieve; hold over the pan and press out the juices with the back of a wooden spoon, then discard the stones.

5 Remove the pan from the heat and add the Armagnac. Allow the jam to cool sufficiently to prevent the pecans floating on the surface.

6 Pot the jam while still warm, cover with waxed paper discs. Do not seal the jars with cellophane or screw lids until cold.

COOK'S TIP
Do not stir the jam vigorously or the fruit will break up completely. Simply stir the corners and base of the pan gently to prevent the jam burning.

Rosehip Jelly

PREPARATION TIME:
25 MINUTES, PLUS
STANDING
OVERNIGHT

COOKING TIME:
ABOUT 1 HOUR
15 MINUTES

35-40 CALS PER
15 ML (1 LEVEL
TBSP)

MAKES 2 KG (4½ LB)

A beautifully coloured jelly to make when rosehips can be gathered.

900 g (2 lb) cooking apples
450 g (1 lb) ripe rosehips

1.25-1.5 kg (2½ -3 lb) sugar (see method)

1 Remove any bruised or damaged portions from the apples, then roughly chop without coring or peeling.

2 Put the apples and rosehips in a preserving pan with just enough water to barely cover. Bring to the boil on the BOILING PLATE, then cover and transfer to the SIMMERING OVEN for about 45 minutes or until the fruit is soft and pulpy. Crush well with a potato masher.

3 Spoon the fruit pulp into a jelly bag suspended over a large bowl and leave to drip through for at least 12 hours.

4 Discard the pulp remaining in the jelly bag. Measure the extract and return to the preserving pan with 450 g (1 lb) sugar for each 600 ml (1 pint) extract.

5 Heat gently, stirring, on the SIMMERING PLATE until the sugar has dissolved, then bring to the boil and boil rapidly for about 15 minutes or until setting point is reached. Remove any scum with a slotted spoon, then pot and cover in the usual way.

Seville Orange Marmalade

PREPARATION TIME:
30 MINUTES

COOKING TIME:
ABOUT 2½ HOURS

35 CALS PER 15 ML
(1 LEVEL TBSP)

MAKES ABOUT
4.5 KG (10 LB)

The Aga can lose a tremendous amount of heat when making marmalade by the traditional method with double the water. By cutting the liquid, cooking with the lid on and cooking inside the oven as much as possible, you can make perfect, trouble-free marmalade.

2.7 kg (6 lb) sugar   **juice of 2 lemons**
1.4 kg (3 lb) Seville oranges

1 Place the bags of sugar at the back of the Aga to warm. Halve the oranges and squeeze out the juice and pips. Tie the pips, and any membrane that has comes away during squeezing, in a piece of muslin. Slice the orange peel thinly or thickly, as preferred, and put it in a preserving pan with the fruit juices, muslin bag and 1.7 litres (3 pints) water.
2 Bring to a fast boil on the BOILING PLATE, then cook in the SIMMERING OVEN for 2-2½ hours or until the peel is really soft. Remove the muslin bag, squeezing it well and allowing the juice to run back into the pan. Add the sugar. Heat gently, stirring until the sugar has dissolved.
3 Transfer half the marmalade by ladling it into a second ovenproof pan and place on the floor of the ROASTING OVEN. Meanwhile bring the remainder to a rapid boil on the BOILING PLATE for 15-20 minutes until setting point is reached.
4 Remove any scum with a slotted spoon. Leave to stand for 15 minutes, then stir to distribute the peel. Meanwhile place the marmalade from the oven on the BOILING PLATE – this will take only about 5 minutes to reach setting point. Pot and cover in the usual way.

COOK'S TIP
Setting point for marmalade is 105°C/224°F if you are using a thermometer. The marmalade drops off a wooden spoon held well above the pan in a 'flake' or heavy double droplet. If testing on a cold plate, a good skin should form when cold, wrinkling up when pushed with a teaspoon.

Brandied Cherries

PREPARATION TIME:
15 MINUTES

COOKING TIME:
ABOUT 15 MINUTES

50 CALS PER 15 ML
(1 TBSP)

MAKES ABOUT
450 G (1 LB)

Imported cherries or peaches are available in the winter and taste delicious brandied. They make quick and easy desserts and are wonderful with ice cream.

450 g (1 lb) cherries   **1 cinnamon stick**
225 g (8 oz) sugar   **about 150 ml (¼ pint) brandy**

1 Prick cherries all over with a sterilised fine skewer. Put 125 g (4 oz) of the sugar and 300 ml (½ pint) water in a saucepan and dissolve on the SIMMERING PLATE to make a light syrup.
2 Add the cherries and cinnamon stick, bring to the boil on the BOILING PLATE, then poach gently for 4-5 minutes in the SIMMERING OVEN. Remove the pan from the oven and drain the cherries, reserving the syrup but removing the cinnamon stick. Cool, then arrange fruit in jars.
3 Add the remaining sugar to the reserved syrup and dissolve it slowly. Bring to a fast boil on the BOILING PLATE and boil to 110°C (230°F), then allow to cool.
4 Measure the syrup and add an equal quantity of brandy. Pour over the cherries. Cover and store for about 1 month before eating.

AGA TIP
The SIMMERING OVEN is ideal for the traditional bottling of fruit, so it is well worth buying screw lidded or clip-topped bottling jars which can be used time and time again.

Bottled Spiced Pears, Peaches and Nectarines

PREPARATION TIME:
20 MINUTES

COOKING TIME:
ABOUT 20 MINUTES

55 CALS PER
SERVING

MAKES 900 G (2 LB)

Beautiful bottled fruits – picked when in their prime and poached in a sweet-sour and spiced sugar syrup – make lovely Christmas gifts. They are particularly delicious served with hot or cold ham. Use whole spices for optimum flavour and effect.

2.5 cm (I in) piece fresh root ginger
I lemon
450 g (I lb) golden granulated sugar
300 ml (½ pint) white wine vinegar
300 ml (½ pint) clear malt vinegar
15 ml (I level tbsp) allspice berries

15 ml (I level tbsp) cloves
I large cinnamon stick or several pieces of cassia bark
1.25 kg (2½ lb) ripe but firm unblemished William pears

I Thinly slice the ginger and pare the rind off the lemon in three strips. Put the sugar and vinegars into a saucepan and dissolve on the SIMMERING PLATE. Add the ginger, lemon rind and spices. Slowly bring to the boil.

2 Carefully peel the pears. Halve or quarter them, then remove the cores. Place in a pan and bring to a fast boil on the BOILING PLATE.

3 Lift out the pears with a slotted spoon and pack into three 500 ml sterilised jars, with an even distribution of the cooked spices.

4 Reduce the syrup to about half on the BOILING PLATE for 10 minutes until syrupy. Pour over the pears, making sure they are all covered. Seal and store in a cool dark place for up to 6 months.

COOK'S TIPS
Do not use over-ripe fruit or it will discolour and disintegrate during cooking.

For spiced peaches or nectarines, prepare in exactly the same manner, but skin, halve and remove the stones from the fruit. Use orange instead of lemon rind and omit the ginger.

Tomato and Apple Chutney

PREPARATION TIME:
10 MINUTES

COOKING TIME:
45-50 MINUTES

25-30 CALS PER
15 ML (I TBSP)

MAKES 1.4 KG (3 LB)

This recipe is ideal for using up a glut of tomatoes.

1.4 kg (3 lb) tomatoes
2 apples, peeled, cored and roughly chopped
I medium onion, finely chopped
2 garlic cloves, crushed
250 g (8 oz) light, soft brown sugar

10 ml (2 level tsp) fresh ginger, finely chopped
5 ml (I level tsp) turmeric
250 g (8 oz) sultanas
100 ml (4 fl oz) white wine vinegar
10 ml (2 tsp) salt

I Scald the tomatoes for 7-8 seconds in boiling water. Peel, quarter and squeeze out the seeds. Roughly chop.

2 Combine the tomatoes in a large, shallow pan with all the remaining ingredients. Cook briskly on the BOILING PLATE for 5-7 minutes, stirring constantly when boiling. Transfer to the floor of the ROASTING OVEN and cook, uncovered, for 15-20 minutes until thick and well reduced. Cover the pan and transfer to the SIMMERING OVEN for 30 minutes to complete cooking.

3 Pot while still very hot and screw down lids immediately.

RHUBARB, GINGER AND ALLSPICE CHUTNEY

Rhubarb, Ginger and Allspice Chutney

PREPARATION TIME:
15 MINUTES, PLUS
STANDING TIME

COOKING TIME:
1¼ HOURS

30 CALS PER 15 ML
(1 LEVEL TBSP)

MAKES ABOUT
1.6 KG (3½ LB)
CHUTNEY

This spiced chutney is a useful preserve to have in the storecupboard and tastes especially good with mature cheeses, hot goat's cheese salads and cold meats.

1 kg (2¼ lb) thick rhubarb stems, trimmed and cut into 5 cm (2 in) pieces
20 ml (4 level tsp) salt
225 g (8 oz) red onions, cut into thick slices
700 g (1½ lb) soft dark brown sugar

450 ml (¾ pint) white wine vinegar
25 g (1 oz) fresh root ginger, coarsely grated
1.25 ml (¼ level tsp) ground allspice
125 g (4 oz) raisins

1 Place the rhubarb in a non-metallic bowl, mix with 10 ml (2 level tsp) salt, then cover and leave in a cool place for 12-24 hours.

2 Drain and rinse the rhubarb, then place in a preserving pan with all the other ingredients except the raisins. Cook on the SIMMERING PLATE until the sugar has dissolved, then transfer to the floor of the ROASTING OVEN for 45 minutes-1 hour or until well reduced and pulpy. Add the raisins and bubble, stirring constantly, on the SIMMERING PLATE for 5 minutes until thick. Pot hot or cool (not warm), then cover and label the jars.

COOK'S TIPS
This recipe can be made with end-of-season rhubarb. Use the tender stems from the centre of the crown. New season forced rhubarb has too high a water content for the best chutney.

Salting rhubarb in this recipe reduces the amount of liquid that must be boiled off.

Index

almond Bakewell tarts, 122

anchovy and caper tapenade roast beef, 50

apples: apple and blackberry oat crunch, 107
apple and mincemeat tart, 113
apple strudel, 114-15
butter and rum-baked apples, 111
spicy apple mincemeat, 100

apricots: apricot and cardamom crumble, 109
spiced apricot cake, 130

aubergine and chickpea pilaff, 70

Bakewell tarts, almond, 122

banana muffins, wholemeal, 137

beans: Tuscan bean soup, 18
Tuscan bean stew, 67

beef: anchovy and caper tapenade roast beef, 50
beef and beer stew, 54-5
beef jambalaya, 52
chilli beef with salsa, 55
mustard and peppered beef stroganoff, 49
slow-braised beef, 54
spiced beef and noodle soup, 14

biscuits, 126-7

blackberry, apple and cardamom jam, 138

bread, 134-6

bread and butter pudding, chocolate, 121

broad bean and lemon risotto, 70-1

broccoli and goat's cheese soup, 18-19

Brussels sprouts: chiffonade of sprouts, 78
creamy Brussels sprouts, 94

bûche de Noël, 101

cakes, 101-3, 129-31, 136

cannelloni: mushroom and ricotta, 72
with roasted garlic, 62

carrots: buttered fennel and, 77
glazed carrots and turnips, 93

cheese and apple bread, 136

cherries, brandied, 141

chestnuts: bûche de Noël, 101

chicken: chicken and artichoke pie, 35
chicken and champ, 28
chicken and leek pilaff, 30-1
chicken breasts with courgette and herb stuffing, 34
chicken casserole, 30
chicken roasted in a lemony vinaigrette, 34-5
chicken soup, 15
roast chicken with spiced orange sauce, 31

chickpeas: pasta and chickpea soup, 16

chilli beef with salsa, 55

chocolate: chocolate and orange truffle torte, 106
chocolate bread and butter pudding, 121
chocolate meringue roulade, 116
chocolate mousse cake, 131
chocolate pancakes, 114
chocolate, prune and orange soufflés, 118
chocolate puddings, 108

Christmas, 84-105

Christmas cake, 102-3

Christmas morning muffins, 86-7

Christmas puddings, 96-7

chutney, 142-3

cinnamon and orange stack, 112

coconut squares, 124

cod fillet with a herb crust, 22

couscous and herb stuffing, 91

curries, 61, 71

dried fruit: cinnamon and orange stack, 112

duck: duck and juniper cassoulet, 39
duck breasts with cinnamon plum sauce, 38

Eccles cakes, citrus, 132

fettucine with spicy seafood sauce, 23

figs in cinnamon syrup, 116-17

fish and shellfish, 20-7
creamy fish gratin, 20-1
fish tagine with couscous, 25
Provençal fish fillets, 27

flapjacks, sticky ginger, 124-5

fruit cake with glacé fruits, 128

game pie, 40

garlic, cannelloni with roasted, 62

ginger: gingerbread tree decorations, 84
sticky ginger flapjacks, 124-5

granary and rosemary batch loaves, 134-5

gravy, 61, 89

guinea fowl with Madeira, 36

herb and soured milk scones, 133

honey and yogurt muffins, 137

jams, 138-40

Jerusalem artichoke soup, 14

kumquat compote, 97

lamb: herb-scented lamb, 56
lamb and bamboo shoot red curry, 61
lamb and chestnuts en croûte, 60
roast leg of lamb, 58
spaghetti with lamb ragu, 59

lasagne, vegetarian, 75

leek soup, cheesy, 19

lemon seed loaf, 136

liver: crisp chicken liver risotto, 32

manhole cover biscuits, 126-7

marmalade, Seville orange, 141

meatballs with olive and pesto pasta, 51

meringues, 110, 116

mincemeat: apple and mincemeat tart, 113
old-time mince pies, 99
spicy apple mincemeat, 100

muffins, 86-7, 137

mulled wine, 105

mushrooms: mushroom and olive stuffing, 92
mushroom and ricotta cannelloni, 72

mussel and smoked haddock chowder, 17

nuts, spiced, 85

olives, marinated, 85

onions: roasted onion and coconut soup, 16

orange: orange biscuits with Seville curd, 127
Seville orange marmalade, 141

pancakes, chocolate, 114

pannetone, 104

Parmesan crisps, 12

parsnips: parsnip soup, 12
parsnips in a lime glaze, 93

pasta and chickpea soup, 16

pasta with smoked haddock and spinach, 24

pears: bottled spiced pears, 142
pears in Malmsey Madeira, 117

peppers: roast sweet pepper with sage, 83

pheasant with cider and apples, 43

pies, 35, 40, 95, 99

pizza, tomato, artichoke and prosciutto, 63

plums: plum and Armagnac jam with pecans, 140
plums with caramelised fruit bread, 108-9

pork: meatballs with olive and pesto pasta, 51
pork and spinach pots, 48-9
pork steaks with sage and apple, 47
roast pork with apple and saffron chutney, 44
sweet and sour spiced pork, 46

potatoes: chicken and champ, 28
creamy baked potatoes with mustard seeds, 67
crumb roasted rosemary and garlic potatoes, 92
crunchy topped mash, 80-1
pommes Anna, 76
potato and celeriac puffs, 66
potato 'spiders', 43
roast new potatoes with garlic and Parmesan, 79

prawns: fettucine with spicy seafood sauce, 23
prawn and lemon risotto, 26

Provençal fish fillets, 27

prunes: prunes in brandy, 118
sesame prune slices, 125

pumpkin and cheese bake, 81

raisin puddings, spiced, 120-1

ratatouille, roasted vegetable, 82-3

red cabbage timbales, 68

red mullet, spiced, 22-3

rhubarb: rhubarb and raspberry meringues, 110
rhubarb, ginger and allspice chutney, 143

rice: aubergine and chickpea pilaff, 70
beef jambalaya, 52
broad bean and lemon risotto, 70-1

chicken and leek pilaff, 30-1
crisp chicken liver risotto, 32
prawn and lemon risotto, 26

rigatoni baked with spicy sausage, 64

rosehip jelly, 140

rum, spiced, 105

saffron scones, 132-3

sausages: rigatoni baked with spicy sausage, 64
sausage and bacon rolls, 91
wine-braised sausages with lentils, 65

scones, 132-3

seafood, puff-topped, 26-7

sesame prune slices, 125

Seville orange marmalade, 141

smoked haddock, pasta with spinach and, 24

soufflés, chocolate, prune and orange, 118

soups, 12-19

spaghetti with lamb ragu, 59

stars, savoury, 87

strudel, apple, 114-15

stuffings, 91-2

swede and carrots with mustard seeds and ginger, 79

sweet potatoes, purée of, 78

tarts, 74, 113, 120, 122

Thai vegetable curry, 71

thyme and port gravy, 61

tomatoes: tomato and apple chutney, 142
tomato and basil tarte Tatin, 74
tomato and harissa soup, 13
tomato, artichoke and prosciutto pizza, 63

treacle tart, 120

turkey: lemon and herb roasted turkey, 89
roasted turkey, 88
turkey gravy, 89
turkey pot pie, 95

Turkish yogurt cake, 129

Tuscan bean soup, 18

Tuscan bean stew, 67

vegetables: roasted vegetable ratatouille, 82-3
Thai vegetable curry, 71
vegetables à la Grecque, 82
winter vegetable roast, 76

vegetarian lasagne, 75

venison and cranberry daube, 42-3

walnut bread, rustic, 134

wine, mulled, 105